Ecology and Popular Film

THE SUNY SERIES

HORIZONS of CINEMA

MURRAY POMERANCE | EDITOR

Also in the series

William Rothman, editor, *Cavell on Film*

J. David Slocum, editor, *Rebel Without a Cause*

Joe McElhaney, *The Death of Classical Cinema*

Kirsten Thompson, *Apocalyptic Dread*

Francis Gateward, editor, *Seoul Searching*

Michael Atkinson, editor, *Exile Cinema*

Bert Cardullo, *Soundings on Cinema*

Paul S. Moore, *Now Playing*

Ecology and Popular Film

Cinema on the Edge

Robin L. Murray

and

Joseph K. Heumann

Cover art courtesy of Photofest.

Published by
State University of New York Press, Albany

© 2009 State University of New York

For information, contact State University of New York Press, Albany, NY
www.sunypress.edu

Production by Marilyn P. Semerad
Marketing by Michael Campochiaro

Library of Congress Cataloging-in-Publication Data

Murray, Robin L.
    Ecology and popular film : cinema on the edge / Robin L. Murray and Joseph K. Heumann.
        p. cm. — (Horizons of cinema)
    Includes bibiographical references and index.
    ISBN 978-0-7914-7677-2 (hardcover : alk. paper)
    ISBN 978-0-7914-7678-9 (pbk : alk. paper)
    1. Nature in motion pictures.   2. Ecology in motion pictures.
I. Heumann, Joseph K.   II. Title.

PN1995.9.N38M87 2009
791.43'66—dc22   2008008873

10 9 8 7 6 5 4 3 2 1

Contents

Illustrations

Acknowledgments

First of all, we convey our heart-felt thanks to our series editor for his exquisitely clear editorial eye and pointed advice. Without his guidance, our book would have been a dim reflection of the product presented here.

We also would like to thank Lola McElwee for her helpful commentary on the original manuscript. She helped make this book more accessible for a broader base of readers. We want to thank Lola and Jessica Pickering for their help formatting both the bibliography and filmography.

Thanks also to Julia Lesage and Chuck Kleinhans, editors of *Jump Cut*, for their unending support for our work. They provided comments on much earlier drafts of chapters in our manuscript but, more importantly, encouraged us to write this book-length project in film and eco-criticism.

We also appreciate the professional climate SUNY Press provided us. Thanks go to James Peltz for his support and professionalism throughout this project. Our experience with SUNY Press has been a pleasant one because of his dedication to this project.

We also are grateful to Chris Hanlon and the English graduate studies committee and Bob Augustine and the Graduate School for their support for our work. Support from colleagues like our English department's acting chair, Linda Coleman, and continuing department chair, Dana Ringuette, has also encouraged us.

Most importantly, we would like to thank family and friends for their support and understanding throughout this project.

Chapter 1 is an expanded and revised version of "The First Eco-Disaster Film?" published in *Film Quarterly* 59.3 (Spring 2006): 44–51, and is used with permission.

Cover art, image from *The Day After Tomorrow* courtesy of Photofest—DAT-277.jpg.

Introduction

Reading the Environment in Popular Cinema

WRITING ABOUT NATURE IN LOS ANGELES, Jenny Price not only seeks to redefine nature writing but also argues it has lost its relevance. "The core trouble is that nature writers have given us endless paeans to wildness since Thoreau fled to Walden Pond, but they need to tell us far more about our everyday lives in the places we live," she argues. "Perhaps you're not worrying about the failures of this literary genre as a serious problem. But in my own arm-waving manifesto about L.A. and America, I will proclaim that the crisis in nature writing is one of our most pressing national cultural catastrophes" (Price). She believes nature writing has failed because it ignores the urban world in which most of us live, especially the urban world of Los Angeles, and because it disregards the products of our everyday lives now seen as necessary: from concrete to electricity.

This same problem permeates eco-films and the film industry that produces them. Films blatantly seen as environmental—documentaries and fictional films that tackle ecological issues—are discussed as "nature writing" or, as David Ingram calls them, "film vert." Examples are Al Gore's *An Inconvenient Truth* (2006) and Leonardo DiCaprio's *The 11th Hour* (2007). Films with more hidden environmental messages, however, receive short shrift in ecological film festivals or award contests. And discussions about the film industry itself and its impact on the environment are all but erased in explorations of environmental films. Onscreen, eco-films articulate environmental messages as powerful as the anti-global

1

warming manifesto *An Inconvenient Truth*, yet the environmental impact of the film industry and its Los Angeles setting is all but ignored.

For example, in spite of Al Gore and Leonardo DiCaprio's announcement at the Oscars "that ecologically intelligent practices had been integrated into the planning and execution of the Oscar presentation and several related events" (Academy Statement), the film and television industry "is responsible for a significant amount of both air pollution and greenhouse gas emissions" (Corbett and Turco 5). Charles J. Corbett and Richard P. Turco's November 2006 UCLA Institute of the Environment study found that the film and television industry in greater Los Angeles "make[s] a larger contribution to conventional air pollution than four of the other sectors" they studied (8). The film and television industry contributed less than petroleum refining but more than aerospace manufacturing, apparel, hotels, and semiconductor manufacturing in the five-county Los Angeles region. Coming in second among these six sectors rated the film and television industry a grade of "A" for environmental best practices (based on isolated cases), and a grade of "C" for industrywide actions, even in California where control of emissions is the tightest in the United States.

The UCLA Institute report called for both a monitoring of progress toward "more environmentally sustainable operations" (Nichols quoted in *Southern California Environmental Report Card 2006*) and action within the film and television industry to "foster environmentally friendly approaches" (Corbett and Turco 9). Corbett and Turco note challenges within the industry: "work is controlled by short-lived production companies rather than by long-lived firms in stable supply chains, making it difficult to institutionalize best practices" (9) and " 'stop-and-go' practices impede "consider[ing] and implement[ing] environmental mitigation policies" (9). These challenges, according to Corbett and Turco, should be and can be addressed to overcome the "environmental impacts of filmmaking." The environmental destruction is rather massive and amounts to emissions of about eight million metric tons of carbon dioxide due to energy consumption, as well as waste, air pollution, and greenhouse gas generation (Corbett and Turco 7–8). Transportation on and off the set uses fuel, and explosions for special effects emit toxic chemicals as they erupt in polluting clouds of black smoke.

Still, some film studios and projects integrate environmental best practices into the process in effective ways. Corbett and Turco note recycling programs for both waste and set materials implemented by a few studios and television series, as well as attempts to implement "energy efficiency and green building practices" (9). For example, both *The Day After Tomorrow* (2004) and *Syriana* (2005) were carbon-neutral productions, in which carbon dioxide generated by machinery and vehicles during production is offset by the planting of trees or investing in climate-friendly technologies. The sets from both *The Matrix 2* (2003) and *The Matrix 3* (2003) were recycled, as well (9). In spite of these isolated cases, Corbett and Turco admit that "policies to mitigate environmental impacts remain to be implemented in a more systematic and transparent manner" (40).

Yet, progress has been made, even in publications like *The Hollywood Reporter* and *Variety* where there has been an increase in stories centered on the environmental content of productions (11). The Environmental Media Association Awards (EMA) now not only include categories related to content of films and television shows with environmental messages, but also (since 2004) include "a separate category for environmental 'process' improvements based on EMA's Green Seal checklist" (11). In 2006, *Ice Age: The Meltdown* (2006) and *An Inconvenient Truth* (2006) won awards for environmental content. Productions from *10,000 BC* (2006) to *The Dukes of Hazzard* (2006) won Green Seal Awards for best environmental practices, and corporate offices like Dualstar and United Talent Agency (UTA) won Green Seal Awards for Industry Corporate Offices.

The UCLA Institute Report notes that the number of environmental messages highlighted in films and film industry publications has increased significantly from 2002 to the present (Corbett and Turco 40), an increase we see as a hopeful reason to explore films in relation to the environmental messages they present. The film and television industry continues to contribute to environmental degradation, not only in Los Angeles but around the world. For example, Corbett and Turco note the "environmental impacts of filmmaking, which involve energy consumption, waste generation, air pollution, greenhouse gas emission, and physical disruptions on location" (5). Yet some of the films produced in Hollywood embrace a powerful environmental rhetoric that moves audience members to action.

Other films merely reflect changes in our culture, but we see these films as indicators of real changes in worldview and, as in the case of earlier films, a change at least in our own views as audience members. Contemporary popular environmentalist films like *Happy Feet* (2006), *Ice Age: The Meltdown*, and *The Day After Tomorrow* (2004) provide obvious ecological messages couched in comedy or melodrama. These films indicate a move in Hollywood toward "film vert," as David Ingram explains in his "Preface" (vii), toward a greening of Hollywood. In his *Green Screen*, Ingram "seeks to identify the complex ways in which both nonhuman nature and the built environment have been conceptualized in American culture, and to analyse [sic] the interplay of environmental ideologies at work in Hollywood movies, while ultimately keeping the debate over environmental politics open and provisional" (x). In other words, Ingram concentrates on overt environmental ideologies presented in the content of Hollywood movies, a focus we seek to build on in *On the Edge*.

Readings of recent ecological films, including *The Day After Tomorrow*, have emphasized their ecological messages, as Ingram does in *Green Screen*. Instead, our text attempts to illuminate ecological themes underpinning more obvious surface readings. *The Day After Tomorrow*, for example, argues vehemently that we need to combat global warming as quickly as possible to avoid the apocalyptic consequences on display in the film. But the film conveys this message in ways that many find so hyperbolized it becomes nearly laughable, because in the story, consequences some scientists argue might result from global warming arise almost instantaneously rather than over the course of decades or even centuries.

Critiques of *The Day After Tomorrow* point to its exaggerated claims regarding global warming not as a way to highlight the film's environmental ideologies but to highlight one of its biggest weaknesses. In fact, the environmental message is all but lost because it rests on such a poor interpretation of climatology. Instead, critics valorize the film's spectacular effects and faithful execution of the eco-disaster formula. A surface reading of the environmental politics on display in the film, then, deconstructs the film's environmental leanings.

For example, in an Internet Movie Database (IMDB) review of *The Day After Tomorrow*, Roger Ebert calls the film "silly" but "scary" and enjoys the adherence to formula while noting the lack of scientific grounding for the cataclysm on display:

> Of the science in this movie I have no opinion. I am sure global warming is real, and I regret that the Bush administration rejected the Kyoto Treaty, but I doubt that the cataclysm, if it comes, will come like this. It makes for a fun movie, though. Especially the parts where Americans become illegal immigrants in Mexico, and the vice president addresses the world via the Weather Channel. *The Day After Tomorrow* is ridiculous, yes, but sublimely ridiculous—and the special effects are stupendous.

Peter Bradshaw of *The Guardian* agrees, in another IMDB review of the film, asserting that:

> There are some great special effects showing New York under the waves, with hints of Spielberg's *AI* and, of course,

Planet of the Apes. You have to get through an awful lot of
terrible dialogue and acting, however, plus a lot of fantasti-
cally insincere waffle about the environment, to get to those
spectacular scenes. I felt the waters of silliness and boredom
close over my head.

These critiques of the bad science driving the ecological disasters in the film are supported by the multiple plot holes and revealing
mistakes in the film, including an impossible yet heroic journey led by
father and climatologist Jack Hall (Dennis Quaid), in which Jack and
two colleagues tramp through seventy miles of subzero blizzards in less
than two days' time.

Frederick and Mary Ann Brussat give a different reading, one that
may resonate with the wide range of viewers captivated by the film. In
a review in *Spirituality and Practice Magazine,* they assert, "Whatever you
think of the scientific explanations given for the phenomenon, the movie
deserves praise for making one thing very clear: humans, especially in the
industrialized countries, are the evil-doers who are responsible for the
destruction of the good earth." For the Brussats, ecological messages, no
matter how ineffectively they are presented, serve to educate the public,
showing viewers that humans have contributed to environmental devastation. Yet the Brussats use a religious envelope for couching their critique
and invoke evil and apocalyptic visions that, again, veil the environmental
politics of the film. They, like *The Day After Tomorrow,* hyperbolize their
assertions and, therefore, may invalidate them because they rest on irrational emotional arguments rather than rational and logical evidence.

Director Roland Emmerich's assertion that the film's climate-change
exaggerations were intended as a way to add to its dramatic appeal points
to another consequence of the "sublimely ridiculous" ecological disasters:
large box office sales. All of the 258 reviews on the IMDB admit that
the environmental catastrophes on display in the film are spectacularly
powerful, drawing audiences who crave the entertainment value that a
highly special effects-driven disaster movie provides. The special effects
paid off: *The Day After Tomorrow* grossed $528 million worldwide and
earned a stunning $85.8 million during its opening weekend.

For us, more appealing are ecological themes beyond the surface
meaning, themes that help us answer questions like, how is this eco-
disaster? And how is this eco-disaster film different from those that have
come before it? In ecological disaster films from the 1970s (for example,
Soylent Green [1973]) and eco-comic disaster films from the 1980s forward
(such as *Eight Legged Freaks* [2002]), disaster plots are driven by two different kinds of heroes: tragic pioneers and comic community builders.

The Day After Tomorrow, on the other hand, relies on a different kind of hero, one that arguably combines both tragic and comic characteristics. Our reading of *The Day After Tomorrow* attempts to make the idea of the new ecological (eco)-hero more transparent rather than rearticulating the obvious ecological messages on display in the film.

Both *The Day After Tomorrow* and *Children of Men* (2006) illustrate similar visions of the new eco-hero. In both films, heroic roles are filled not by tragic pioneers or even bumbling comic heroes, but by fathers seeking to save their own children or children they adopt as their own from an environment that humanity has made toxic in multiple ways. In *The Day After Tomorrow* Jack Hall attempts not only to save the world from global warming but to save his son Sam (Jake Gyllenhaal) from a flooded and frozen New York City library. In *Children of Men*, Theo Faron (Clive Owen) agrees to help an activist group transport Kee (Claire-Hope Ashite) and her soon-to-be-born child to a group of benevolent scientists on the coast, saving the only surviving baby in a dying world. In fact, in the film's opening, crowds of people mourn the loss of the youngest living person, a teenager murdered by a fan.

This new breed of eco-hero fails to fit in categories of tragic or comic heroes as defined by either Aristotle or Joseph W. Meeker. Meeker expands Aristotle's categories to include the natural world in his eco-critical approach to Classic literature. Meeker's tragic heroes in the natural world are the ecological pioneers, "the loners of the natural world, the tragic heroes who sacrifice themselves in satisfaction of mysterious inner commands which they alone can hear" ("The Comic Mode" 161). His comic heroes build community. Meeker argues that once ecosystems mature, heroic solitary pioneers become not only unnecessary but also subordinate to the group. In a mature or climax ecosystem, "it is the community itself that really matters, and it is likely to be an extremely durable community so long as balance is maintained among its many elements" (Meeker "The Comic Mode" 163). Comic heroes emerge from these climax ecosystems.

Jack Hall and Theo Faron serve the community while maintaining solitary quests, however. These two new eco-heroes combine the best qualities of the tragic and comic heroes to build a better world community while also saving children who are closest to them. Our first view of Jack Hall highlights his more traditionally heroic features. We first see him working as a climatologist at the North Pole, cutting samples out of the ice to study the impact of greenhouse gases on the environment. One of his colleagues continues to drill until the ice collapses, leaving a giant canyon into which he and a large vehicle fall, but Jack saves him and then jumps the canyon to retrieve the equipment on the other side.

Jack leaps back, makes it to the edge and hands his equipment to another colleague, but he too falls into the ice canyon and this time saves himself, grabbing the wall of ice with an ice pick.

This physically challenging feat allows Jack to serve as another kind of hero, one who is intellectually driven and seeks to save the world from the consequences of climate change he endured at the North Pole. Jack, looking like Al Gore in *An Inconvenient Truth*, explains global warming to a world delegation considering the Kyoto Accord and encourages all nations, including the United States, to approve it. In spite of these two daring acts—one physical and the other intellectual—Jack's many weaknesses are also on display in the film. When he returns from his latest Arctic trip, his house plants have nearly died, his son has failed calculus, and his ex-wife has lost faith in his ability even to pick up his son in time to get him to the airport for a scholastic bowl tournament.

These everyday events, however, are juxtaposed with images of worldwide eco-disaster. Professor Terry Rapson (Ian Holm), an oceanographer, discusses the possibility of a new ice age, and reports of its oncoming effects soon come in from all over the world. Pieces of ice fall from the sky in Tokyo, destroying cars and killing any people they strike. Snowstorms drift into New Delhi. Storms hit Jack's son Sam's flight, on its way to New York. And when Sam and his friend Laura (Emmy Rossum) reach the city, they watch from their taxi as flocks of birds migrate away from the city, seemingly disturbed by climate change.

More storms, golf ball-sized hail, and tornadoes hit Los Angeles. The LA tornadoes blow across highways, knocking over cars and rolling them down the road in a spectacular effect. A weather station building is cut in half vertically, so a reporter falls to his death when his office collapses, and only a janitor survives, opening a door to empty space left by the crashed rooms. All of these spectacular events are explained by Professor Rapson, who reveals that the delicate balance between fresh and salt waters has been destroyed, dramatically changing the North Atlantic current. When Jack enters Professor Rapson's data into his climate model, the results are devastating. According to their conclusions, the Earth will be in a full-scale ice age in six to eight weeks.

More disastrous events point to this upcoming ice age: frozen helicopter pilots in Scotland, and massive flooding in New York City with tidal waves catapulting down its broad avenues. Sam and the rest of his scholastic bowl friends make their way into the New York Public library, and the father/son narrative takes center stage. Sam finds a water-logged pay phone in the library, calls his father, and hears his father's promise: "Wait it out and burn what you can. I will come for you. I will come for you."

Figure I.1. *The Day After Tomorrow*: A wall of water in New York City.

The rest of the film revolves around Jack's quest to save his son, and his son's evolution into a new eco-hero like his father. Jack makes one more attempt to sway the government machinery into action and finally succeeds, packing up his arctic gear and taking off to save his son, with two colleagues, Jason Evans (Dash Mihok) and Frank Harris (Jay O. Sanders), tagging along. The way is treacherous, and their long walk from a crashed car near Philadelphia parallels the escape attempt made by a police officer and some followers from the library, with the freezing deaths of two followers aligning with the death of one of Jack's friends, Frank, when he falls through the glass ceiling of a mall.

Jack's ex-wife Lucy's (Sela Ward) heroism is highlighted after Frank's death, when an ambulance arrives to save her and a young patient, Peter, whom she has refused to leave alone. The family melodrama becomes the main focus until the film's end, even though it is occasionally broken with more global concerns, like the death of the President and the fate of American refugees in Mexico. So after Lucy's heroic act, it comes as no surprise that Sam too might act heroically. He has shown some signs of heroism when he grabs Laura and drags her into the library and away from the tidal wave, but he gains cunning when a cut on Laura's leg festers and penicillin is needed. With some ingenuity, Sam makes snowshoes out of chair seats and makes his way toward a Russian ship that has somehow drifted up the street in front of the library. He and two friends, Brian (Arjay Smith) and J.D. (Austin Nichols), fight off wolves, the cold, and an oncoming vortex to gather penicillin and food, which they drag back to the library in spite of J.D.'s bite wounds.

Then, in a blatant link between father and son, Sam and his father, Jack, escape the vortex into the door of their shelters at the same time,

Figure I.2. *The Day After Tomorrow*: New York harbor after global warming's aftermath.

closing the doors behind them with an almost simultaneous slam. Jack has found warmth with fires in a Wendy's restaurant; Sam in a library reading room. Jack explains, as he tramps back out into the cold, "I made my son a promise. I'm going to keep it," and the storm dissipates over North America, just in time for Jack and Jason to find the library and the heated inner room where Sam and a few stragglers remain. "Who is that?" Laura asks. And Sam tells them, "My father. You found us." "Of course I did," Jack replies, and a helicopter saves them and other New York survivors waving their arms wildly on the roofs of high rises. The film ends with images of the Earth from a space station—"I've never seen the air so clear," one of the astronauts exclaims.

Figure I.3. *The Day After Tomorrow*: New eco-hero saves family.

And the eco-drama ends, with father and son reunited (and possibly husband and wife). The eco-disaster looks like most disaster films in every way other than the way the image of the hero is constructed. In *The Day After Tomorrow*, the hero is a true eco-hero, attempting to save the world from environmental disaster, but his most heroic act is localized and less than self-sacrificial. Jack makes his heroic journey not to save the world—as we might expect an eco-hero and a climatologist to do—but to save his son. And both Lucy and Sam act heroically for similar reasons—to save the individuals they love, not the world, the nation, or even the community.

In *Children of Men*, Theo transports Kee to a haven at sea to save her child and, ultimately, the world. But Theo chooses to act because his ex-wife, Julian Taylor (Julianne Moore), reminds him of the loving family life they shared when his own son lived. In *Children of Men*, both mother (Julian) and father (Theo) die during the undertaking, but our last glimpse of life in the movie shows us Kee and her baby floating in a boat while a ship in the distance comes closer to save her. The focus is local rather than global in this well-shot film, with long-takes emphasizing the individualized perspective of the hero and his acts.

None of these heroes act like pioneers attempting to conquer an opponent, even if that opponent is the environment or an ecological disaster. They don't fight against the disaster but against the forces that caused it. And they fight most intensely not for all those affected by the disaster—as do most eco-heroes—but only for sons, friends, and a helpless child. The new eco-hero is not a tragic pioneer who sacrifices him or herself for a species. Nor is this hero a comic hero who bumbles and succeeds only communally. This hero acts alone, but only at a local level, not seeking control of a landscape or species but seeking to save new and renewed relationships. This local view corresponds to the ecocritical approach we take with other environmental themes represented in films from 1896 to the present. Representatives of what David Ingram calls film vert, with blatantly environmental messages, are only a small sample of films with possible ecological themes.

In *On the Edge: Ecology and Popular Film* we look at narrative films organized around a variety of themes but all driven by either intentional or unintentional environmental messages as products of a complex cultural context that includes ecology. Popular narrative movies respond to the culture in which they are embedded—they also contribute to that same culture, even in relation to the environment. To reveal representations of environmentalist issues sometimes obscured by spectacle, filmic technology, and conflicting messages, we read a selection of films in relation to a variety of what we call eco-critical readings. Our selection is limited and opens up opportunities for further readings of multimedia, including television and advertising. Here, however, as a way to demonstrate the possible scope of eco-critical film studies, we focus our readings on popular films that correspond with the following wide-ranging environmental themes: the spectacular, environmental politics, eco-terrorism, reconstructing underground space, ecology and home, tragic eco-heroes, comic eco-heroes, urban street-racing culture, film ecology, and evolutionary narratives, themes we see as not only far-reaching but ongoing.

Our eco-critical lens responds to analyses of eco-criticism Lawrence Buell outlines in his *The Future of Environmental Criticism*. This approach aligns most closely with what Buell defines as second-wave inquiry in eco-criticism:

> the exegesis of environmental subtexts through historical and critical analyses that employ ready-to-hand analytical tools of the trade together with less familiar ones eclectically derived from other disciplinary bailiwicks and . . . the identification or reinterpretation of such thematic configurations as pastoral, eco-apocalypticism, and environmental racism. (130)

This project examines representations of nature in mainstream film, broadens definitions of nature writing to include film, and reads a selection of films embracing a variety of themes. Our work is far from exhaustive. The films we have chosen primarily illustrate the broad range of themes available for such a reading. Our eco-critical approach reads movies in relation to themes, but it also examines each film's context in a localized and aesthetic way.

Most eco-critics valorize an essential view of nature and the natural world, a view that excludes a situated post-modern view of nature. "Postmodern Natures," views of nature that suggest its representation is relative, are often seen as problematic. In *Reinventing Nature?* for example, the majority of the articles suggest that we should fear the consequences of viewing nature through a postmodern lens. Gary Lease's introduction asserts that "Postmodern answers, to date, have ignored certain actors and obscured certain questions" (vii). Donald Worster's "Nature and the Disorder of History," argues that postmodern historians are excessively relativistic and that they distort reality. N. Katherine Hayles' "Searching for Common Ground" insists that the "deconstructionist paradigm, if accepted broadly, would . . . destroy environmentalism, since the environment is just a social construction" (viii). And Stephen R. Kellert's

"Concepts of Nature East and West" asserts that "The deconstructionist notion that all cultural perspectives of nature possess equal values is both biologically misguided and socially dangerous" (103).

Eco-critics suggest that immersing perceptions of nature in their historical context would "distort reality." In fact, any form of relativism—viewing nature relative to history, culture, or individual perceptions—is seen as problematic by many eco-critics. For these eco-critics, the consequences of viewing nature and the natural through a postmodern lens become frightening because such a perspective paralyzes the viewer, eradicating any possibility of socially or environmentally conscious activism. These eco-critics, then, take an ahistorical view of nature.

Eco-critics like Patrick Murphy and Dana Phillips argue that relative views of nature and its representations need not silence nature. By empowering nature at the local, culturally and historically situated, level, its essential value can be valorized. Dana Phillips describes a movement from modernist dualistic thought to a postmodern world of representation (205, 6). Patrick Murphy contends in a 1999 *PMLA* Forum that in a postmodern eco-criticism, "Environments . . . are seen instead as a fundamental feature of the ideological horizons of literary works" (1099). Dana Phillips' view of postmodernism, unlike that espoused in either the Western Literary Association discussion or the *Reinventing Nature?* anthology, does not lead to a lack of agency or inability to take an activist stance toward the environment. Instead, Phillips concludes in his "Is Nature Necessary?" that postmodern thought offers a way to "green our society" from a local level. Our approach looks to both Buell and Phillips for a way to reveal environmental themes and aesthetics obscured by the technology presenting them.

A brief reading of a Warner Brothers short, Goofy Gophers and the *Lumber Jerks* (1955), demonstrates how we might apply such a localized postmodern approach to less blatantly ecological media. This seven-minute cartoon lacks the obvious environmental melodrama found in *The Day After Tomorrow* or *An Inconvenient Truth*. Yet it gains resonance as an eco-cartoon when it and its production are historicized and culturally situated. *Lumber Jerks* may stem from an attitude in 1950s America that Norman M. Klein calls "Consumer Cubism" (210), "an obsession with the efficient, angular plan." The faster a consumer could gain access to goods, the better. Klein asserts that "individualism and democracy were being redefined in terms of consumer desire. The homogeneous surface, open and 'free,' came to stand in for America's imperium" (210). These attitudes were reflected in both narrative and aesthetics of some cartoons after 1954.

Lumber Jerks first focuses on saving one tree in a forest. Two cheerful gophers, Mac and Tosh, scurry toward their home, but when they

Figure I.4. *Lumber Jerks* (1954): The Goofy Gophers' home is destroyed.

go up into the hollow of their tree, they find it has been cut down and carried away. The two gophers take steps to retrieve their tree—what they call their property—tracking it to a river and then picking it out of the hundreds of logs floating on the water. They climb on their tree and row away but cannot fight the current and nearly go over a waterfall. Once they escape, one gopher exclaims, "I'm bushed," and the two fall asleep, waking up only after entering a lumber mill and living through a saw blade cutting their tree trunk in two.

After seeing the devastation around them, the gophers state the obvious about the repercussions of consumerism. One of the gophers explains, "It looks like they are bent on the destruction of our forests," and the scene shifts to the mill's workings. One "shot" shows trees ground into sawdust being made into artificial fireplace logs. Another shows an entire tree being "sharpened" to produce one toothpick. Then the gophers discover what had happened to their own tree: "They're going to make furniture out of our tree," states one of the gophers.

But the idea of ownership of consumer goods extends to the gophers and their tree home. They wish to reclaim their property, their own possession, so the other gopher exclaims, "That is definitely our property. We must think of a way to repossess it." The gophers siphon the gas out of the furniture truck and, when it breaks down, "steal" their tree's furniture from the truck. They build a tree house with the furniture, adding branches for good measure and topping the tree off with a television set. The cartoon ends with one of the gophers telling the other, "Isn't our home much better than it was before . . . [we have] Television . . . and just think how much better it will be with electricity!" Because the gophers view their tree home as a possession not unlike the furniture produced from its wood, they seem pleased with their "repossession." But the enviro-toon leaves viewers feeling ambivalent about the price of progress.

Lumber Jerks combines a critique of consumerism with a statement about its source—natural wilderness—but it also endorses interdependence between humans and the natural world (and between progress and conservation), at least to the extent that furniture built from a tree trunk can return to the forest as the Goofy Gophers' home. With its overt focus on consumerism, however, the cartoon goes further. It leaves viewers questioning the Goofy Gophers' conclusion: "Isn't our house much better than it was before?"

Figure I.5. *Lumber Jerks*: The gophers' new home built from lumber mill furniture.

As Klein suggests in his discussion of Tex Avery's *The House of To-morrow* (1949), *The Car of Tomorrow* (1951), and *Farm of Tomorrow* (1954), consumers may become "victimized by the very machines that promise an easier, more extravagant life" (211). After all, the consumer goods that make up the trunk of one tree were built from the trees of an entire forest. *Lumber Jerks*, especially, reflects an increasing ambivalence toward technology and post–World War II progress in an increasingly more complex (and anxiety-ridden) nuclear age. Here the Goofy Gophers successfully negotiate between the wonders of modernism and its impact on both natural and human worlds. But it's a negotiation that's impossible in the world outside cartoons. Still, Klein's argument that "cartoons [are] ever the barometer of changes in entertainment" (211) may also include changes in mainstream American culture. Unlike cartoons that maintain the nature/culture binary or those that seek to reconcile it through the intervention of a controller, classic shorts that critique our treatment of the natural world respond explicitly to changes in the American cultural context and illustrate an ambivalence toward modernism and its ramifications.

The period during and after World War II is commonly associated with a drive for technological advancement, from constructing needed military equipment during the war to building highways and freeways and entering the space race after the war ended (See Rothman, *Saving the Planet* and Shabecoff, *Fierce Green Fire*). There were noteworthy inclinations toward conservation prior to World War II, such as Teddy Roosevelt's creation of the National Park System and Franklin Delano Roosevelt's New Deal programs, and noteworthy exceptions after World War II such as William Vogt's best-selling conservation book *Road to Survival* and Fairfield Osborn's book *Our Plundered Planet*, which came out in 1948. Aldo Leopold's *Sand County Almanac* was published a year later and proved to be one of the most influential eco-works ever written. Leopold's work had a positive influence on both Supreme Court Justice William O. Douglas and Secretary of the Interior Bruce Babbitt. Douglas began protesting what he saw as exploitation of nature as early as 1954, when he successfully opposed the building of a proposed highway that would have destroyed the Chesapeake and Ohio Canal and its towpath. Babbitt, who served under President Clinton, is still a tireless advocate of environmental issues, but he traces the origin of his stances to Leopold's 1949 *Sand County Almanac* in the preface to the 2000 edition he wrote in memory of Leopold and in honor of Leopold's work for the conservation movement.

After World War II, Americans gained enough economic stability to not only purchase cars in record numbers but also use them for traveling across the United States on cross-country highways like Routes 40 and 66. Americans took to the road, towing trailers behind them, so they could experience some of the nature they had left behind when they moved to the cities and concrete suburbs surrounding them. According to Rothman, Americans increasingly vacationed in national parks and forests after 1945. And, "as more of them vacationed, exemplified by record numbers of visitors at Grand Canyon National Park each month after August 1945, they had an impact on the natural world that soon caused them to take notice" (85–86). Rothman asserts that "what Americans found in many of their national parks and forests shocked them: decrepit and outdated campgrounds, garbage piled high, and a lack of facilities and staff to manage them" (86).

Vacationing Americans noticed the devastation in national parks and forests, however the Wilderness Act that served to protect and preserve them wasn't passed until 1964, almost 20 years after the end of the war. Alexander Wilson argues that Americans in the late 1940s and 1950s saw "the open road [as] a metaphor for progress in the U.S. and for the cultural taming of the American Wilderness" (34). Wilson even suggests that "What we saw out the window of a speeding car . . . was the future itself" (34). These views of nature through the window of a car—or even the window of a camper in a national park—skewed Americans' vision of the natural world. Such confusion between seeking pristine nature and embracing progress at any cost complicated ideological views of the environment and environmentalism. In "Conservation Esthetic [sic]," a section of his *Sand County Almanac*, Aldo Leopold describes late 1940s' views of nature and wildlife recreation as a destructive search for meaning in an altered "natural" world:

> The automobile . . . has made scarce in the hinterlands something once abundant on the back forty. But that something must nevertheless be found. Like ions shot from the sun, the week-enders radiate from every town, generating heat and friction as they go. . . . Advertisements on rock and rill confide to all and sundry the whereabouts of new retreats, landscapes, hunting-grounds, fishing-lakes just beyond those recently overrun. Bureaus build roads into new hinterlands, then buy more hinterlands to absorb the exodus accelerated by the roads. A gadget industry pads the bumps against nature-in-the-raw. . . . And now, to cap the pyramid of banalities, the trailer. To him who seeks in the woods and mountains only those things obtainable from travel or golf, the present situation is tolerable. But to him who seeks something more, recreation has become a self-destructive process of seeking but never quite finding, a major frustration of mechanized society. (165–66).

The *Lumber Jerks* illustrates the consequences of rampant consumerism that serves as a sign of progress—devastation of the natural world. Instead of looking at nature from the skewed perspective of a speeding car, this cartoon shows us what's wrong with what Wilson calls "the cultural taming of the American Wilderness" (34) and provides real reasons for embracing Aldo Leopold's conservation esthetic [sic]. Post–World War II optimism faded quickly because of similar binaries—this time between those that strengthened the Cold War and fostered a skepticism toward "progress" that diminished the power of individuals. These changing attitudes in the United States had an impact on cartoons after World War II, as well as on the cartoon industry itself. In 1948, according to Klein, the studio system changed. Studios were no longer allowed to maintain vertical monopolies, so their theater chains were sold out, and film (and cartoon) distribution was transferred to "independent jobbers" (206).

By 1953, Jack Warner "ordered the animation units [temporarily] to close down, to make way for 3D movies" (Klein 206). Television became a new medium, and fewer movie screens were available for audiences. All of these factors led to what Klein calls a "stripped-down" version of cartoons. Klein argues that a "mixture of ebullience and paranoia can be seen very clearly in fifties cartoons, in the stories and the graphics" (207). According to Klein, this mixture "is particularly evident in cartoons about consumer life" (207).

A rich reading of *Lumber Jerks* must take into account all of these elements, structural and aesthetic, historical, ideological, and technological. The environmentalist message in the cartoon, however, gains strength for us because it is not explicitly environmentalist. In fact, a straight reading of the cartoon might suggest that modernism has improved the lives of these goofy gophers.

This multifaceted approach also gains strength when juxtaposed with the film industry itself. The technology necessary to produce films—even those with an environmental bent—conflicts with the environmental messages sometimes on display. Such a contradiction exists even in film productions of blatantly environmentalist films like *An Inconvenient Truth* or *Happy Feet*. Instead of erasing or obscuring the technology behind all the films discussed here, this text rests on the belief that, like humanity itself, the film industry both uses and critiques technologies that potentially abuse nature. In a sense, this text offers a space to explore what happens when nature serves as the center of an analysis of a medium (film) that has traditionally been aligned with nature's opposite, technology. Such contradictions hold true in relation to many of the binaries critiqued in film—sexuality, race, gender, class, among others. Instead of denying this conflict, we suggest it calls for further exploration.

This book examines films foregrounding multiple environmental themes. Chapter 1, "Ecology and Spectacle in *Oil Wells of Baku: Close View*: The First Eco-Disaster Film?," explores how the spectacular fires on display in oil well fire films from as early as 1896 sometimes obscure the environmental disaster on the screen. Chapter 2, "Environmental Politics: Pare Lorentz's *The River* and the Tennessee Valley Authority," offers a reading of the environmental politics surrounding New Deal Tennessee Valley Authority dam projects along the Tennessee River as they are valorized in *The River* (1936) and *Wild River* (1960). Chapter 3, "Reconstructing Underground Urban Space in *Dark Days*," explores the complex structure of a 2000 narrative documentary built on a new idea of progress, this time in New York City's Amtrak tunnels where homeless people have established and constructed homes. Chapter 4, "Ecology, Place, and Home in *Dark City*: Is It Our Nature to Live in the Dark?" provides a space in which to explore a 1998 multi-genre film that seeks to determine the best ecology for human and nonhuman life.

Chapter 5, "Environmental Nostalgia and The Tragic Eco-Hero: The Case of *Soylent Green* and the 1970s Eco-Disaster Film," highlights the tragic eco-hero in a blatantly environmental film whose rhetoric rests on nostalgia. Chapter 6, "The Comic Eco-Hero: Spoofing Eco-Disaster in *Eight Legged Freaks*," explores how images of the eco-hero have changed as our cultural context has evolved to allow us to laugh at the results of toxic waste dumping meant to both satirize and spoof serious science fiction films like *Them!* (1954).

Chapter 7, "Eco-Terrorism in Film: *Pale Rider* and the Revenge Cycle," discusses the effectiveness of eco-terrorist techniques as a way to combat corporate hydraulic mining practices. Chapter 8, "Car Culture and the Transformation of the American Landscape in *The Fast and the Furious*," highlights transformations of already de-naturalized urban landscapes in contemporary inner-city car-racing films. Chapter 9, "Film Ecology: Simulated Construction and Destruction in *Hooper*," looks at both filmic representations of nature and environmental effects of film production itself. And Chapter 10, "Apocalypse as a 'Return to Normality' in *28 Days Later* and *28 Weeks Later*," expands on notions of the eco-hero and examines two different evolutionary narratives, one tragic and the other comic.

We conclude our book with a reading of *An Inconvenient Truth* as a film not unlike *Soylent Green*, since its rhetoric is also driven by differing versions of nostalgia. Together, these chapters offer multiple thematic readings of potentially environmental films.

Ecology and Spectacle in
Oil Wells of Baku: Close View

The First Eco-Disaster Film?

Blazing oil gushers make marvelous cinematographic material . . . only cinema can capture the thick oil stream bursting forth like a fiery monster. Only cinema can display such an awesome inferno in its terrifying beauty and majesty.

—Rahman Badalov, "Oil, Revolution, and Cinema," 1997

W HEN BERTRAND TAVERNIER asserts that an 1896 Lumière Brothers' film, *Oil Wells of Baku: Close View*, "may be the first ecological film ever made" (*The Lumière Brothers' First Films*), he is, to a certain extent, reading the footage of burning oil wells from an eco-critical perspective. The film invites such a reading, one that centers on environmental concerns, because of what looks like devastating effects of drilling for oil. This thirty-six second "view," shot by Kamill Serf with a stationary camera, shows huge flames and black smoke streaming from burning oil wells in Baku, Azerbaijan, seemingly sure signs of environmental disaster. But disaster looks more like spectacle in this closely shot scene, and both Serf and the film's viewers serve as attentive spectators.

Although the camera never moves during the film, the vibrant image it captures also captures its viewers.

The film appears to be strategically framed. The oil wells in the frame look like miniatures until the immensity of the oil derricks is emphasized by a human figure moving in the front of the center well. This figure looks minuscule as it walks away from the center derrick and out of the frame of the shot. The two tall derricks in the view behind the tiny striding male figure show us that the view was shot from a distance. This extreme long shot accentuates the power of both the tall derricks and the rising flames and smoke, smoke that darkens into the distance from the right side of the frame. We see enormous flames shoot up and clouds of heavy black smoke plume from the fire, but more smoke comes from similar oil well fires offscreen. To the right of the center derrick, as far away as the horizon line, two blazes flame up from what look like vertical pipes. Gray and black smoke flows out of the fires in a plume that covers the sky.

The enormity of these flaming plumes mesmerizes because their powerful blaze shocks us. But the raging flames also bring forth images of phoenixes rising from the flames and hearths stoked by Hestia, broaching the question, "Is this beautiful?" Within the context of our Western culture, such a scene looks fabulous because it is based in a mythology in which fire and its power are associated with beautiful rebirth.

The center derrick serves as the focus of the shot. This derrick is placed inside an enormous pit, as if to capture any excess oil flow. A platform connects the derrick to its outside enclosure and what looks like a pipeline to transport oil from these interconnected wells. A roofed building serves as the derrick's foundation. In front of the derrick are what look like the frames of new derricks under construction. Vertical pipes that resemble bare trees pop up in every corner of the shot, usually in rows of four or five. A set of wooden stairs leads up to a scaffold on the left side of the center derrick. The second completed derrick sits on flat ground, with no scaffold—and only an enclosed building at its bottom. The center derrick, though, sets off the tall derrick to the left and the gray and black smoke to the right. The left derrick hides the source of the fire that bursts out from behind it. This fire is just one of three fires in the view: one to the left of center, the other two to the right and offscreen. Smoke from the fires fills the background in the view.

All this smoke and uncontrolled fire supports Tavernier's assertion of this as an eco-disaster film. Such a disaster, from a current point of view, begs for an ecological reading. Today we have become committed to considering the consequences of uncontrolled oil well fires and gushers, and the fire and smoke look destructive to humans and their environment. More than just spectacle, these burning oil fields, these obfuscating clouds of smoke, this general conflagration of the natural world, signify humans' rape of the landscape for personal gain—oil at any price to the natural world.

But the figure walking in front of the derricks suggests another reading altogether. He moves without the urgency an ecological reading might spur. In fact, he walks in front of the derricks and the burning oil fields with quite a normal gait, as if he's unconcerned about anything. We'll see this again in two films shot one hundred years later: David Douglas's *Fires of Kuwait* and Werner Herzog's *Lessons of Darkness* (both 1992). But as the Lumières' brief film offers no explanation for its fires, nor does its title: *Oil Wells of Baku: Close View*, it leaves today's viewers wondering, is this a picture of business as usual or an account of eco-disaster?

It is possible, then, to be caught in a conundrum with a film like this, forced to struggle in uncertainty as to whether the extremity of the screen depiction is meant to say something about our environment and our way of living in it, or merely show with a certain casualness the world as received.

What the Lumière view "means" may be different now than it was in the late 1890s, but spectacular events continue to overpower environmental statements on film. So, what does the view tell us about what we would now call our "concerns about nature"? And what did the view tell its original viewers? This is an issue, to be sure, that has itself changed in meaning since the beginning of the twentieth century and that has come to have a principal focus for scholars, citizens, and viewers of entertainment today. Also, what sets this view—comprising one of the first films produced—apart from other images of fires in Baku found in photographs, on postcards, and in narrative descriptions found in texts? When (if ever) does the destruction "wrought" by gushing oil wells—"monsters," according to explorer and historian Abraham V. W. Jackson (40)—become seen as something other than a "spectacle" "surpassed only by the awful grandeur when fire adds terror to the scene" (40)?

When, in other words, does a burning oil well gain the status of ecological disaster? When does it come to be perceived that the costs of such flames include not only money and human lives but also nature? This brief view can certainly be read as stating a message, and this more powerfully than did photographs, postcards, and textbooks that came before it, but if we are to presume there is a message here, that message at first is subsumed by its context. That is, the spectacular event serves as the context of a possible environmental message—oil well fires and gushers not only waste resources; they also destroy the surrounding ecology. Yet, this view, like that in later films highlighting oil-driven eco-disasters, begs a question: How does disaster come to be turned into a spectacular image that leaves spectators struck more with awe than with concern?

Baku

Oil production in the region around Baku goes back to Hammurabi and the Babylonian Dynasty—and so, it appears, do perspectives that see oil well gushers and fires as spectacle. According to Sarah Searight, "Baku, on the sandy south-west shore of the Caspian Sea, has been renowned for its oil for some 3,000 years" (46). Evidence from Herodotus and Vitruvius demonstrates that crude oil (bitumen) from around Baku was being used as "mortar in the walls of Babylon" and "as a binding agent, mixed with clay" (Searight 46). In 700–600 BC, "oil was being extracted for use in everyday life, both for medicinal purposes and for heating and lighting in homes. 'Fuel oil' was known for being transported from Absheron Peninsula (where Baku is located) to Iran, Iraq, and India" (46). Plutarch, as well, talks about oil in northern Iraq. But "the oil and gas of the Absheron peninsula, on the southern side of which lies Baku, was sufficiently well known for a Zoroastrian fire temple [a temple built to worship spectacular oil fires] to be built at least 2,500 years ago over a gas seepage at Surakhany" (Searight 46). The fire temple remained in Baku as late as 1911, when Jackson published his *The Oil Fields and The Fire Temple of Baku*, a reminder of the oil fields that prompted the temple, where an eternal flame shone, fueled by the oil below it until, according to Jackson, the oil boom drained the reserves below the temple (40). The praise worshippers brought to this flame parallels Jackson's awe at the sight of such a magnificent spectacle as a burning oil well.

Oil from the Absheron Peninsula provided resources for everyday life in the region, but it also became a source of revenue—indeed, of prosperity—especially in the late nineteenth century when the Nobel family of Sweden invested in the region. Under their auspices beginning in 1874, the oil fields at Baku flourished. According to an 1882 statement by Ludwig Nobel, "Russia could light all the world, lubricate all the world, and paint all the world" (quoted in Searight 47). Hazards like heavy smoke from kerosene refineries and gushing oil wells did not decrease economic gains for the Nobel family and smaller oil producers like Viktor Ragozin, and, again, were seen more as spectacle than disaster. Instead, Baku's smaller oil producers formed the Baku Petroleum Association and sought "continued development of the industry" (McKay 613), so that, as Searight argues, "pollution seemed a small price to pay" (47).

In fact, hazards in the oil field translated into environmental damage that looks horrific by today's standards. According to Searight, "when drills reached the deeper strata, violent eruptions of gas, oil and sand were sometimes sent sky high," creating a gusher (47). Searight explains, "In 1886 a particularly ferocious gusher in Bibi-Eilat, Baku's richest field, is said to have produced more oil in one day than all the rest of the world's wells put together" (47). Gushers spewing out tons of oil were common in late nineteenth-century Baku. And in 1896, the year *Oil Wells at Baku: Close View* was shot, "Another well produced close to 12 million poods (60 million gallons), and engineers could not get it under control for 15 days. Most of the oil flowed into the Caspian Sea because there were no adequate means to contain it" ("The Development of the Oil and Gas Industry of Azerbaijan"). Such spillage would have destroyed aquatic ecosystems and inhibited aviary reproduction along the coast. Yet soon after the gusher, oil production, transporting, and refining increased by thousands of poods with little concern for the environmental consequences of either oil gushers or fires. The spewing turned the area around oil wells and refineries into "Black Town," a town still black as late as the 1980s when oil spillage and overuse of oil resources still caused "sand storms and flies" (Searight 48).

This disregard for environmental consequences continued into the twentieth century. When explorer and historian Abraham V. W. Jackson visited the oil fields near Baku around 1910, his primary concern regarding oil as pollutant seemed to be sartorial. Jackson explains, "On all occasions when visiting the petroleum fields it is advisable to wear old clothes." When wells gush, he goes on, they "fill [. . .] the air with a deluging rain from whose greasy downpour there was no escape." In spite of Jackson's warning, he describes each well as "a source of revenue that is a fortune" and uses adjectives like "thrilling" to describe gushing wells. For Jackson, the main challenge with gushers related to loss of revenue: "Sometimes the boring [drills] strike 'fountains,' and then a tremendous 'spouter' is the result, belching up its concealed contents with the force of a geyser, and perhaps bringing ruin instead of fortune to its owner unless the giant can be speedily throttled and gagged" (Jackson 40).

Jackson compares gushers to monsters and geysers, but the description he provides emphasizes their sublime rather than their destructive force. The wells, whether burning or gushing, may seem "awful," but they are mostly seen as a magnificent "spectacle." Although unavailable for viewing, the photographs and film footage from A. H. Mishon, a French photographer and cinematographer who lived in Baku for twenty-five years, included footage of some of these oil fields (footage that still exists was shown in France in 1995, according to Aydin Kazimzada, director of Azerbaijan's Cinema Museum). Kazimzada states that "from 1879 to 1905 [Mishon] documented landscapes, episodes from oil extraction, the refining process, as well as the oil gushers' eruptions and terrifying fires that broke out in the oil fields." Writing in 1997 about Mishon's footage of fires in 1898, Kazimzada called the oil field fires "terrifying," raising us to an alertness entirely absent from the person in *Oil Wells of Baku: Close View*, who appears blithely unconcerned with them.

A decade after both the Lumières' oil fire film (with Kamill Serf as cinematographer) and Mishon's, environmental damage caused by gushing or burning oil wells was still being ignored. Jackson's book notes attempts made to protect Baku oil derricks (and what he calls their "precious liquid") from fire, but those preservation attempts are based on economic rather than environmental concerns. These pyramidal wooden structures were "covered with gypsolite or iron plating as a protection against fire," to save the oil reserves, "one of the richest articles of commerce," according to Jackson (39). Yet, as Searight asserts, despite these precautions, in late nineteenth-century Baku, "The dense forest of tall, wooden oil-soaked derricks resulted in frequent fires, especially since everyone smoked heavily." In the 1880s, British journalist Charles Marvin explained that over Baku "hung a dense cloud of smoke and long before you reach it you perceive the all-pervading smell of oil, which you will breathe everywhere and taste in everything so long as you remain in Baku" (quoted in Searight 47). According to Searight, "Pollution seemed a small price to pay" to have such a bounty from oil production (49). In 1890, George Curzon described Baku as "a town of crude and undigested wealth" (quoted in Searight 49). The only contemporary negative consequence of fires and gushers that Searight (writing in 2000) notes, however, is their impact on revenue: "too many gushers depressed the price of oil, thereby adding to the economic and political fragility of Baku" (47).

The Baku of the 1890s has been compared to an American frontier town, with oil instead of gold inviting outsiders to compete for economic gain. Depressed prices exacerbated racial and political discord brought on by this influx of foreigners.

Jackson's first description of Baku after entering its "handsome station" also at first suggests that around 1911 pollution was viewed in a negative light. According to Jackson,

> Oil is in the air one breathes, in one's nostrils, in one's eyes, in the water of the morning bath . . . , in one's starched linen— everywhere. . . . The very dust of the streets is impregnated by the petroleum with which they are sprinkled; the soil of the

home garden is charged with oil; and if flowers are really to thrive, it is said that earth must be imported from Lankuran farther down on the Caspian. (25–26)

But Jackson's impulse is to defend the town's drinking water and connect oil to prosperity in the region rather than to destruction of the environment. Immediately after what amounts to a criticism of the town, he continues, "The busy wheels of commerce that roll out of Baku are lubricated with the native product; the engines and steamers are propelled by it; the coffers of the great petroleum companies are filled with it; and the bourse of the city's exchequer is governed by its rise and fall." Jackson "look[s] back with pleasure to each visit" to Baku and says he "shall gladly welcome the chance to see this busy metropolis again if another opportunity takes me to the Caspian" (25, 26, 27). Although journalists such as Marvin and historians such as Jackson do take note of the pollution produced by the oil wells, Jackson, especially, interprets smoke, dirt, and grease as necessary annoyances that are outweighed by the economic boom that oil has provided Baku and the Azerbaijan region.

Spectacular Destruction

Oil Wells of Baku captures on film the exact sort of fire noted by Jackson, as well as smoke from burning oil wells described by both Jackson and Marvin, with the addition of "sensuous elaboration" that, as Susan Sontag argues, filmic representations provide (212). The view also reflects the same purely fiduciary perspective on oil production and its consequences—that because oil catalyzes an economic boom in the region, pollution and debris are a small price to pay. The nonchalant figure in the Lumière view acts as if the fire and smoke caught on film are quotidian, the same reaction Jackson has when re-entering Baku's oil-covered streets and breathing its smoke-filled air a decade later. At least as late as 1911, most Westerners saw burning oil derricks and gushing wells as signs of progress, not ecological disaster.

Most essentially, however, *Oil Wells of Baku* is a film, a construction that works by capturing a spectacle for a viewing public. The 1896 Lumière *View* may have been the first film of Baku's oil well fires, but many others followed: *Fire at the Oil Gusher in Bibi-Heybat* (1898), *White City/Black City* (1908), *In the Realm of Oil and Millions* (1916), and *Symphony of Oil* (1933) to name a few, all of which caught oil fires, like flaming monsters, as centerpieces in one way or another (see Kazimzada and Badalov). All filmic displays of burning oil highlight their spectacular—if terrifying—effects, even if these fires are shot for purposes other than entertainment. Yet the rhetoric of entertainment provides a license for especially extravagant displays, as, for instance, in *Cimarron* (1931), *Spoilers of the Plains* (1951), *Comes a Horseman* (1978), and *Jarhead* (2005). As museum curator Rahman Badalov explains, "Blazing oil gushers make marvelous cinematographic material . . . only cinema can capture the thick oil stream bursting forth like a fiery monster. Only cinema can display such an awesome inferno in its terrifying beauty and majesty."

Later filmic representations of oil gushers and fires sometimes achieve a spectacular quality without invoking the glory of wealth. Documentary and newsreel footage of oil fires during World War II, for example, foregrounds loss of fuel and supplies more than profit. The film series *WWII Road to Victory* (1941–1945) highlights battles won by both the Allies and their enemies. Some of these films show us the frequency of oil fires during the World War II, from those on allied ships and oil tankers devastated by the Germans in *Commerce Raiders* (1940) and *U Boat War* (1940–1941) to the German/Rumanian oil fields destroyed by allied bombers in *Bombing of Ploesti* (1943). Even on newsreel film, oil fires erupt with the same hot flames and black smoke as in *Oil Wells of Baku*, but now they are in color, presaging the kind of electrifying aesthetic vision presented in such contemporary films as *Jarhead*. None of these films mentions loss of oil profits, because for World War II combatants, oil meant fuel for military vehicles, not money. Yet the images remain spectacular. Flames flaring up from oil tankers and bombed oil fields provide us with violent and mesmerizing views, especially since film footage of oil fires tends to be shot from above. Looking down on erupting fires distances us from them and enhances their monstrous, yet spectacular, power. In *Jarhead*, the angle is reversed, since the oil has become rain that is blackly misting soldiers as they slog through the Kuwaiti desert.

Although both the oil well fire films from Baku and the documentary footage of exploding oil tankers and fields from World War II are unconstructed, perhaps only to seize and record actual events, they still play on what Nick Browne calls the "rhetoric of the spectacular." Browne asserts that "formally, the rhetorical parameters of the spectacular work by modulation of cinematic scale, repetition, and perspective." Here, filmed oil well fires take on spectacular qualities when they assume the large-scale dimensions that such fires produce, when they are shot repeatedly or for a long duration, and when they are shot from an angle that emphasizes the fires' force. Considerable documentary footage we viewed does all of these things without any creative special effects. According to Browne, the goal of spectacular effects in action films like the *Die Hard* and *Batman* series (1988–2007; 1989–2008) is to "recreate [an event] experientially, namely in a mode that displays the force, that is the physics of the event, but not its meaning." But *Oil Wells of Baku*, too, hardly an action film, displays the force and physics of an event—not its meaning.

Spectacle conflicts with the historically based environmental messages in these films, and what Nick Browne calls the "big bang" overpowers any possible ecological leanings in *Oil Wells of Baku* and masks and deludes environmental concerns raised in later oil well fire films. Browne suggests that an "analysis of the spectacular explosion as an event and the movies which feature it pose a larger sociological question about entertainment's simulation of the war-like foundations of modern economies." Browne argues that when we watch such spectacular events, "we are meant to be aware of the expense and take pleasure in the simulation of destruction," a paradox evident in *Fires of Kuwait*. We are aware, generally, that there is expense to the environment when watching burning oil wells and black-clouded skies on the screen; but we also take pleasure in the spectacular events on display and do not pause to calculate the effects.

Resolving such a contradiction may require a negotiation. Geoff King argues that the spectacular features of a film do not necessarily erase "the kinds of underlying thematic oppositions and reconciliations associated with a broadly 'structuralist' analysis of narrative" (25). He suggests that spectacular events presented on film and the narratives that drive them can work together to illustrate and reinforce "the opposition between the 'frontier'—or its contemporary analogues—and a version of technological modernity" (25). King's reading reinforces the eco-critical reading on display here. King's argument suggests that by making the workings of spectacle transparent, the underlying environmental issues on display in *Oil Wells of Baku*, as well as the later oil fire films, can gain more force. Yet the conflict between the spectacular and the environmental degradation on display is not resolved, even from King's perspective; it is merely revealed. Knowing the conflict exists makes possible a double reading of the event both as spectacular and sublime splendor and eco-disaster.

In fact, the filmic production of the spectacular event becomes part of this technological modernity on display. Nick Browne even suggests that when it is turned to spectacle, at least in cinema, destruction can be evidence of a certain active social spirit. "Spectacular destruction," he writes,

> is one of the opaque signs of life and types of pleasures evident under late, some would say, post-modern capitalism's commodi-fication and marketing of the mass visual event, one whose in-vestment sustains cinema as providing an experience of a certain

scale and intensity in its struggle with television's miniaturization
and sentimentalization of the contemporary world.

We cannot deny these spectacular events put on display precisely because they are so eye-catching, so undeniable; such spectacles are made
more transparent, their causation more evident, through the structural
and ahistorical lens cinematic drama provides. When placed within their
cultural context, such events demonstrate the paradox that a highly
industrial medium (film) provides a framework for unearthing possible
environmental ideology. But can these environmental leanings, further
revealed by historicized readings, also be explored when these seemingly
contradictory approaches are applied together? Eco-criticism, inherently
interdisciplinary in nature, may work in tune with such readings to reveal
the environmental ideology concealed by the spectacular. Here Browne's
and King's arguments contradict one another. Browne argues that spectacle itself can provide the social action an eco-critical reading of the
event behind the spectacle should reveal. King suggests that spectacular
events cannot erase or veil environmental issues behind them. Instead,
we suggest that spectacular events and the issues behind them are always
already in conflict, so an eco-critical reading can only reveal the conflict
itself, neither erasing nor valorizing either the spectacular event or the
message behind it.

Fighting Hell

Feature films with oil well fires at their center go even further to show
the force of fire while minimizing displays of environmental costs. Stuart
Heisler's *Tulsa* (1949), a post–World War II film about the Oklahoma oil
boom of the 1920s, seems at first to bypass spectacle and foreground the
prosperity that oil revenues can bring to a region. But after an opening
that shows us an aerial view of the bustling prosperous city of Tulsa in
1949, the film backtracks to the 1920s conflict between ranchers and oil
producers in Oklahoma, a conflict that climaxes in a tremendous oil fire
spectacle. The first 1920s scene highlights the pollution that exploitation
of oil reserves causes: a stream polluted with oil kills cattle on a ranch
owned by the protagonist Cherokee's father, Lansing (Lloyd Gough), who
throws a match in the stream and ignites the oil floating on its top. And
when Lansing "trespasses" on his rival Tanner's (Robert Preston) land
to protest his oil production, he is killed running from a spectacular oil
gusher that blows up in a tornado of wood and metal. Both the stream
fire and the exploding oil well are shot first in close-up and then from
a distance to heighten their force. Yet although *Tulsa*'s opening spectacle

Figure 1.1. *Tulsa* (1949): Oil field fire.

foregrounds pollution for a current audience, the film's main conflict is between cattle ranchers and oil producers, not between environmentalists and land exploiters. Lansing originally attacks Tanner not because he polluted the stream, but because the pollution has killed his cattle, a sign that Lansing cares more about the impact of oil on his cattle ranching than on the water and landscape itself.

The film's ending outdoes the beginning with an even more spectacular oil fire that, according to Hal Erickson, "must have cost as much as all the other Eagle-Lion releases of 1949 combined" ("*Tulsa* Review" *All Movie Guide*) Framing the burning stream opening, the film's Native American lead, Jim Redbird (Pedro Armendariz), his cattle lying dead from drinking the poisoned water, lights an oil-laden stream on fire and waves it into flame with his jacket. The ensuing oil field fire blasts up in red flames and black smoke that fills nearly half the frame. As in the opening sequence, erupting flames are shot first in close-up, for spectacularizing magnification, and then from a long shot that distances the viewer and adds force to the fire. Repeated shots of the heightening flames intensify the oil fire's force.

Although the film resolves its conflicts in favor of both Native Americans and conservation, it is the massive fire scene that sells the film.

Even though the film's narrative foregrounds Lansing's daughter Cherokee (Susan Hayward) and her rise to power as an oil queen, it also enacts a battle between white oil moguls and Native Americans, and between greed and conservation. But it is the film's spectacular ending that resolves both conflicts. Jim Redbird chooses to destroy oil fields that supplant cattle ranches—a choice that, ironically, results in environmental destruction more massive than that caused by drilling oil wells too close together to accommodate cattle. Redbird's action reinforces the film's emphasis on spectacle rather than on environmental devastation. Although events point toward a conservation message, spectacular effects obscure or even erase the meaning of that message. What stays with us, in other words, is the intensity of the magnificent fire itself, and not the message about the conflicting demands that oil drilling and cattle ranching place upon the ecology and society.

A filmed oil well fire can serve as spectacle for an audience even when the principal object of a film or scene is extinction of the flames. A veteran of World War II, Paul N. "Red" Adair served as a firefighter controlling oil well fires and blowouts from 1945, when he left the army, until his death in 2004. His expertise contributed to two oil fire films, Andrew McLaglen's *Hellfighters* (1968) and *Fires of Kuwait* (1992). Adair served as a consultant for *Hellfighters*, which highlighted a hero like him—Chance Buckman (John Wayne). According to film critic Dan Pavlides, Adair and his assistants "provided excellent and credible information for the film and the pyrotechnic team headed by legendary special-effects expert Fred Knoth" ("*Tulsa* Review" *All Movie Guide*). In his role as consultant, Adair ensured that authentic techniques were used to extinguish oil fires in the film, from Texas to Sumatra and Venezuela. But he also helped authenticate the spectacular visual effect that flaming oil wells provide.

According to the *Hellfighters* production notes, in the film, John Wayne "had his most formidable battle—taking on giant, billowing towers of searing flame." Based on the experiences of Red Adair and his assistants, the film put fire at its center, so that "John Wayne had to take a back seat to explosive pyrotechnic effects." As special effects engineer, Knoth created a pyrotechnic mixture that "provide[d] a maximum of spectacle." As in other oil well fires, spectacular flaming plumes inspire awe, but here the fires, while enormous, are simulated and deftly controlled by the filmmaker and his crew.

Looking for authenticity, Knoth and his team produced oil well fires using oil and propane, thereby reproducing some of the same environmental consequences flowing from actual oil fires. The opening scene shows them a drilling operation that is "coming in wild." Shot from the

Figure 1.2. *Hellfighters* (1968): John Wayne fights fires.

point of view of a worker (who is ironically smoking a cigarette), the scene looks like documentary footage of a gushing well in extreme long shot. Oil workers struggle to contain the gusher, but the whole derrick operation explodes into flames, throwing off gray and black smoke. Fire and smoke fill the frame, as burning oil field workers run away from the disaster.

As with the *Oil Wells of Baku* view, erupting red flames fill the sky with a heavy black smoke. And like the Lumière view, this opening scene is an extreme long shot, providing the viewer a safe distance from which to take pleasure. While it is filmed in Technicolor, this scene from *Hellfighters*, because it is shot at night, looks as dark as *Oil Wells of Baku*. Other scenes show flaming oil stifled by courageous firefighters. As McLaglen explains, the special effects also have consequences similar to actual oil well fires. Smoke fills much of the frame. To produce such powerful effects, special effects engineers burned 350,000 gallons of diesel oil and 60,000 gallons of raw propane. For example, in the final scenes of five oil wells in Venezuela rigged for fire by special effects men, fires and explosions produced "tremendous" heat: "I had to bite my tongue every time I sent Duke Wayne into the scene because I knew the heat was almost unbearable. . . . As soon as he went near the fire he started steaming, like a boiled egg" (*Hellfighters* Production Notes). With "geyser[s] of flame 125 feet high" and temperatures so extreme they melt the plastic on the director's chair, special effects replicate the awesome power of an actual oil well fire (*Hellfighters* Production Notes).

Gushing and flaming oil creates a spectacle especially powerful when caught on film. In *Hellfighters*, the five oil well fires McLaglen discusses provide visions of fire and smoke that are exacerbated by rebel attacks from Colombian Communist insurgents combating the Venezuelan dictatorship. While the hellfighters attempt to ignite and extinguish the fires, two rebel snipers attack, shooting one of the workers (Jim Hutton) in the process. The Venezuelan military intervenes in a battle scene that contributes to the spectacle produced by the fires and smoke shooting up through the rainforest. The fires and dangerous atmosphere also serve as the catalyst for Wayne's character's return to firefighting—and give us monstrous images of heroic "hellfighters" extinguishing flames and skirting bullets. *Hellfighters* thus combines spectacular eco- (and economic) disasters with heroic (and successful) firefighting strategies onscreen in a series of stimulating visual effects. The ecological work of the firefighters is all but lost in the spectacular hell where they battle.

In 1992, almost a century after the *Oil Wells of Baku: Close View* was produced, the IMAX documentary *Fires of Kuwait* foregrounds that same spectacle—this time in a documentary produced for a fifty-foot screen. Although it follows a traditional narrative that moves from a problem to a solution and foregrounds firefighters' heroism, *Fires of Kuwait* heightens the effect of monstrous spectacle, not only because of the immensity of the Kuwaiti fires but also because, as it was designed to do, the IMAX format displays the colossal, the sublime, and the spectacular. Film technology, then, heightens the impact of the spectacular, even as it documents environmental destruction.

Fires of Kuwait opens out of blackness broken only by red flames. Red light flickers as the camera tilts down to show the burning flame. It tilts up again and reveals a series of four flaming oil well fires in perspective receding into the distance. Then the film cuts to a second shot of a river of molten burning oil on the ground. A third shot shows oil well fires pushed by wind to reveal the sun—which looks like a red moon since the sky is so black. The last shot before the film's title parallels the Lumières' *Close View*: an extreme long shot of a row of burning oil wells that stretches into the distance. The dark smoke nearly fills the screen; the sky goes black.

The film cuts to a map of the Persian Gulf region, and the origin of these hellacious fires is revealed. The rest of the film exposes the devastation caused by these hundreds of fires and valorizes the miraculous cleanup efforts of firefighters from all over the world. *Fires of Kuwait* takes a stand against damaging nature that is primarily based on values other than economic. For David Douglas, the director and cinematographer, and for the firefighters who contain the blaze, burning oil well fires should be extinguished not only because the fires waste money but also because they destroy the natural environment and pollute the air and soil. However, Douglas filmed his documentary in the IMAX format, which, when projected, provides viewers with breathtaking views of the projected images, from all angles and with a 3-D effect. Douglas was struck by the fires' enormity, when sent to Kuwait to get footage for another film, and filmed the post-Gulf War destruction instead. Desson Howe suggests that "On a normal screen, 'Kuwait,' directed by David Douglas, would rate only as a passably engaging 'Frontline'-type documentary. But in the IMAX format (ten times larger than 35mm film), it becomes a titanic, archetypal man-versus-nature clash" (4 December 1992, *Washington Post*).

The first 25 minutes of the 34-minute DVD version of *Fires of Kuwait* provide such spectacle—glimpses of fire, black smoke, and firefighting teams stemming the flames. Fantastic fires and battles to curb them are the highlight. Awesome views of towering flames with enormous plumes of smoke are strengthened by aerial views through the darkness invoked by black smoke. From a distance even the sand is black from spilled oil. Only after Red Adair's team detonates an oil gusher and snubs the well 25 minutes into the film does the narrator turn to environmental consequences of the fires and oil spills, explaining that costs to the environment may be "devastating" and "global" so firefighters are helping "wildlife," too. The film shows oil-covered desert sands, and the voice-over explains that the "ecosystem is damaged." A black oasis appears on the film, and the narrator tells us "oases are under lakes of oil." Trees are "encrust[ed]" with oil mixed with poisoned chemicals. "Migrating birds" are lost in "poisoned air." The water is polluted, and the beaches are still strewn with mines.

The devastation is "an environmental assault." But the film ends on a hopeful note: Gushers are under control and a blue sky is visible. People work in teams, highlighting the need for cooperation, as they extinguish the last of the fires, stop oil gushers, and find and destroy all land mines. To demonstrate the re-growth of the land—and of nature—the last shots show signs of life: green leaves grow out of the oil-covered ground in oases. *Fires of Kuwait* successfully demonstrates a nation's recovery from a vengeful and tyrannical act of eco-terrorism. But the film relies on a rhetoric of spectacle intensified by the use of the IMAX format, which provides viewers with breathtaking views of the projected images, from all angles and with three-dimensional effect, all but erasing the environmental message blatantly proclaimed by the film's narrator.

The effective use of documentary footage to create spectacular sequences in *Fires of Kuwait* becomes even more evident when lined up against the cinematography and narrative of Werner Herzog's *Lessons of Darkness*. Herzog's film uses images from the same Gulf War and the fires that erupted after it to create a multi-genre 54-minute film that is part documentary and part science fiction, a meditation on the nature of the spectacle that the filmmaker encountered as an "outsider," a "visitor"

Figure 1.3. *Lessons of Darkness* (1992): Beautiful fires in Kuwait.

sensitive to the environmental destruction. Herzog also takes the time to explore intimate details of Kuwaiti citizens who have been brutalized by the Iraqi invasion. But both films depend on the nature of the fires that only images can fully describe.

As a way to clarify the power of the image of an oil fire, it is important to reiterate that *Fires of Kuwait* was originally shown on enormous screens using either the IMAX or OMNIMAX format that hyperbolizes the physical impact of the visual. Herzog's meditative, more metaphysical art piece, however, adds weight to spectacle without IMAX effects. In both films, because these fires are deliberately ignited to create an environmental disaster of unimaginable proportions, they have no rival as visual presentations. Whether presented in narrative or poetic form, they become all the more spectacular, both because their scope can only be illustrated through sweeping overhead shots from a helicopter and because they are projected onto large screens.

Despite their narrative difference, *Fires of Kuwait* and *Lessons of Darkness* both give us the scale of the distance between the oil wells that are burning. They both emphasize the utter darkness caused by smoke from the fires, a smoke so thick the sun is blacked out. The epigraph from Blaise Pascal that opens Herzog's film helps illustrate how devastating fires might take on the role of spectacle: "The collapse of the stellar universe will occur like creation—in grandiose splendor," the same splendor on display in *Oil Wells of Baku*.

Conclusion

This brings us back to our initial questions about the 1896 view—and about perspectives on oil fires then and now. There is no definitive answer to the first question: Is the fire depicted in *Oil Wells of Baku: Close View* business as usual or an eco-disaster? Although it looks like an eco-disaster to its retrospective commentator, Bertrand Tavernier, and, perhaps, to other twenty-first-century viewers, to historical observers such as Jackson, the fires recorded in the Lumière view and elsewhere in the late 1890s seem typical, if not "natural," and unthreatening. The only disastrous result mentioned by historians of the period relates to financial loss, not environmental consequence.

The second set of questions, however, requires a more complex set of answers. The most complex of these questions becomes, when do burning oil wells gain the status of ecological disaster? When do the costs begin to include not only money and human lives but nonhuman nature? The answer turns on another question: When, how, and why does disaster become a spectacular image? In this context, the notion of spectacle obscures or even erases ecological readings. In Baku itself, meanwhile, neither the rhetoric nor the real pollution have changed dramatically in the century since *Oil Wells of Baku*. Postcards and photographs heightened the effect of the Lumière Brothers' view, providing viewers around the world with a monstrous spectacle that inspired awe. The Baku that Jackson describes in 1911 looks and feels pretty much the same seventy or eighty years later. As Searight describes it, "when arriving by train in the 1980s, one was struck by the grimy desolation of the Bibi-Eilat field on the approach to the city, with its ancient 'nodding donkeys' wearily bringing oil to the surface, and the pipelines leaking over the sandy soil. Black Town was still black; sandstorms and flies were still a blight" (48).

Whether oil fires flare up by accident, as they did in the late 1800s (and still do today) or are set deliberately, as they were during the Gulf War (and still are today—in Colombia and Iraq, for example), their erupting plumes of fire and smoke and gushing rivers of oil still spark the same awestruck response. Photographs of burning oil wells and pipelines in 1896 and shots of Iraqi pipeline sabotage in 2006 provide the same universal force. *Hellfighters, Lessons of Darkness, Fires of Kuwait,* and *Jarhead* attest to the continued popularity of this particular form of spectacle, of the sublime. Spectacular flaming explosions inspire awe.

Oil Wells of Baku: Close View highlights what looks like a horrific eco-disaster, but the view of oil fires spurting up in 1896 sparks immediate visual attention and blunts attention to the ecological impact of the fires. *Oil Wells of Baku* stands out as an ecological film, an environmental film, and a view highlighting a history of wealth garnered from resources around the world. It also foregrounds a history of spectacle, and the history of one of the most contentious modern currencies. Images of gushing oil in later films like *Giant* (1956) and *Oklahoma Crude* (1973) and in television series such as *The Beverly Hillbillies* (1962–1971) demonstrate the pervasive power of oil. And contemporary images of oil well and pipeline fires on the covers of newspapers and magazines attest to our continuing appetite for the spectacle that burning oil may produce. Reading these images through an eco-critical lens, however, can make the workings of the spectacular events transparent.

2

Environmental Politics

Pare Lorentz's *The River* and the Tennessee Valley Authority

We built a dyke a thousand miles long.
Mules and mud a thousand miles up the Mississippi.
A century before we bought the great Western
    River, the Spanish and the French built
    dykes to keep the Mississippi out of New
    Orleans at flood stage.
In forty years we continued the levee the entire
    length of the great alluvial Delta

— Pare Lorentz, *The River*

Taking away people's souls, puttin' electricity in place of 'em ain't progress. . . . I like things runnin' wild, like nature made 'em. There's always enough dams locking things up, tamin' 'em, makin' 'em' go against their natural wants and needs. I'm again' dams of any kind.

—Ella Garth, *Wild River*

HURRICANE KATRINA HAD A devastating effect on the levees and flood walls protecting New Orleans and its surrounding communities. The Mississippi River Outlet breached its levees in approximately

20 places, flooding nearly 80% of the city. But engineering was as culpable as the weather in producing this catastrophe. According to engineers' investigations reported in newspapers from *The Houston Chronicle* to *The Washington Post*, the levees and flood walls shifted and were breached not just because a storm surge had overtopped the levees but because a major design flaw had been made during their construction. The breached levees and flood walls devastated New Orleans and the region. Yet, as with flooding that spurred New Deal programs like the Tennessee Valley Authority (TVA) dam projects, some of this was clearly due, at least in part, to human hands.

Hurricane Katrina's destruction of New Orleans in 2005 was an environmental disaster just like those along the Mississippi River in the 1920s and 1930s. These flooding disasters are foregrounded in Pare Lorentz's *The River* (1937), a New Deal rhetorical documentary drawing on historical memory to make a case in favor of dam projects implemented by one of Franklin Delano Roosevelt's most successful programs, the TVA. These dam projects would, according to the TVA, halt rising waters along the Mississippi and its tributaries while also producing electricity for the rural regions around them.

More importantly for our eco-critical reading, the aftermath of the Katrina disaster also broaches issues of historical memory and cultural context like those that drive the message of *The River*. The levee malfunctions in New Orleans have already led filmmakers like Spike Lee, in *When the Levees Broke* (2006), to examine the impact of flooding on the city and its residents and to critique the responses from local, regional, and federal governmental agencies. But the Katrina disaster and the films that document its breadth already rely on historical memory, memory that soon fades. If we don't remember, Spike Lee argues, all this is going to happen again.

The arguments surrounding the need to remember Katrina are similar to those driving the rhetoric of *The River*. *The River* documents the history behind the rivers' floods, a shifting and situated historical memory manipulated to drive the film's argument for environmental action. Through its recurring images of progress and destruction and accompanying musical score and narration, the film describes the work mankind has done to keep the Mississippi River and its tributaries' waters in their banks to impede devastating floods. But *The River* also argues that our exploitation of the land has contributed to these floods and, consequently, to the need to control them. Flood waters must be controlled because humans have overused lands and overdeveloped flood plains, causing damage humans can only repair by building huge dams to reroute the wild river waters.

Elia Kazan's *Wild River* (1960), on the other hand, as a fictional-ized feature film about the TVA projects during the New Deal, focuses on one consequence of the damming projects that *The River* promotes: individual property loss. Pare Lorenz directed *The River* as a tool for the policies of the Roosevelt administration, under the auspices of the U.S. Farm Security Administration, policies that might be seen both as socialist and as appropriate for eradicating some of the problems caused by the Great Depression. The film also promotes "the Tennessee Valley Authority (TVA) as the solution to problems of flooding, agricultural depletion, and electrification" (Bordwell and Thompson 58). Although also influenced by his own work for New Deal programs years before, especially as the director of *The People of the Cumberland* (1937), Kazan offered *Wild River* as both fiction and personalized historical memory instead of a mandate for TVA programs.

In spite of their environmental leanings, both films respond explicitly to their own cultural contexts (1930s and 1960s, respectively), so they fail to address critical long-term ecological concerns. *The River* argues that there is only one solution to the problem of flooding, the Tennessee Valley Authority Dam Projects. *Wild River* asserts that rerouting the river to battle flood problems counters individual rights and liberties fought for during the Civil Rights period in which the film was produced.

Since they make assertions based in their contexts, neither film fully discusses the catastrophic consequences of flooding along the Mississippi and its tributaries. Nor do they underline either the massive human loss caused by the floods, especially in 1927, or the political consequences of Republican policies before, during, and after the 1927 flooding of the Mississippi and its tributaries.

Because both the floods and the Depression occurred so close to filming *The River*, Lorentz is able to exploit the historical memories surrounding these events in the film to serve New Deal policies, setting these policies up as problem-free solutions to the economic crises facing the Deep South. In *Wild River*, Kazan has the luxury to examine the TVA from a distance of more than twenty years. In 1960, the TVA is a fact, and the South now has electricity and a growing industrial base, in large part because of the success of the TVA; the floods of the 1920s and 1930s are a distant memory. *Wild River* can now focus on the drama surrounding individual rights versus the needs of the federal government.

Both *Wild River* and *The River* assert that the TVA represents prog-ress without interrogating environmental and economic arguments still debated to this day: Should the production of electricity be controlled by public or private agencies? Should the river and land be transformed by forces like the TVA or be allowed to restore themselves naturally, as

Ella Garth (Jo Van Fleet) argues in *Wild River*? Should the environment (especially the Mississippi River system) be controlled by governmental agencies like the Army Corps of Engineers, or should environmental groups or even private enterprise intervene and provide a more broad-based restoration project?

In spite of each film's failures, however, *The River* and *Wild River* stand out as films—eco-films, if you will—that explicitly address and support a viable solution (TVA dams) to consequences (flooding) of real environmental exploitation (overuse and overdevelopment of land).

The River as Eco-film

Lorentz's *The River* asserts that the best way to solve the problems humans have caused by their degradation of nature is to implement technological projects driven by human ingenuity and innovation: the TVA's construction of enormous dams like the Norris Dam, started in 1933 and finished on 4 March 1936, at the head of the Tennessee River. As the film's narrator argues, "The old river *can* be controlled. We had the power to take the Valley apart. We have the power to put it together again." According to the narration that accompanies images of a working dam near the conclusion of *The River*, the TVA's dams "will transform

Figure 2.1. *The River*: Overuse of land on display.

the old Tennessee into a link of fresh water pools locked and dammed, regulated and controlled," resolving any problems associated with overuse and overdevelopment of lands along the river system.

But as Bordwell and Thompson point out, "Here is a case where one solution [building large dams like those on the Tennessee], because it has been effective in dealing with the problem, is taken to be *the* solution" (61). Bordwell and Thompson describe several alternatives to the TVA project and its possible negative repercussions, but they do not point out the economic reasons behind the FDR-led project: The federal government could not tell people threatened by catastrophic years of flooding and impoverished by the Great Depression (and, perhaps, by their own abuse of the landscape) to let their land lie fallow for at least fifty years, nor could they deny themselves the economic (and cultural) benefits that work on the projects and electricity produced by the dams brought them.

While *The River* accurately highlights the environmental problems of the Tennessee Valley and offers a definitive solution, it depends on recent historical memory for the force of its argument. The catastrophic floods of 1927, '36, and '37 were still fresh in the nation's memory when the film was produced. But this film only provides a generalized portrait of the human hardships before the TVA project and can only speculate about the future benefits the hydroelectric dams would create.

The River builds to a climax, showing us signs of historical progress in the Southern states along the Mississippi—staged scenes of slaves loading bales of cotton onto steam boats in dramatic low-angle shots and lumbermen maneuvering loads of lumber down the river, for example. The film builds sympathy for the South after the Civil War devastation but foregrounds a more moderate view of progress (with a combination of recreated scenes and documentary film footage). The goal in *The River* is not to halt progress but to control its aftereffects, flooding still remembered by the film's contemporary viewers.

Wild River as Eco-film

On the other hand, Kazan's *Wild River*, a 1960 narrative film deriving its plot from the TVA's work on the Tennessee River, lacks the recent historic memory reflected by Lorentz's *The River* but tells a more human, although fictionalized, story about the repercussions of the TVA project—the displacement of individuals by the "controlled" flooding caused by the dams themselves.

Set in 1936 Tennessee, during the height of New Deal programs like the TVA, Kazan's film has been called "an anomaly—a social-issue film from a major Hollywood studio that refuses to take sides" (Chase 1). Yet critics define that social issue not in terms of the environmental (and economic) reasons behind the TVA project the film highlights but in relation to the class structure called into question by the romance between the northern TVA representative, Chuck Glover (Montgomery Clift), and the rural Southern widowed daughter-in-law, Carole Garth Baldwin (Lee Remick) of Ella Garth, the Southern island landowner Chuck has come down from the North to "relocate."

The film, however, highlights the environment and the consequences of environmental catastrophe almost immediately: it opens with black-and-white documentary footage of flooding along the Tennessee River which, according to the film's voice-over narration, will be eliminated with the help of TVA projects comprised of a series of dams intended to stop the loss, devastation, and waste caused by the Tennessee River floods.

Yet in *Wild River* it is the river that is blamed for the devastating flooding, not humans' overuse of the land. And the federal government, represented by the TVA projects, is the only possible savior for the South. In *Wild River*, a film shot around 1960 but foregrounding problems and solutions from the mid-1930s, the TVA brings rural poor people out of poverty, provides them with housing wired for electricity, and finds jobs for all men, no matter what their race happens to be. Here the benefits of TVA projects are highlighted, especially in relation to economic and race issues. TVA projects will extend civil rights to the oppressed and underprivileged rural Southerners, according to the film's narrative. Positive consequences of TVA projects rather than human causes for the flooding these projects curtail are the focus of *Wild River*.

The success of the TVA has been valorized in texts like John Moore's *The Economic Impact of the TVA*, a volume of essays that highlights the impact both historical memory and cultural context have on definitions of success and the means to gain a successful end. In the booming U.S. economy of the 1960s, when industry along riverfronts like the Tennessee were at the height of their production, the TVA is seen as a successful model for building a mature economy, for stimulating progress other "agencies and institutions with a broader focus than that conceived by the founders of TVA a generation ago" (Moore xv) can develop even further.

Kazan's *Wild River* shares this same perspective of the TVA and its successes. After providing the documentary black-and-white footage of people avoiding flood waters, even on their rooftops, the film switches perspective to a color view of the landscape from the window of the plane that is carrying Chuck to the Tennessee River region to take over the local TVA office. Such a contrast suggests that the technologically advanced North must rescue Southerners from not only Tennessee River flooding but also from the stagnant rural life that stifles progress.

Because *Wild River* looks back on the devastation caused by the flooding of the Tennessee River from a perspective influenced by post–World War II prosperity that has seemingly transformed the Tennessee River Valley, the film establishes several binary oppositions in which Chuck, who represents the TVA and all it stands for, acts as the superior end of each, especially those in which nature and the environment play a role. Ella, Carole's mother-in-law and the owner of an island that will soon be flooded by waters from a dam, most represents nature and the natural, since she argues that taming the river goes against nature. She refuses to leave her land and clear the way for the river's dammed waters, an act she sees as unnatural and soul-wrenching. The TVA, on the other hand, is seen as a civilizing influence, giving Southerners the chance for a soul by providing them with electricity, jobs, and economic freedom.

Ironically, however, reliance on such skewed historical memory hides the human reasons behind the flooding and incorrectly defines both nature and the natural as based on private ownership because they are shown from the perspective of Ella's own misinformed historical memory. The film does underline some of the negative ramifications of a flooding Tennessee River—loss of homes and homeland and of human life—but unlike *The River*, the film does not explain the reasons for the river's flooding—humans' overuse of the land. Instead of demonstrating that the troubles characters like Ella are enduring happened because they exploited nature, *Wild River* highlights Ella's personal and individual struggles. An old woman living with her family and her black laborers on a small island, Ella refuses to leave her land, seemingly to undermine the TVA's plan to dam the river and flood her island, a plan she sees as going "against nature."

The Films, Politics, and the TVA

These two films, one a rhetorical documentary and the other a fictional narrative, also focus on similar events set in similar cultural contexts: a TVA project led by 1930s New Deal politics. And they both provide a vision of the economic devastation caused by frequent flooding of the Tennessee and, to a certain extent, the Mississippi Rivers. The connections between the two films are also rooted in the ties both Lorentz and Kazan had to the Farm Security Administration, the federal agency that in 1937 produced Lorentz's *The River* and Kazan's Frontier Film, *The People of the Cumberlands*. And even though Kazan's *Wild River* does give Southern racism some attention and the narrator of Lorentz's *The River* mentions blacks and shows portraits of slaves picking cotton, neither director grounds either the romanticism of *Wild River* or the rhetoric of *The River* in a clear view of the real results of catastrophic flooding.

John Barry's *Rising Tide: The Great Mississippi Flood of 1927 and How It Changed America* and Nancy L. Grant's *TVA and Black Americans: Planning for the Status Quo* illustrate not only the results of such flooding but also some of the human causes of ideological changes that prompted Franklin Delano Roosevelt's election and the New Deal policies his administration implemented. Although *The River* and, to a certain extent, *Wild River*, acknowledge the great flooding of the Mississippi and its tributaries from 1903 until 1937, when *The River* was produced, neither focuses particular attention on the greatest of those floods—the 1927 flood that changed voting patterns of African Americans and helped, in part, fuel the Democratic Party's rise to power in 1932.

Barry's research reveals some startling statistics about this devastating flood. According to Barry, during this flood year, the Mississippi River expanded to 125 miles across and covered 127,000 miles of what was arable land in the South. As a result of the flood, more than one million people's homes were washed away, which, at the time, accounted for almost 1% of the population of the United States. Almost 700,000 of these people were forced to subsist on rations from the Red Cross for months. Most of those affected were African Americans, more than 300,000 of whom fled to refugee camps where the National Guard ensured that no one could enter or leave without a pass and all were forced to work for no wages (285–86).

Barry argues that those African Americans served as slave labor to maintain the economy of the Mississippi Delta. Since at the time the Republican Party was in power at both the federal and state levels, African Americans reacted against a government that nearly enslaved them by shifting party allegiances from Republican (the party of Lincoln) to Democratic, a shift still maintained today. The abandonment of the Republican Party by black voters first in 1928, and to an even greater extent in 1932, was a direct result of the 1927 flood. Hoover lost about 15% of the black vote in 1928 because black newspapers endorsed the Democratic candidate, Al Smith, over Hoover, who, as Vice President under Calvin Coolidge, had betrayed them after the flood. Since Al Smith was Catholic, however, Southerners who were historically Democrat (the party that destroyed Reconstruction and enacted Jim Crow laws) voted Republican and helped provide Hoover with a landslide (Barry 414).

According to Barry, blacks' defection from the Republican party was a direct result of "uncertainty in many sections as to [Hoover's] attitude toward the Negro in the Mississippi disaster" (413). Barry argues that before the floods, the Mississippi Delta provided blacks with a relatively safe haven, where whites actually protected blacks from vigilantes and refused to tolerate the Ku Klux Klan. The flood and the economic devastation it spearheaded changed all of that, leading blacks back into a state close to slavery and, consequently as of 1932, away from the Republican party and its representatives that had oppressed them. In rebellion, blacks moved to the Democratic Party led by FDR (Grant). This monumental flood and its aftereffects are all but forgotten, even in these two films meant to highlight the ramifications of humans' exploitation of nature and the solution to the flooding human abuse had caused. Only subtle signs of these consequences remain.

Wild River and the TVA

The opening of *Wild River* provides a view of some of the human consequences of the floods along the Tennessee River. This black-and-white documentary sequence includes an aerial tracking shot of homes flooded by the river, an interview with a man who lost his wife and children to the waters, and the only voice-over narration of the film. The voice-over informs us that this is the Tennessee River flooding and that on "May 18, 1933, the TVA was created and authorized to build a series of dams along the river." To carry this out, the federal government, led by the TVA, must "buy up land along and islands in the river." This brief documentary introduces us to the problem (flooding) and the solution (TVA intervention). It also suggests one of the complications of the TVA solution—the need to relocate those living on lands purchased by the TVA because dammed waters will flood them. The footage, however, only provides the year the TVA was established, not the year of the floods or of the TVA intervention highlighted in the film. It also blames flooding only on the river, on nature, not on humans' overuse of the land.

After this opening, resistance to relocation becomes the center of *Wild River*. As the voice-over narration concludes, a color view of the lands surrounding the Tennessee appears, this time from the view of Chuck (and the TVA he represents). The narrator reveals that Chuck is the third representative sent to evacuate Ella Garth from her island, an island we see from Chuck's plane—highlighting the contrast between the technologically advanced North and the agrarian premodern South. Ella is constructed as a rugged individual, as a woman resisting the homogenizing forces of the federal government, forces reinforced by the New Deal programs in place in the Tennessee River town on shore: signs outside buildings announce the WPA, the NRA, and, of course, the TVA, signs Chuck sees from the bus that drops him off at his office.

Progress, however, as exemplified by Chuck and these programs, demands that America's individualistic agrarian roots be left behind to ensure equal access to prosperity.

The film's narrative suggests that Ella, then, must be uprooted from her home and relinquish some of her freedom, to help save the environment and economy of the Tennessee Valley. The balance between freedom and equality, between Ella's rugged roots and the more federalist agenda of Chuck and the TVA, is a delicate one in the film. When Chuck enters the TVA office, he asks the secretary, Betty (Barbara Loden), how best to remove Ella from her island home. Betty's reaction is to "let her drown." But Chuck must maintain positive public relations to ensure the New Deal programs work effectively, especially in a South where many in power were suspicious of big government and the solution it promised to both frequent flooding and the Depression economy.

Chuck's introduction to Ella's premodern island demonstrates the extent of the contrast between North and South, between the technological progress promised by the TVA and the stagnant rural economy of stolid unchanging Southerners. Chuck leaves his TVA car behind and reaches the island by rope-driven ferry.

On the island Chuck walks through rows of corn, and the camera shows us not motorized vehicles but horse-drawn carts driven by black sharecroppers, all from Chuck's point of view. At Ella Garth's house, we see Ella look through a window at her crops, but she won't speak with Chuck about leaving to avoid the imminent flooding of her island by the dam waters. And when Chuck speaks with Ella's sons, they make clear that "Ma knows all about floods down here" before throwing Chuck into the river, suit and all. When Chuck is asked to return to the island and speak with Ella, she clarifies her perspective on damming the river: "There's always enough dams locking things up. Taming 'em, making 'em go against their natural wants and needs. I'm again' dams of any kind."

Ella and her sons see damming the river as going against nature rather than healing damage caused by human overuse of land. But Chuck's encounter with both Ella and her sons demonstrates the racial inequalities that serve as a cog in Southern agrarian economic life, the economic ecosystem on which what Ella calls "natural" is built. Ella and her sons' "freedom" is gained only at the expense of blacks and poor whites with no property. Chuck's inquiry to Ella's sons about who does the work on the island demonstrates who bears the cost of that freedom. While lazily reeling in catfish from the river, Ella's sons nod toward the black sharecroppers, who work laboriously around them. Ella's sons don't work because, as they put it, they "just never started."

Ella the landlord, in turn, tells her parable of the land among her own serfs, using one of her most loyal serf's, Sam's (uncredited), attachment to his dog as a tool to teach Chuck about her connection to the island: "Sam and me, we don't sell. Sam don't sell his dog, and I don't sell my land that I poured my heart's blood into." In the midst of her sharecroppers, Ella argues, "I ain't goin' against nature and I ain't a crawling for no damn government," but her land has provided her with a livelihood only because blacks work for her willingly for slave wages.

Ella's personal history, her own historical memory, goes back to her husband's founding of the Garths' island kingdom. After teaching Chuck her lesson about property, Ella shows Chuck what will happen to her after the flood gates close—in the cemetery where her husband, Woodbridge, is buried. According to Ella, Woodbridge found the island while floating in a flat-bottomed boat. And Ella has lived there since her marriage and reigned there since Woodbridge's death. Carole, Ella's daughter-in-law, establishes the strength of Ella's connection to the island as a site of her personal history and historical memory: If Ella had to leave the island, "it'd kill her," Carole explains.

Ella's connection to the island relates directly to her connection to the black serfs who maintain its economy. The connection between Ella and her sharecroppers, though, now seems reciprocal to the black families living in shacks around Ella. Although Sam seems interested in learning more about how the dam will produce electricity, one of the black women near the ferry when Chuck leaves anxiously asks him, "Who's going to look after us?" if they are forced to leave. Chuck replies with "Wouldn't you rather look after yourselves?" But after so many years working for the Garths in return for room, board, and a small wage, the black sharecroppers seem unprepared for independence within the film's context. The film suggests that Ella's self-sufficiency is an illusion built on the backs of her serfs, but Ella's patronage has limited their own growth as individuals.

Ella's role as benevolent landlord, however, parallels that of the white land owners on shore. Blacks work the land owned by whites for less than half the wages of their white counterparts. Propertied whites argue that paying blacks as much as whites would "ruin our economy down here," an agrarian economy depending on near-slave labor because the land and all it produces are worth so little. But Chuck, constructed as a representative of both the TVA and the technologically advanced modern North, replaces Ella's patronage with good wages and homes lit by electricity. Most of Ella's serfs leave her to clear land for the TVA and move into tenant homes on shore, but Chuck and at least one black laborer suffer at the hands of one of the propertied whites—Bailey (Albert Salmi), who owns 400 acres of cotton farmed by black sharecroppers. One of his workers, Ben (Robert Earl Jones), joins Chuck's TVA work gang for $5.00 rather than the usual $2.00 per day and is beaten so hard with a stick that he can't work for at least two days. Bailey demands that Chuck pay the $4.00 he needed to pay Ben's replacement and, when Chuck refuses to pay, Bailey beats Chuck and takes the money "owed" him.

Chuck's reaction to such violence, however, is not to combat racism tied in with beating Ben and paying blacks less than whites for equal work. Instead, Chuck finds jobs for Ella's blacks not simply to free them but so he can evacuate Ella more quickly because she has lost the black labor on which she depends. Chuck drowns his wounds in alcohol with Carole's fiancé, Walter (Frank Overton), and comes to an understanding not about blacks' exploitation but about Ella's reasons for staying on the island. In a drunken stupor he tells Ella that he knows why she refuses to leave: You're "fighting for your dignity," he exclaims before passing out below Ella's porch. Chuck even counters Ella's sons, who, as he had suggested earlier, now seek to find her legally incompetent, so they can sell her land and force Ella off the island. Chuck argues that he'd "rather have her put off at the point of a gun."

So with the TVA's approval, since "It'll be a lot worse publicity if she starts getting wet," Chuck gets the sheriff to evict her. "I guess it all comes under the general heading of progress," the Sheriff asserts, but he carries out Chuck's orders and warns Ella that she must leave by the next day or be forcibly evicted. Sam, the only remaining black sharecropper, plows a field that will soon be flooded, defying the TVA and demonstrating his loyalty to Ella, the landlord, but in the end he and the rest of the black serfs leave lands that will soon be flooded in tug-pulled boats. Before the final eviction, Chuck is torn about whether or not Ella's eviction is just: "When I first came here, I thought, how can any one person go against this country. . . . Now I have to make sure I get her off the island, but I don't know."

Carole's reply complicates Chuck's choice even further: "You're gettin' awful human, aren't you, Chuck," she says, suggesting that the TVA and the progress it signifies lack humanity and are mere mechanisms of culture separate from the nature that for Ella, the river and her black serfs represent.

The film's narrative resolves in favor of Northern progress, but Ella leaves her island only by force, while, in long-shot, waters rise toward her home. And, still the rugged individual, she watches black workers cut down her large trees as she floats away, in a shot from her point of view, ever more distant from the island she leaves behind.

The last shot of Ella is on her new home's front porch, where she refuses to sit in a rocker, refuses the services of her black servant, and asks Carole to pay off her last debts: "That's all I owe anybody," Ella says, just before she dies, alone and unencumbered by obligations.

Our last view of Ella's island is from the boat where Chuck looks on in dismay as Ella's island house burns down. An American flag flies on the boat, as Chuck and the crew watch, a clear sign that they and the U.S. government they represent are responsible for the fire and flooding, flooding so widespread that only the cemetery where they bury Ella beside her husband remains above the rising waters.

Carole and her children leave Tennessee and the South with Chuck, and they all look down on the island as they fly away in a shot similar to Chuck's first view of the area from the air. But the film closes on a bird's-eye shot of the dam, with an iris in to highlight its prominence and perhaps suggest that Chuck, or at least other TVA representatives, plan to continue the work of the TVA.

Wild River, then, argues for the benefits the TVA produces: electricity, work for both blacks and whites, and revitalization of a failing agrarian economy. But at the same time, because of its reliance on a dimming historical memory, the film fails to show the human reasons behind the flooding and instead asserts that taming the river with dams goes against nature—as Ella proclaims—and creates problems for white Southerners and, perhaps, the lands the Tennessee River floods when the dam is closed. Although the film illustrates that racism serves as an essential cog in the Southern economic ecosystem, it does not offer a viable alternative for slavelike labor. In fact, Chuck uses blacks to serve his own purposes, just as Ella and the other propertied whites did. The environmental message here is confused and unexamined.

The River and the TVA

In Lorentz's *The River*, however, ecology is foregrounded at the expense of race. This 1937 film provides a clear government-sponsored argument for intervention by programs like the TVA. But it also examines the reasons for widespread flooding before offering this solution; this is the historical memory missing from *Wild River*. *The River* illustrates the impact of human settlement along the river and efforts to combat flooding that erosion caused by stripping the land for farming encourages, at least from the early nineteenth century. The film illustrates how impoverished the South became after the Civil War not only because of the "tragedy of war" but because "already the frenzied cotton cultivation of a quarter of a century had taken toll of the land." It also demonstrates the ramifications of lumbering in the North, mining in Pennsylvania, Ohio, and West Virginia and urbanization along each river shore in the poetic narration of Thomas Chalmers:

> We built a hundred cities and a thousand towns—
> But at what a cost!
> We cut the top off the Alleghenies and sent it down the
>   river.
> We cut the top off Wisconsin and sent it down the river.
> We left the mountains and the hills slashed and burned,
> And moved on.
> The water comes downhill, spring and fall;
> Down from the cut-over mountains,
> Down from the plowed-off slopes,
> Down every brook and rill, rivulet and creek,
> Carrying every drop of water that flows down two-thirds
>   the continent
> 1903 and 1907,
> 1913 and 1922,
> 1927,
> 1936,
> 1937!

The River shows the extent of the battle against the floods and the number of flood victims through both the images on display and the powerful narration: Flooding left 750,000 without "food and water and shelter and clothing," the cost of exploiting the lands for their resources. To meet these victims' needs, the narration explains that "We sent armies down to help the engineers fight a battle on a two thousand mile front: The Army and Navy, / The Coast Guard and Marine Corps, / The CCC [Civilian Conservation Corps] and the WPA [Works Progress Administration], / The Red Cross and the Health Service," programs that were part of FDR's New Deal. Here we see levees and sandbags holding back water that is narrowing and picking up strength before overflowing its banks before New Deal programs intervened. With the musical score of Virgil Thomson emphasizing tone change and climactic results, the ecological power of these New Deal programs is reinforced.

And *The River* offers numbers to support its claims about the cost of exploiting the land:

> For fifty years we plowed for corn, and moved on when the
> land gave out. / Corn and wheat; wheat and cotton—we

planted and plowed with no thought for the future—/and four hundred million tons of top soil . . . have been washed into the Gulf of Mexico every year." It also highlights not only the immediate repercussions of flood damage but also the consequences of losing top soil—"poor land makes poor people." According to *The River*, as of 1937, "forty percent of all farmers in the great Valley are tenants. / Ten percent are share croppers. . . . But a generation facing a life of dirt and poverty, / Disease and drudgery; / Growing up without proper food, medical care, or schooling . . . /And in the greatest river valley in the world.

The images that accompany the narrator's statements about environmental, human, and economic costs, however, point out an important element missing from *The River*: blacks bearing the greatest burden of flood-induced poverty and homelessness. In fact, all of the images of tenant farmers impoverished by poor soil and flooding are of whites. Blacks are only shown in footage where slaves work the fields and load barges with bales of cotton before the Civil War. Only in the epilogue to *The River* are blacks even mentioned—because their labor contributed

Figure 2.2. *The River*: Human costs of flooding.

to the degradation of the land: "We got blacks to plant the cotton and they gouged the top off the valley," the narrator explains.

Like *Wild River*, *The River* seeks to valorize the TVA and other New Deal projects, this time from the perspective of the federal government that commissioned the film. Like *Wild River*, *The River* ends with a long-shot of a Tennessee Valley dam producing electricity to bring "a Soul"—and progress—to the South, effective when coupled with "soil conservation" and "model agricultural communit[ies]" built by the Farm Security Administration, programs highlighted even further in *The Power and the Land* (1940) and *The New Frontier* (1934), two other New Deal documentaries. The narration ends by arguing that, unlike past attempts, New Deal projects can successfully control rivers and land of the Mississippi delta:

> For you can't wall out and dam two-thirds the water in the
>   country,
> We built dams but the dams filled in.
> We built a thousand mile dyke but it didn't hold;
> So we built it higher.
> We played with a continent for fifty years.
>
> *Flood control? of the Mississippi?*
>
> Control from Denver to Helena;
> From Itaska to Paducah;

Figure 2.3. *The River*: Tennessee Valley Authority dam and hydroelectric power as solution.

From Pittsburgh to Cairo—
Control of wheat, the corn and the cotton land;
Control enough to put back a thousand forests;
Control enough to put the river together again before it is
    too late . . . before it
has picked up the heart of a continent and shoved it into
    the Gulf of Mexico.

This powerful narration aligns perfectly with the powerful hydroelectric dam on display, a dam that promises both flood control and electricity for the rural South. The conclusion also adds support to the film's rhetorical stance in favor of TVA programs as a solution to multiple problems associated with uncontrolled development of lands in the name of progress.

Conclusion

Both films, then, argue for federal intervention and public control of land and water. The long political battles begun in the 1920s over whether dams built in the South would be publicly owned or privately controlled were finally resolved in 1933, when Roosevelt established the TVA (Hubbard 312–315). Manmade environmental and economic disasters vitiated debates of the 1920s, especially after the 1927 flood, and helped bring in Roosevelt and a Democratic-controlled government in 1932. Coolidge and Hoover's Republican policies of the late 1920s and early 1930s depended on a vision of private solutions to large-scale social problems. This philosophy was replaced in 1933 by the new civic outlook ushered in by FDR and Democrats.

Both films suggest that individual actions have led to collective disaster so great that government social planning must intervene for the good of all. But government intervention on such a grand scale was continually tested in the courts throughout the 1930s and beyond, pointing again to some of the important questions neither film interrogates, but which are still being interrogated today after disasters like Hurricane Katrina.

Historic memory and cultural context clearly affect both films' approach to the race question. *Wild River*, which came out in 1960, emphasizes the plight of black sharecroppers much more fully than does *The River* because the civil rights movement was in full swing. *The River*, on the other hand, seeks to sell the TVA and other federal projects to a general (white) public in 1937, when whites, especially the Southern whites most affected by the projects, would resist images of black slaves and sharecroppers carrying the greatest burden in the Southern agrarian economy.

Both films rely on the notion of historic memory to provide the power to their arguments in favor of the TVA, but the actual devastation of the floods—especially the 1927 flood—is glossed over. Neither film reveals that this devastation was so far-ranging that political as well as social, economic, and environmental effects, are still being felt today. See for example the controversy surrounding the Mississippi flooding after the levees broke during the Katrina catastrophe and the ongoing attempts to maintain the river's flow and dispose of its muddy residue.

Neither film clearly addresses the arguments made in the 1930s for private enterprise or support of private property, either. This remains key for today: the policies of the New Deal versus the continuing call to private intervention—a central debate from the beginning of the Republic. Although *Wild River* does foreground problems that arise for individuals when the federal government more or less demands they sell their private property to the TVA, because of its focus on valorizing the TVA, the film does not examine private alternatives to public intervention. In other words, when the TVA imposes eminent domain on lands that will soon be flooded by dam waters, the film demonstrates some sense of individual loss for Ella, but only for the benefit of all Southerners. The TVA is constructed as not only the definitive solution to flood problems but also as a benefactor bringing progress (and electricity) to the South.

Neither *Wild River* nor *The River* explores problems particular to public control of flooding along the Mississippi and its tributaries, then, because they both seek to valorize New Deal projects like those established by the TVA. John Barry's *Rising Tide*, however, suggests that even massive public plans put into place to eliminate great floods like that of 1927 might fail because they were inadequately funded, limiting the abilities of organizations like the Army Corps of Engineers. Barry argues that

Figure 2.4. *Wild River*: Clearing the island.

the Corps' assertion that "its plan will handle a flood greater than that of 1927" (425) is built on false information that may lead to catastrophic flooding in the future, especially since in 1928 the Army engineers were ordered to design an inexpensive plan (Barry 425). Such flaws could be eradicated with further funding and interaction with civilian engineers. Otherwise, "many engineers believe that sooner or later, no matter what man does, the Mississippi will shift its channel. . . . And a finger of the sea will climb past New Orleans, north to Baton Rouge" (426). After the devastation of New Orleans in August 2005, Barry's premonition gains even more strength.

Two big questions missing from the films emerge from this examination: Should an inadequately funded federal program led by the Corps of Engineers be asked to halt the flooding? Or should "civilian engineers" and representatives from private enterprise invest funds necessary to stop the Mississippi from shifting its channel? But these questions, like both *Wild River* and *The River*, rest on either/or binary oppositions that break down under scrutiny. The films argue that either the South accepts TVA interventions or catastrophic flooding (caused by either humans or the rivers themselves) will continue when, as Bordwell and Thompson make clear, alternatives to government intervention might be more effective solutions to flooding and its causes and consequences.

The questions Barry raises suggest that the Army Corps of Engineers, a public agency, is in conflict with civilian engineers of the private sector. In reality, public and private agencies and programs have worked together to control rivers like the Mississippi since the nineteenth century when Andrew Atkinson Humphreys, chief of the U.S. Army Corps of Engineers after the Civil War, and James Buchanan Eads and Charles Ellet, Jr., civilian engineers, proposed plans to control flooding along the Mississippi (Barry 21–22) that were eventually combined (Barry 424).

Merging of public and private interests, as solutions to the Tennessee and Mississippi Rivers' flooding, however, is only one way these binaries disintegrate under examination. Environmental interests also contribute to arguments surrounding flooding in the Tennessee Valley (as well as along the Mississippi and its other tributaries). In the 1937 of Lorentz's *The River* and the 1936 setting of Kazan's *Wild River*, however, only the TVA and other federal New Deal programs offered hope to an impoverished South desperate for the technological and economic progress the electricity created by dams would provide.

Historical memory allows a positive view of public works projects like those implemented by the TVA—and of other New Deal Programs. Although few currently recall the disastrous environmental and economic repercussions of flooding along the Mississippi and its tributaries, especially following the great flood of 1927, *The River* and *Wild River* give us a glimpse of these disasters and some of their costs. And even though the films leave important questions either unanswered or uninterrogated, they draw on historical memory lost to most of us today and, perhaps, provide grounding for arguments still being debated, including the politics of disaster aid and the privatization of control of rivers like the Mississippi for both environmental and economic benefits. They also show us what happens when we forget why the levees broke, as they did in 2005 New Orleans.

Whatever the case, together, Lorentz's *The River* and Kazan's *Wild River* highlight the consequences of humans' overuse of land—loss of life and property—and offer a solution that demonstrates the interconnectedness of humans and their natural environment. The films further argue that in order for humanity to prosper, they must not only control nature but also rebuild it. As *The River*'s narrator proclaims, "We had the power to take the valley apart—we have the power to put it together again." These films, then, argue for a more moderate and scientific approach to land production and for a more equitable approach to ecology and racial politics, assertions currently under debate because of the ecological, economic, and racial repercussions related to Katrina's aftermath. Although the films fail to fully demonstrate political and economic consequences of massive floods of the 1920s and 1930s, they make their main environmental arguments clear: We made a mess, but we can clean it up.

3

Reconstructing Underground Urban Space in *Dark Days*

I N MODERN MYTHOLOGY, THE underground has served as the site of technological progress where excavation produces not only the means of production—coal and oil, for example—but also the foundation for the urban infrastructure—sewage and water systems, railways, gas, and lines for electricity, telegraphs and telephones. What, then, happens when humans not only enter this technologically driven underworld but also reconstruct, domesticate, and humanize it as a space to escape from the savage city above them? Historically such adaptive living practices have gone on for a long time in New York City; according to Margaret Morton, finding living spaces underground began there with the arrival of the Hudson River Railroad in the mid-1850s (*The Tunnel* ix) (see also, *Fragile Dwellings*).

In a documentary film set in a contemporary mode, *Dark Days* (2000), Marc Singer records the lives of several "homeless" people living in subway tunnels underneath New York City. As this documentary enters the "domesticated" underground, where those with little economic stability struggle to make a home, it traces the inhabitants' lives using what we call a narrative of environmental adaptation. In a move toward a more sustainable view of urban environments and their development, the homeless subjects Singer documents adapt a seemingly lifeless environment into an underground home.

As Henry (one of the older homeless people in the film) puts it, the homeless people in the tunnels have built themselves shanties there to "stop you from being helpless, not from being homeless." From the film's opening forward, we see little houses that have become homes with domestic comforts like electric lights, hot plates, and coffee pots, all in a reconstructed urban underground space left by Amtrak.

Like Robert J. Flaherty's subjects in films like *Nanook of the North* (1922), Singer's homeless have adapted the environment to meet their needs. But also like Flaherty, Singer shapes his subject romantically. He further transforms his subjects' context both by physically altering it and by manipulating his subjects' stories into a traditional narrative. In this framework, we assert that Singer's ethnographic portrayal of eight of the homeless people living beneath the city complicates images of the underground either as hell or as technological foundation. Within the romantic narrative Singer constructs, these homeless have transformed their underground environment just as American pioneers transformed the western landscape two hundred years ago. Singer argues that by re-constructing the "hell" beneath the city, these homeless redefine notions of progress in relation to community rather than individual growth.

In her interview with Singer at the 2000 Sundance Film Festival, Amy Goodman argues that Singer's *Dark Days* "is unique among docu-mentaries because while it is not an advocacy film with an overwhelm-ingly sagging political agenda, the subjects' stories and their sensitive treatment by Singer are testament to more creative, gentler solutions to the problem of homelessness." Goodman sees the underground Singer enters as "possibly America's most damnable version of hell" and finds Singer's decision to live with the homeless in their underground homes as an "abandon[ment of] comparatively opulent lives on earth." For more than two years, Singer lived in the New York subway tunnels with the homeless, and eventually intervened as an ethnographer seeking to document their stories.

Singer's own story about the making of *Dark Days* demonstrates that he acted as more than an objective observer. He not only entered the world of the homeless; he altered it by including the homeless in the filmmaking process. Singer argues that involving the homeless in the process helped them in at least two ways: It gave them a way to earn their way out of their homeless state, and it provided each with employ-ment that helped prepare them for the world above ground—a world Singer suggests thrives more when it rests on community values rather than on the alienation caused by the homeless state. To facilitate this new way of thinking, Singer not only helped build community by providing a common cause among the homeless; he also manipulated film footage to create a narrative of community below ground.

Dark Days illuminates urban underground adaptation as it is fed by stolen technology: electricity and (at least for a time) running water from

Figure 3.1. *Dark Days* (2001): Homeless shanty in the Amtrak tunnels.

above ground is accessed cost-free by the homeless living in the tunnels built for the New York subway system. However, documentary realism or facticity is complicated as Singer's *Dark Days* provides a realistic representation of homeless New Yorkers living in shanties built under the city—in an underworld created by the subway tunnel system.

Here, Singer controls not only the perspective and point of view of his camera but also the world above ground, which the homeless enter to "earn" a living before returning to their underworld homes. The city streets Singer shows are nearly devoid of human activity, even during the daylight hours when several of the homeless forage for cans, bottles, compact discs, books, and discarded television sets to sell for an income. It looks like Singer has constructed this above-ground city as a "wilderness" the homeless must escape because they cannot tame it. And they only reenter this "wild" urban world to acquire subsistence. Below ground, however, domestic life flourishes in a world the homeless, according to Singer's perspective, have adapted to serve their needs. Singer, too, then, takes a "hands on" approach to filming *Dark Days* because he represents the city as virtually devoid of the human (and natural) life that thrives (or shall we say, prospers) below.

Singer interviews subjects to reveal back stories, and they both build narratives out of individual tales of environmental compromise. To construct this narrative, Singer and his subjects create a world in which the city is a dangerous place, a wilderness, and the homeless seek shelter where no one else will go. Singer and his subjects work together to alter the underground landscape to accommodate filmmaking, as well. In Singer's discussion about the making of *Dark Days*, he explains how involved the homeless he interviewed became. Singer had lived with these homeless long enough to learn about their skills and the jobs they had worked above ground, so the homeless became both cast and crew in the film. For example, "one of the guys" ("Making of *Dark Days*"), who had worked on the railroad, built the dollies that facilitated the film's tracking shots. And Henry "tapped into" the city's electrical system, so Singer and the crew could construct power lines with sockets throughout the tunnels. Ralph took on the most responsibility, acting as Singer's primary assistant, helping with every step of the process—from filming to editing. Homeless people who had adapted the underground environment to serve their domestic needs altered it even further for their own documentary, a film built on a traditional narrative that advocates both interdependent living and progress.

Romantic Narrative Structure of *Dark Days*

The narrative of *Dark Days* follows a three-act structure:

1. going underground (with introductions to each character),

2. living like a family in the relative domestic bliss below, and

3. after a forced removal by Amtrak officials overseeing the tunnels near Penn Station, climbing back up above ground to begin living isolated lives in single-person apartments.

Act one begins with a representative of the homeless, Greg, descending out of a dark urban landscape into the relative domestic comfort below. The normalcy of living in shanties built in subway tunnels is first emphasized by portrayals of each of the "main characters" waking up in their shanties and getting ready to go to work, but this first act only shows us a glimpse of the ordinary lives Greg, Ralph, and Tito lead. The first act focuses instead on the individual tales the homeless tell, which explain not only how they ended up homeless and why they moved underground, but also how they escaped from a certain kind of hell above ground by entering this underground world.

Greg's first comment after descending into the subway through a hole in the city's concrete establishes this bifurcation between the urban wilderness and the domesticated tunnels below it. Greg calls the tunnel dangerous because "it's so dark," but argues that "it can't be as bad as it was up top." Greg's comment aligns with the first dimly lit shot in the tunnel, a pan of the shanties the homeless have built underground. A train comes in at an angle, bringing up the title, "Dark Days," but Singer's focus on individuals living ordinary lives deconstructs notions of darkness as entirely bad. Immediately after the title, the ordinary lives of the homeless living in those shanties come to the fore, so we first see each subject waking up and getting ready to go to work. Tommy, Tito, Ralph, and Greg—with captions announcing their names—get out of bed one by one, each stating his working aims for the day. Greg is "ready to hit the street." Ralph is, as Tito puts it, "always workin' on the house." Greg tells us, "I got to get paid. Got to make that almighty dollar. Find me something to sell."

The introductions to the characters include not only their immersion in the middle-class values exemplified by emphasizing work and, especially, workin' on the house—civilizing the underground. The opening also provides a space in which each subject can tell his or her story, which explains how each ended up homeless but fled the city—first, as Greg puts it, to "get out of the public eyesight," but then "this fuckin' became home." Even though Henry tells Tommy that "houses stop you from being helpless, not from being homeless," according to their narratives each subject has made a home underground that would be impossible on the streets above. Ralph explains how crack made him homeless and lost him his family. And Tommy tells about his escape from a family that "couldn't treat me like a human being." These introductions move the narrative forward because they allow us to view the contrast between the hell of living on the street and the homes and families they have built below ground.

Ethnography and *Dark Days*

Singer's *Dark Days* first presents an ethnographic reading of particular homeless under New York, using film as his tool. He adheres to the criteria Karl Heider outlines for ethnographic filmmaking, when explaining that "the most important attribute of ethnographic film is the degree to which it is informed by ethnographic understanding" (5). According to Heider, first of all, "ethnography is a way of making a detailed description and analysis of human behavior based on a long-term observational study on the spot," (6) a technique Singer applied by living with the homeless before, during, and after the shooting of his film. Secondly, Heider suggests that ethnography should "relate specific observed behavior to cultural norms" (6). Singer demonstrates well how even these homeless individuals are immersed in American middle-class–driven culture in which goals like building a house and community prevail. He also shows us how middle-class norms are refracted to fit the subhuman underground environment in which the film's subjects live.

The individual narratives Singer provides us also support Heider's third criteria for an effective ethnography: "holism" (6). The stories of these poor individuals are presented in not only their context as narrations unique to each individual but also in the context of an overarching story about the movement down into the world beneath New York, the growth of a community below ground, and then the movement back to a brighter life in apartments above ground. These interconnected stories are "truthfully represented" (Heider 7), Heider's last criterion for an effective ethnographic film.

Dark Days fits into Heider's definition of the genre: "Ethnographic film is film which reflects ethnographic understanding" (8). Like Flaherty's *Nanook of the North* in which archaic Inuit hunting practices are re-enacted to highlight a romanticized, more natural state, and Merian C. Cooper and Ernest Schoedsack's *Grass* (1925) and *Chang* (1927), which show us how civilization has corrupted the native, Flaherty's film reconstructs (both literally and figuratively) the stories his subjects tell, providing viewers with a romantic narrative that foregrounds progress. Heider argues that Flaherty's and Cooper and Schoedsack's works "reflect the romanticism of the period" (26). *Dark Days* suggests that the U.S. middle-class values highlighted in this film rest on such "romanticism," a foundation of the American dream.

The contrast between the hell found above ground and the American dream found below it also illustrates the complex combination of documentary and ethnographic strategies Singer draws on in *Dark Days*. The film not only follows the approaches taken in ethnographic films, it also integrates elements of at least two other types of documentaries. The first of these answers the question, "How do they do that?" which focuses on the details of human skill or ingenuity practiced in unusual circumstances. This is the focus and the appeal of films like *Dogtown and Z-Boys* (2001) (which documents how skateboarders learned their craft practicing in empty swimming pools) and *Riding Giants* (2004) (which shows us how the forerunners to skateboarders upped the ante for surfers). The other common type of documentary filmmaking illustrates how people cope when they are in a transitional state or moment in their lives, as does the Academy Award-winning documentary *Born into Brothels* (2004), and the earlier Maysles brothers' *Salesman* (1969) and Frederick Wiseman's *Basic Training* (1971).

Dogtown and Z-Boys shows how skateboarding evolved from a dying fad to a competitive sport based on hot-dogging stunts that grew out of surfing techniques. The documentary includes footage of stunts performed in empty swimming pools around Santa Monica and clips of some of the first competitive events sponsored by Zephyr Productions Surf Shop. The film depicts the rise of the skateboarding lifestyle, including how skateboarders like Tony Alva, Jim Muir, and Jay Adams transitioned from surfboard to skateboard, performing similar tricks on land as well as water, as they do in *Riding Giants*.

Born into Brothels represents a second category of documentaries, those that highlight coping skills during fundamental transitions. Although criticized for spotlighting Western intervention as a cure for poverty in India, the film still attempts to show us, as a review from *Newsweek* proclaims, "the power of art to transform lives." In the film, Zana Briski, a photographer first drawn to Calcutta's red light district to photograph women sex industry workers, teaches these prostitutes' children how to take pictures, and she attempts to finance some of their educations through exhibits of their photographs. The film's construction, documenting these children's transition from hopeless resignation to hopeful love of learning, is certainly fabricated through Briski's narrative (and editing) choices, but the film does attempt to show how the children and their mothers cope with changes brought on by both the entrance of the Westerner (Briski) and her camera.

The Maysles brothers' work shows us how Bible salesmen cope in *Salesman*. The film follows middle-aged male salesmen on their day-to-day, house-to-house sales pitches and from the winter in Massachusetts to new territories in Florida. While the weather becomes vacation-like, many of the men question whether they can continue in this line of work, questioning their ability and contemplating a transition not only from region to region but from the stressful profession of Bible sales to something else. In another transitional documentary, Wiseman reveals how military recruits survive in *Basic Training*.

Climax in *Dark Days*

Providing the fascination of the "how do they do that" type of documentary, in the second phase of Singer's film he shows us what these homeless literally do to survive, climaxing with a view of how they cope with a transition from their underground community to a life above ground. The lives the subjects live underground and their means of subsisting are traced by Singer in detail in this phase of his narrative. We see each subject leave home and reenter the city streets to earn a living. Tommy collects plastic empties, proud that he collects enough from selling bottles to take the weekend off. And Greg sells anything he doesn't keep himself, bragging that he had once sold "40 faggot books" and movies. But they all return to their self-built homes for comfort. As Henry cooks country corn bread made with buttermilk (because it makes it go together better) on a hot plate, he clarifies their world:

> Being homeless you can like consider growin' down here. 'Cause if you homeless on the street, you got only [what's] on [your] back. If they got caught in the rain, they ain't got shit. If you're homeless, better to be down here in a shanty than up top, where [you] only have what [you] can carry.

The world these subjects have created has become so civilized that they can own and nurture others, including pets. Tommy talks about his dogs and the pen he has built for them. Julio (with Lee) shows pictures of all of his pets—cats, birds, and a hamster—and tells a story about each one. Ralph plays with his dog in the house and then puts it outside "'cause [it's] too rough." Above ground we see life and light only at a distance with sounds of sirens in the emptiness. The sirens serve as a bridge to the first major conflict below—Dee's house fire, which firefighters attempt to extinguish. But even though Dee is burned out, she does not end up homeless. Instead, she moves in with Ralph, and the two become a family. Dee cooks meatballs on a two-burner hot plate in the well-stocked home Ralph has constructed and explains, "If you know how to cook, cook right."

Ralph and Dee form a relationship so close that Ralph tries to intervene in Dee's crack habit and the two scrap about a mermaid cup Dee left out so long that Ralph threw it away. The cup incident, however, brings up another source of conflict in the underground world—rats. All of the subjects have stories about rats, from Greg's suggesting they "are intelligent enough to tell others to come back," to Henry's stating that the rats "walk at night. I try to sleep at night." The story underground, then, includes conflict with nature. Subjects must contend with rats and must fight to maintain a civilized life in the underground where the city hides not only the source of its progress but also the real consumer products—human and animal waste.

Hygiene and waste center this final scene before the film's climax. Tommy's friend Brian showers in the cold water leaking out of a dirty pipe. Tommy shovels dog waste out of the kennel, and Brian pours a human waste bucket down a sewage crack. "Welcome back to the shit," Tommy says. The last scenes tracing subjects' lives below ground intertwine images of and discussions about food and rats and shit disposal, including even a match-action cut from people eating doughnuts scavenged from

Figure 3.2. *Dark Days*: Male/female relationships thrive underground.

the garbage above ground and wishing for milk to rats drinking milk underground from an overturned carton. Dee's story about losing her children and how she liked "the responsibility of being a mother," another veiled reference to milk, ends this scene, with shots of Dee ending her story preparing a crack pipe. Such narration and imagery foreshadow the end of the underground narrative.

The climax of this narrative occurs when Amtrak intervenes and breaks up the family-like relations and domestic world that the film's subjects have built for themselves below ground. Such a climax also parallels the kinds of the transitional coping strategies documented in films like *Born into Brothels*. The order to dismantle the shanties and leave the tunnels within thirty days destroys the civilization the film's subjects have constructed. As Julio puts it, "You guys are coming down here to fuck me up" at the point of a gun. They all fear the alternative homeless life above ground. Ralph proclaims, "I don't want to go to the shelter—steal all I have. Drugs. They should leave us down here until they get housing." Julio focuses on Amtrak's "breaking up the family" and argues that they should "leave us alone." According to the subjects, "This has been our home. For some twenty years."

This major conflict seems like it cannot be resolved. Amtrak officials like Rich provide ample evidence that the life below is dangerous because of respiratory illnesses, vermin, trains, and exposure. But the film's narrative structure works here, too. A homeless advocate, Mike Harris, provides the story's resolution. He works with Amtrak officials and promises that no one will be left in the tunnel if all the homeless get housing above ground. Amtrak agrees, and the underground pioneers are elated. Tito starts knocking down his shanty and yells, "We're out of here!" Dee, Tommy, Brian, Ralph, and Greg all jubilantly destroy their underground homes. Greg signs a contract, proving that he is actually homeless, in order to acquire an apartment, and the music rises to a crescendo as the walls come down.

Resolution

The film ends as it concludes the underground narratives. But the ending also demonstrates that each subject's story has only just begun, with a clear transition from one life to another. The film subjects' own narratives traced how they evolved from helpless homelessness to pioneering shanty lives below ground, but now the people have entered homes above. The last shots of Ralph, Greg, Dee, and Tommy show each living isolated in apartment homes with windows overlooking sunlit trees filled with birds. Greg cleans windows and fries chicken. Dee puts clothes away in dresser drawers and makes up her bed. Ralph pours out cereal and looks out the window, saying he feels like a baby. Tommy plans his living room decor—sectionals and an entertainment center with a 25-inch TV, a VCR, and cable hookup.

Figure 3.3. *Dark Days*: Ralph above ground in the light.

The brief speech each gives demonstrates they have left both the street and the underground for good. Greg highlights the film's title when he says he's left the dark days behind. And Ralph argues, "It will never happen again . . . Never. I will never go homeless again. It was like I was asleep . . . I'm stayin' awake." Dee's only comment is to yell "Whoopee!" as she falls on her clean-sheeted bed and proclaims, "It feels good."

The *Dark Days* do seem to have ended by the film's end. Subjects have moved from the streets to an underground adapted to meet their needs and up to the isolated but clean apartments above ground. But, as Tommy suggests, the move from pioneer in a dark wild underworld comes at a price: "I've got some good memories here, too," he says. "I'm going to miss the freedom."

Urban Environmentalism and *Dark Days*

Currently, writers, filmmakers, and other purveyors of pop culture seem to be constructing the inner city landscape in terms of seeing the inner city as a wilderness that must either be tamed or escaped. Its inhabitants seem like savages—dehumanized (and inferior) natives from whom "white suburbanites" must separate. If we expand the boundaries of this view of wilderness to include the inner city, the subjects in Singer's *Dark Days* might be viewed as superior humans choosing to separate from the demonized city and its dwellers above ground by entering the more civilized tunnels below. This construction is effective because each subject—Greg, Ralph, Tommy, and Dee, especially—embraces middle-class values like cleanliness and a strong work ethic that are emblematic of the suburban lifestyle. Ronnie, another tunnel dweller, even calls his shopping cart a minivan, the soccer mom vehicle of the 1990s.

And the "city" above ground each subject endured has savage tendencies. Living above ground means suffering the challenges of an environment inhabited by savages, who can't treat Tommy like a human and who steal Greg's and Ralph's possessions, even in what is ironically called a shelter. In this classical view of the wilderness, the wild city holds the resources humans must exploit in order to survive. So each subject goes above ground every day in search of food and items to sell, just as eighteenth- and nineteenth-century fur-trappers killed wild prey both for food and hides to sell.

A more romantic view of the wilderness might also be applied to the film, however, if the underground instead of the city above it is constructed as a wilderness. From this perspective, the subjects in *Dark Days* act like pioneers who leave civilization behind in order to live a freer and, perhaps, more natural life below ground. The city they leave is, as Andrew Ross puts it, "sick, monstrous, blighted, ecocidal, life-denying, [and] parasitical" ("Social Claim on Urban Ecology" 16). Like Huck Finn, who runs from "civilizin' " forces that encourage monstrous practices like slavery and squelch attempts to live a free life outside the status quo, each subject escapes his or her own monstrous conditions when leaving the city to build homes where they can live unique, individual, free, and, thus, more natural lives. Such romantic views of the wilderness are distinctly American, especially in terms of the ideology embedded in such views—freedom, individuality, and hearty self-reliance.

Dark Days challenges views of the homeless as savages and of their underworld homes as a form of hell. Living in and adapting the wilderness to meet their needs in some ways means that this wilderness is necessary. Without a wilderness to tame, a community cannot be built. Although crack addictions and domestic crises isolated them above ground and drove them to the street, in the underground tunnels, subjects form strong relationships that transcend race and gender.

Ralph, for example, is never alone when he tells his story and illuminates his underworld life. Ralph's introduction shows him with his dog beside him and his friend Tito explaining, "He's always workin' on the house." Tito is there when Ralph narrates his homeless story, as well, and laughs as he roughhouses with his dog. Tito returns to Ralph later in the film after going through rehab, to exalt the eggplant parmesan Ralph too had enjoyed. Tito and Ralph share doughnuts and camaraderie above and below ground. Knowing from Singer's commentary that Ralph was Marc Singer's main assistant on the film cements Ralph's rehabilitation.

Race and gender don't hinder friendships formed below ground, since Ralph is a light-skinned Hispanic male and Tito a bi-racial, mostly African American, young man. And Ralph forms another close relationship with Dee, a dark African American female, when her house burns down. Dee shares Ralph's home until Amtrak evicts them, sharing the cooking and helping Ralph out with his hygiene. In one scene Dee shaves Ralph's head with an electric razor, laughing when she shows a clump of hair left at the nape of the neck. Ralph takes the joke, but the scrapping between them here (as earlier over the mermaid cup) demonstrates the closeness of their relationship.

Ralph's close relationships below ground have helped him both kick his crack addiction and gain some insight into his failed relationships above ground. The next shot of Ralph after the laughter over the funny haircut shows him reflecting on the breakup of his family: "I'm bein' punished for every goddamn thing I did wrong. Sometimes I felt like crying. I was so damn selfish," he says before talking about his five-year-old daughter's being raped and burned. Dee, too, has learned the value of close relationships, saying she misses "all those things," when talking about the loss of her own family. Even when dismantling their shanties after Amtrak and the Homeless Coalition find them apartments, Ralph has his friends beside him. Dee and Tito hammer away on the shanty walls with Ralph looking on and then helping out, maintaining these close relationships until the end of their underground lives.

The film highlights close familial relationships not only for Ralph, Dee, and Tito, but also for other characters in the film—anyone who narrates a personal story becomes a central character. Tommy is introduced waking up with a woman lying beside him. He is shown caring for a mother dog and her puppies. And he reunites with a close friend, Brian, early on in the film. Brian shares as close a relationship with Tommy as Dee and Tito do with Ralph. When Brian moves in with Tommy, he shares chores as repugnant as dumping the waste bucket. And when the order from Amtrak is coupled with a promise of above-ground housing, Brian helps Tommy pack up their belongings and dismantle their shanty. Tommy tells Brian, "Don't mix dirty clothes in with clean ones," as they stuff clothing into garbage bags.

Only one main character, Greg, looks like he is isolated below ground, since he is shot mostly alone while shaving or collecting compact disks to sell. But even he talks about selling books and movies with a friend. Singer does show other subjects surviving in the elements—sometimes alone, like the older light Hispanic, Jose—but, they remain peripheral to the film's narrative, as "extras" rather than central characters.

Viewing the underground as a romantic wilderness allows individuals to form relationships naturally, without cultural barriers based on race, gender, and, of course, class. Domestic virtue is valorized. The domestic harmony and relative comfort subjects have created in their underground shanties is clear, since Singer focuses on relationships with pets and other subjects and on domestic symbols like food and hygiene.

Amtrak's eviction order, though, is the first written document shown in the film, and the order is reinforced at gunpoint, according to Julio's recapping of events. Before the Coalition for the Homeless intervenes, Amtrak felt justified in evicting the homeless from the subway tunnels because they viewed them as if they were in a savage wilderness, dangerous and life-threatening. And just as in Ellen Baxter's study of homeless adults in New York, *Private Lives/Public Spaces: Homeless Adults on the Streets of New York City*, the homeless they evict have become so dehumanized that they see no need to offer them alternative housing—until Mike Harris advocates for them.

Any previous opposition between the relationship-bound domesticated wilderness below ground and the city above, where subjects now live isolated lives in one-bedroom apartments, also breaks down under scrutiny. The film shows Ralph, Greg, Dee, and Tommy preparing for their lives as individuals in their new apartment homes and highlights their joyful reconnection with the status quo. But subjects' new lives are only introduced at the film's conclusion, so *Dark Days* fails to reveal the extent of progress that each subject enjoys once they escape the unsanitary conditions below. Furthermore, since the film is shot in black and white, we can't see the extent of the squalor and filth subjects must combat underground, even in scenes foregrounding conflicts with rats and precautions each must make to keep home, self, and food clean. And even though we see human and animal waste in buckets and on the ground, we can't smell the stench that would surely permeate their world with no sewage system in a closed tunnel.

Dark Days combines the romantic views of Flaherty, and Cooper and Schoedsack, all harking back to a more communal and, perhaps, more natural state, a community that *Dark Days* implies that the homeless create for themselves in their underground haven. As with Flaherty, the film also critiques the negative impact contemporary "civilization" has on these pioneers below ground. Yet the film ends with a vision of progress like that recorded in *Born into Brothels*. As in Briski's Indian documentary, the "outsider" view is shown as dominant and superior to that of the "natives." In Briski's case, the "natives" are Calcutta children and their prostitute mothers; in Singer's, the homeless.

Such an "outsider" view also matches the perspectives of what Andrew Ross calls *mainstream environmentalism* ("Social Claim on Urban Ecology" 15), an environmentalism concerned with traditional definitions of "wilderness, water-quality control, land-use planning and control, [and] outdoor recreation" ("Social Claim on Urban Ecology" Ross 15). Because mainstream environmentalists view the city as a monstrous savage (Ross "Social Claim on Urban Ecology" 16), the contrasting idea of an environmentalism grounded in the city—an urban eco-criticism—may be, as Ross puts it, "an oxymoron" ("Social Claim on Urban Ecology" 16). For Ross, urban eco-criticism would embrace "environmental priorities that affect urban residents, like sanitation, rat and pest control, noise pollution, hunger, malnutrition, poor health, premature death, not to mention the conditions that underpin these hazards, like the slashing of public services and the savage inequities of public housing policies" ("Social Claim on Urban Ecology" 15).

By Ross's definition, *Dark Days* could be seen as an *urban environmental ethnographic film*, in which at least some urban environmental priorities are combated, for at least a select group of homeless people. Even the Amtrak official recognizes the priorities Ross outlines, since he notes them as reasons for evicting the homeless from the subway tunnels.

Amtrak easily gives into pressure from the Coalition for the Homeless, as well—perhaps as a public relations ploy but definitely to the advantage of the homeless subjects Singer's film highlights. As in *Born into Brothels*, however, the solution is still provided by benevolent outsiders, who know better than the homeless they relocate. The homes these "pioneer" homeless built and the community they represent are dismissed by even representatives of the Coalition for the Homeless.

Conclusion

But *Dark Days* goes beyond the simplistic message of *Born into Brothels*, where Briski appears to beg for a pat on the back for all of the help she and her program have provided to the helpless Calcutta children and their mothers. *Dark Days* does not suggest that the only solutions to such urban problems are institutional—gained through public organizations' interventions. Instead, the film (and Singer, its creator) foregrounds how well the homeless subjects adapt their environment and themselves not only to survive but prosper in their (perhaps) savage underground world. Individuated through their stories and their uniquely furnished homes, especially Ralph (with friends Tito and Dee) and Tommy (with friend Brian) prove the resilience of humankind and suggest that the best way to solve environmental problems, both rural and urban, is to construct narratives that intertwine humans with each other and with their environments, all through a localized nostalgic vision of home. And *Dark Days* also proves, once again, that the best ethnographic films are those constructed mutually by both filmmakers and their subjects.

4

Ecology, Place, and Home in *Dark City*

Is It Our Nature to Live in the Dark?

A lex Proyas's *Dark City* (1998), opens in darkness, in a space lit only by stars and patches of blue that represent the blue world Dr. Schreber (Kiefer Sutherland) claims the "Strangers" invaded to save their race. This long shot of outer space cranes downward from that blue patch of light to an artificially-lit nighttime noir cityscape crowded with cars from the 1940s and 1950s and lit by a cinema neon sign announcing film titles that serve a prescient role: *The Evil* and *Bo k of Dreams* [sic]. Movement from the hollow emptiness of space, a pristine natural cosmos, to a cacophonous city devoid of nonhuman nature startles us both visually and aurally with its clashes—both of space and of genres. Between the pristine and the decadent constructed spaces, outer space of science fiction meets the noir of the dark city, and the organic galaxies traced in white and blue natural lighting meet a luminescent shadowed urban world devoid of nature other than that created and inhabited by the Strangers.

In what looks like an homage to Fritz Lang's *Metropolis*, the opening to Proyas's film, like many openings to science fiction and noir films, introduces us to its settings and chief themes through visual effects and, as a parallel to *Metropolis*'s epigram and inter-titles, a voice-over, this time through the narration of Dr. Schreber. But it also highlights the most important element in the film, its representation of ecology, literally "the study of homes." The shift from a traditional science fiction setting to one indicative of a carefully laid-out 1940s or 1950s noir world coincides with a swing from the pristine to the decayed and, in a parallel binary, from a natural to a constructed environment. The film seems to agree with Alexander Wilson's assertion (with a few changes) that "the culture of nature—the ways we think, teach, talk about, and construct the natural world—is as important as the world itself" (11). To paraphrase, the culture of the world of *Dark City*, the way this noir world is thought about, talked about, and constructed becomes more important than the world—if it is a world—itself.

Ecology and Eco-criticism

The way we think about, talk about, and construct the natural world serves as the central tenet of eco-criticism. In the Western Literature Association Meeting answering the question, "What is Eco-criticism?" Harry Crockett's definition broaches an issue over which eco-critics, ecologists, and other naturalists informed by the "hard sciences" continue to argue: the impact postmodernist thought has on both eco-criticism and the environment. Crockett contends that eco-critics "reject the prevailing critical assumption that reality is socially constructed" because, as liberal feminists suggest, looking at the world through such a postmodern lens encourages a relativism that makes the activism that promotes real change difficult if not impossible. As Crockett argues, "ultimately, [eco-critics] will be failures in [their] own eyes if [their] labors don't help green our society."

These eco-critics argue that nature must be seen as essential instead of constructed to ensure it will remain universal and unchanging and, thus (according to these eco-critics) more easily preserved and protected. Such a perspective limits our ability to connect with nature, however, since it rests on views from modernist and liberal thought that rely on defining ideas in relation to their opposites. Rational thought is defined in contrast to irrational thought, for example, with rational thought being seen as superior to its opposite. Nature, within this framework, is defined in contrast to culture and humanity, with nature taking the inferior seat in this dualism.

This issue has prompted anthologies like Michael Soule and Gary Lease's *Reinventing Nature? Responses to Postmodern Deconstruction* in which eco-critics argue for a vision other than a modern view that bifurcates humans from nature but usually aver that postmodern thought, especially one informed by deconstruction, "would not only threaten the privileged role of science as a source of truth about reality. It would also destroy

environmentalism, since the environment is just a 'social construction' "
(Hayles viii).

At the same time, however, the scholars discussing the term eco-criticism would also agree with Ralph W. Black and Cheryll Glotfelty, who see nature and culture as interacting with—rather than separate from—one another. Black cites William Cronon, who suggests that "human acts occur within a network of relationships, processes and systems that are as ecological as they are cultural" as a way to justify eco-critics' investment in both the natural world and its literary representations. And Glotfelty asserts that, "Despite the broad scope of inquiry and disparate levels of sophistication, all ecological criticism shares the fundamental premise that human culture is connected to the physical world, affecting it and affected by it" (xix). According to Glotfelty, "Eco-criticism takes as its subject the interconnections between nature and culture, specifically the cultural artifacts of language and literature" (xix).

Black and Glotfelty demonstrate that the old dualism between nature and culture that liberal (and modernist) thought encourages breaks down under scrutiny, since neither nature nor culture transcends the other, leaving room for what Dana Phillips describes as a movement from modernist dualistic thought to a postmodern world of representation (205, 6), but a view of postmodern thought that offers a way to "green our society" from a local level.

Like Dana Phillips's article, "Is Nature Necessary?" *Dark City* offers a space in which to explore whether nature is necessary, especially in relation to the idea of ecology as the study of homes, a place where nature and culture interconnect rather than conflict with one another. The film allows us to examine at least three constructed settings—ecosystems—as possible homes for human (and, perhaps, alien) survival, but the film demonstrates that only one of these three provides any promise for humans, as natural beings, to thrive—the constructed setting in which "nature is necessary." According to Phillips:

> Unmaking history seems to me to be the sober prospect postmodernism offers us, and is more difficult than making it. The special difficulty of unmaking what used to be called natural history is compounded by our ignorance of human complicity in it, and revising it is going to take more than just good writing or vigorous demonstration. But thinking and working our way through the past, and the perhaps unthinkable, impossible future of nature, may be our last best hope for building dwelling thinking here and now. (222)

Dark City offers a space in which Phillips's assertion about agency—building dwelling thinking—in relation to a postmodernist worldview can be examined, since within a science fiction futuristic context, the film delves into the past—in this case that of a 1940s noir city—as a way to examine the future of nature, of both human and nonhuman natures and their environments.

Dark City is about a dying race of aliens, the Strangers, coming to a blue planet, presumably Earth, and capturing some humans in order to examine what makes them able to survive as individuals. The Strangers share a collective mind that is in terminal decay. To study these captured humans, the Strangers construct a 1940s-style city and, in a way, construct their humans by implanting different memories into their brains. To see how these humans react in different situations and with different memories, the Strangers change both the city and its inhabitants' memories each night at midnight, with the help of Dr. Schreber—a human forced to serve them—all while the humans are hypnotized into sleep by the Strangers.

Because these Strangers have an aversion to light, however, the city and its inhabitants never experience day. Within this context, one of the humans, John Murdoch (Rufus Sewell), evolves into a super-human, who can resist the Strangers' will, stay awake and even change the shape of his surroundings in Dark City, just like the Strangers. When John Murdoch first resists the Strangers' will and stays awake, he also resists the implantation of memories, so without memories, Murdoch must search for an identity. While Murdoch searches, however, the Strangers attempt to capture him and use him as their sole source of life. In the end, Murdoch claims his name, "saves" Dark City and its human inhabitants, and defeats the Strangers because they make a series of mistakes. Ultimately Mr. Book (Ian Richardson), the Strangers' leader, fails to notice that Dr. Schreber has switched syringes and implants memories other than the collective memories of the Strangers into Murdoch's mind. This seemingly "simple" story, though, occurs in a mixture of settings that serve as more than mere backdrop—especially the noir city that seems to pop out of the cosmos and the Shell Beach setting John Murdoch creates to replace the dark unnatural world of the Strangers.

Filmic visuals are reinforced by Dr. Schreber's voice-over narration, which was added to the film after its initial production, without Proyas's approval. Without listening to Schreber's voice, however, we can see that the cityscape onscreen into which audience members are plummeted was constructed. We learn later, through Schreber's discussion with John Murdoch, that the Strangers built this city as a way to study humans in a variable-free environment, an environment the Strangers change nightly through a process they call tuning. While the Strangers tune, the humans sleep, but when they awaken, changes in the environment go unnoticed because they too have been changed—this time through imprinting, a process in which new memories are injected into their brains with a gothically-decorated syringe. All of these plot elements coincide with other science fiction films in which aliens (or strangers) study and cohabit humans and their bodies as means for survival—think of *The Hidden* (1987) or the three versions of *Invasion of the Body Snatchers* (1956, 1978, and 1993).

Dark City as Film Noir

Dark City shifts our focus from the aliens (the characters) and the film's narrative to its setting—all because the Strangers' study occurs in a 1940s noir city rather than a site contemporary to the film's date of production. This noir setting is meticulously staged, from the interior and exterior mise-en-scène with its low-key lighting and stereotypical noir figures like the detective, the femme fatale, and the hero/victim to the low-angle deep focus camera shots so prevalent in film noir since *Citizen Kane* (1941). All these noir elements of the mise-en-scene are contrasted with the Strangers themselves and their habitat—shot, lit, and staged in horror style—and with the Shell Beach scene Murdoch creates, complicating views of constructed versus natural space, as well as genre. As in film noir, the most prominent characters in *Dark City* reflect a nearly hopeless world: the displaced hero/victim, the femme fatale, the detective.

It is style, however, that sets film noir apart from earlier detective films. Stylistically, the film acts as homage to noir. Shooting styles draw on those perfected in *Citizen Kane*, which Andrew Sarris sees as one of the first and most influential noirs, calling it one of the "two-pronged noir breakthrough[s]" (104). Low-key lighting, extreme camera angles, deep focus, wide-angle lenses, and depth of field are all drawn from *Kane* and the later noir films it inspired. The arched rooms and hallways shot from low-angle camera positions recall Gregg Toland's cinematography in *Citizen Kane*'s varied locations. And the figures, buildings, and interior props—all precisely replicating a 1940s milieu—are dramatically illuminated to maximize cast and attached shadows, including those figures shot in silhouette. Noirs are shot mostly at night in a decaying—and wet—urban milieu. Many scenes are shot from low-angle camera positions to further set the mood with wide-angle lenses that increase depth of field. Many of these techniques are drawn from German Expressionism, emphasizing the chaotic world in which trapped characters seek meaning. *Dark City*'s urban setting fulfills all aspects of this description of film noir.

The city duplicates the 1940s urban noir atmosphere with its dank, dark and decrepit streets and buildings and sleazy interior hotel rooms and night clubs. Noir figures abound in this dark city, beginning with John Murdoch, the mentally displaced hero/victim in search of salvation and self-realization. Women figures, too, take on the noir roles of either torch-singing femme fatales like Emma (Jennifer Connelly) and prostitutes like May (Melissa George) or virtuous virgins like Anna (also Jennifer Connelly), even though the female roles are so flattened in this constructed space that they look almost sexless. As in many noir films, a police detective, Inspector Bumstead (William Hurt), serves first as Murdoch's (the hero's) pursuer, and then as a source of his salvation. And even Dr. Schreber's character aligns with the corrupt doctors of noir who drug heroes like Phillip Marlowe (Dick Powell) in *Murder, My Sweet* (1944).

Sound, too, in this cityscape, brings to mind noirs like *Fury* (1936), *Kiss of Death* (1947), *Out of the Past* (1947), *They Live By Night* (1948), and *Gun Crazy* (1949). Characters' speech patterns follow those of noir figures, since their reactions to horrific events are almost emotionless. Nightclub music, too, harks back to 1940s and early '50s jazz. Background effects sound hollow and muted, as if heard through penetrating thick fogs and continuous rains.

Dark City's cityscape and the narrative surrounding it most resemble that of films like *On Dangerous Ground* (1952), a Nicholas Ray film in which Jim Wilson (Robert Ryan) finds solace in the rural hills, away from the decaying noir urban setting he escapes. Because Wilson, a hardboiled police detective, has become embittered by his dealings with the heartless criminals of the urban underworld, he begins beating his suspects and is sent away from the city to the "country" to pursue a young girl's killer and curb his violence. In this idyllic pastoral setting, Wilson gains self-awareness, with the help of Mary (Ida Lupino), the murderer's blind sister, and frees himself of his own rage. Urban shots in the film maintain Wilson's cynicism and desperation, but gradually, as his view of the world changes, rural shots brighten, suggesting that Wilson's own blindness about himself has lifted.

The earliest views of John Murdoch in *Dark City* set him up as a lost noir hero/victim in search of himself, a character-type who recalls Jim Wilson. He wakes up in a seedy hotel room, parallel to noir openings in which heroes awaken from drunken stupors and wonder, what happened to me? The interior landscape he views reinforces this noir mise-en-scène that includes noir costuming and interior setting, including his 1940s overcoat and the beat-up interior of his hotel room. An arch dominates the scene, another noir motif repeated in the film, especially in the many low-angle shots of hallways lit from the side as in films like *Crossfire* (1947) and *T-Men* (1947).

Camera shots of Dr. Schreber in the phone booth, too, highlight the noir style with depth and shadow detail. Here lights go on and off for even more dramatic effect. And in Schreber's office, too, lighting and camera angles enforce strong silhouettes. The police station where the Inspector and Emma discuss Murdoch's case also draws on the noir style, this time because hot lights are always in full view, never blocked by the figures, for a forced perspective of frames within frames shot from extreme low angles.

This meticulous set design continues even in shots of the prostitute May's seedy apartment where we see beaded curtains casting moving shadows and, in earlier shots, May's lined stockings casting shadows that look like bars. All these scenes, even though shot in color, simulate the black and white of noir by finding patterns of dark and muted color that amplify the noir mood.

But like Jim Wilson, John Murdoch seeks to escape the decay of the city and the empty seediness of his role there. Like many characters in film noir, Murdoch feels trapped by forces beyond his control, in this case literally trapped by the city the Strangers have constructed to study him and the other captured humans. And like Jim Wilson, Murdoch seeks solace in a nonurban setting, the Shell Beach depicted on the post card he finds in his suitcase. Devoid of memories and, it seems, of a sense of self, Murdoch, like Wilson, frantically battles the city and its makers while searching for salvation outside the city and its underworld. As in *On Dangerous Ground*, a virtuous woman contributes to the salvation Murdoch eventually gains, but unlike Wilson, Murdoch must create the "natural" ecosystem that eventually saves him and the rest of the city's inhabitants, a change that puts the eco-edge on this multi-genre film.

The battle Murdoch does eventually win, however, forces him into another ecosystem that proves unsuccessful, the underworld of the Strangers that draws on the visual motifs of the horror genre. In this realm, faces are lit from below and colors of the lighting change from browns and yellows to ghastly blues and greens, and other darker tones, exaggerating the whiteness of the all-male Strangers' faces. This underworld, with its assembly lines and baroque torture chamber wheels out of a Frankenstein lab, draws on both German Expressionist films like *Nosferatu* (1922) and *Metropolis* (1927) and Hollywood's *Frankenstein* (1931) and *Bride of Frankenstein* (1935).

Science fiction plays a role in this realm, as well, since the Strangers act like the parasites depicted in films like *The Hidden* and control humans through the technology of their machines and their memory-filled syringes, but the underworld still looks like a horror film, perhaps as a way to highlight the Strangers' alien presence. Yet both the noir and horror settings prove to be ecological nightmares for the Strangers seeking rejuvenation through their human studies. Shifts from outer space to the constructed spaces of the city and the underworld controlling it demonstrate that these Strangers are dying, and this death state is emphasized by the Strangers' choice to inhabit only male human corpses, seemingly avoiding female bodies with life-giving reproductive capabilities.

Nature in a Lifeless Constructed Space

The shift in the film from the natural but inscrutable emptiness of outer space to the constructed space of the dark city and its underworld underlines perhaps the most important role conflicting settings play in the film—a marker of humanity's relationship with the natural world. The film opens with a wide view of dark space lit only by stars, all presumably created naturally for no particular purpose. Life may exist in this void, but none is perceivable at this distance. When the camera moves downward, the first tangible evidence of life emerges—blue light shimmering in the midst of the stars, a blue that signifies the presence of water, which, for life as we know it, is necessary for survival. But the closer the camera cranes toward the city, the less natural the environment becomes.

Viewed from above, the city's architecture serves as landscape, with skyscrapers peaking out of concrete unbroken by green space. A closer view reveals lines of moving cars from the late 1940s through the 1950s, headlights shining their forward march toward some unknown destination. When these cars stop their march, human life is shown, but these humans are sleeping, in their cars, in a diner, and on a subway—all artificially lit and surrounded by concrete and steel. Sounds, too, reflect this halt, with city sounds evolving into orchestral music that ends in silence. The unnatural exterior world of the city looks like it is devoid of the organic, and the dark noir atmosphere emphasizes its lack of uncontrolled life. The carefully staged exteriors and interiors of the city, then, not only signify the film's noir themes but also the lifelessness of constructed space.

This lifelessness is drawn from the noir, science fiction, and horror genre elements that are evident in the film. The urban noir setting the Strangers have constructed to study humans provides them with a world nearly devoid of nonhuman nature. This nearly lifeless cityscape looks staged and inorganic because it is a constructed urban space instead of a thriving ecosystem. This noir setting also provides the backdrop for the stereotypical characters in the film, especially the flat bifurcated roles represented by the few women present in the film: Women either serve as pure virgins or whores, extreme binaries usually signifying women's inferior and, consequently, more natural state, according to eco-feminists like Annette Kolodny and Gretchen Legler.

But science fiction elements also contribute to the constructed lifeless state of the film, since the Strangers (as aliens) survive in this city only as inhabitants of human corpses. The dead, then, serve as homes for the parasitic Strangers, a sign that these aliens lack the individuality and agency that a human life presumes. These Strangers, too, enact a theme common in science fiction films: If they can construct a world and the memories they believe make humans who they are, then they can duplicate both humanity and their living world—a premise proven false by the end of the film.

Even though these Strangers have created a noir-influenced world in which to study their human specimens, their own world, an underground lair, is even more lifeless. It is the stuff of horror, a Hades where the undead—Strangers housed in human corpses—construct and reconstruct their city and interchange the city's captured humans' memories as a way to save themselves and their own race. This underworld realm of the Strangers looks like another nightmare, with Strangers only able to think with one collective mind and only able to live as parasites housed in the bodies of the dead. Although the Strangers seem oblivious to their failure until the very end of the film—and of their race—Murdoch recognizes (as do we) that the Strangers are looking for their own salvation, for what makes someone human and thus able to survive as an individual, in the wrong place—the dead noir world rather than a more natural irrational ecosystem that houses the soul.

This distinction between what is completely controlled, artificial, and "dead" and what is natural and alive springs from Empirical philosophy of the eighteenth century's "Great Awakening," a view which, according to Gary Lease, "led inevitably to an opposition between reason and nature, a position which Kant in his idealism effectively exploited" (8). In the nineteenth and twentieth centuries, this struggle between a culture controlled by reason and an irrational nature became further complicated by a focus on scientific pursuit that eliminated Spinoza's identification of nature with God.

But, as Lease suggests, "After wrestling with the notion of nature for well over two thousand years, Western tradition had come up dry: Neither an identification of the human species with nature nor a strict dichotomy between the two proved ultimately successful" (8, 9). *Dark City* and its many settings demonstrate not only that such a strict dichotomy proves unsuccessful but also how a constructed space, this time one that agrees that nature is necessary, can serve as a successful site in which human and nonhuman nature can coexist in a web of interconnected relationships.

The first interior view shown in the film demonstrates, just as does Michael Bennett's and David W. Teague's anthology *The Nature of Cities*, that life exists even in a constructed noir cityscape. The hero, John Murdoch, unlike the anonymous sleeping people outside, awakens like a newborn in a milky water-filled bathtub, which Proyas compares to a womb (Commentary). Then he rises and looks at his reflection in a mirror as if searching for himself there. Blood on his forehead proves Murdoch lives, and the pan of the room from Murdoch's point of view shows his awareness of himself and his environment. In other words, unlike others in this world, John interacts with his physical environment, with his (ecological) "home" or "household," enough that he shudders when he notices a bloody mutilated female corpse he observes without recognition. Murdoch lives, but he has no memories to explain his surroundings. Murdoch's self-awareness disproves the Strangers' claim that humans are a product of their memories, since he reacts consciously to his surroundings without remembering them, showing us his more natural uncontrolled state.

Murdoch's interaction with nonhuman nature, too, reveals much about his difference from the rest of the inhabitants of Dark City. When he by accident shatters a goldfish bowl because of a ringing phone, Murdoch quickly places a fish—now on the floor—in his bath water, a sign of his ability to interact with other species, to nurture nonhuman nature. Even more telling, though, is the change Murdoch makes to the bath water, so that the fish will be more likely to survive. Our first view from above shows us Murdoch is in a bathtub full of white, soapy water, but when he places the goldfish in the same bath, the water has completely cleared.

From the beginning, then, Murdoch is aligned with the natural world with which he instinctively knows how to interact. He looks out of place in the controlled environment of Dark City. In fact, the first image he views, other than his own reflection, is that of Shell Beach, another emblem of nature, embossed on a post card. At Shell Beach, according to this card, a summer sun shines brightly on blue water and white sands—signifying the possibility of life, just as Murdoch's awakening demonstrates the presence of his own life force.

Three repeated motifs aligned with nature emerge in this early interior scene: water and its sustaining ability revealed by the goldfish in the bathtub (and, perhaps Murdoch's control over the water's clarity), Murdoch's blood and waking life, and Shell Beach—a place of life and hope for Murdoch and even other humans still controlled by the Strangers.

Water is everywhere in Dark City, even though the Strangers claim to fear and avoid it in the same way they do daylight. Streets lined with dimly lit decaying buildings are filled with it; the seedy Turkish bath where Dr. Schreber hides from the Strangers steams with water vapor, and the canal leading to "Shell Beach" and the edge of Dark City streams with water. The exterior air looks heavy with rain, not only dark but dank and thick, so much so that sometimes fog emanates from the ground, and Neptune's Kingdom, to which John Murdoch escapes, houses numerous saltwater tanks full of exotic fish.

Ultimately, it is water that destroys John Murdoch's chief enemy and leader of the Strangers, Mr. Book, and it is water that helps to transform Dark City into a light-filled world surrounded by sea at the end of the film. The fish tanks and goldfish bowl clearly function as life-giving homes to the fish within, but it is an unnatural life. The people and their memories are trapped in Dark City like goldfish in a bowl, but the Strangers have denied them any real contact with a nonhuman natural world. But only water, in this case from rain and in a swimming pool, serves to ward off the Strangers who seek to literally suck the life out of the humans they have captured. Water acts as a source of life and as a sign of both nature and of an undirected life.

Water serves as the source of life as we know it. According to David Burne, it is the "medium of life" (18). Burne asserts that "at some point, all biogeochemical cycles involve water, because water forms the fluid environment inside all living things [to our knowledge]. But water also moves in a cycle of its own. [On Earth] every year, half a billion cubic kilometers of sea water evaporate into the air, creating the rain that allows land-based life to survive" (18). Water, then, both sustains and is contained by life—and, of course, it contains life forms of its own, as an ecosystem—a biogeochemical cycle—in which plant and animal life thrives.

The Strangers' aversion to water, which we see as necessary to life, signifies their own difference from humanity. In spite of their aversion, however, the Strangers create a cityscape streaked with water, perhaps because they are so wedded to this noir world's construction that they cannot avoid the contradiction. As proof of the Strangers' recognition that humans thrive on water, they include an ominous indoor swimming pool that serves as Dr. Schreber's haven. Proyas recreates this noir motif just as precisely as any of the other noir sets, with careful attention paid to both cinematography and set design.

But water not only literally but also figuratively and thematically signifies life and, consequently, irrational nature. Except for the rat maze in Dr. Schreber's office, water—in fish bowls and tanks—provides a home for the only nonhuman life evident in the city, that of the tropical fish and the plants of their natural habitat. These fish tanks serve as symbols of hope for an escape from the controlled environment of the city, since they illustrate the possibility of a light-filled life free of concrete and urban decay. Murdoch's search for self and his journey from the city's streets, first to Neptune's Kingdom, then to the Strangers' underworld realm, and, finally, to his ultimate destination, the sea he creates, springs from the realization that water means life. John Murdoch recreates the scene depicted in the fish tanks at Neptune's Kingdom and on a constructed home movie and sketchbook, creating a sea now surrounding the city, with life-giving water lit from above by a bright sun.

Water symbolizes life and hope, but it also serves as a repeated motif signifying both an uncontrollable and a cyclical nature. Water wards off the Strangers who constructed a city full of it, so these Strangers may have less control over the cityscape and its inhabitants than it originally appears. Even John Murdoch, who defeats the Strangers, only follows the watery trail to Shell Beach (and to the Strangers' lair) rather than controlling it. Even when he creates Shell Beach and the sea it lines, Murdoch cannot completely control the ecosystem he has put into place. He opens up the pipes and creates the space, but the rest of the city and shore are now out of his control. Even though humans impact both positively and negatively on water and its ecosystem, water, according to Burne, "isn't destroyed by being used" (119)—water signifies an ecosystem in which even Murdoch must take chances rather than take charge because water, in a sense, has a mind of its own.

Shell Beach and the sea it lines, then, serve as symbols of the life-sustaining power of water and, ultimately, of irrational nature, the only successful ecosystem presented in *Dark City*. The noir cityscape fails both the aliens and the captured humans. The underworld and its machinery fails the Strangers, since they cannot control the one life force that might save them with their technology—John Murdoch. Only Shell Beach brings hope to the captured humans as a source for their own survival as a species with free will and agency.

Shell Beach is the only memory all of the captured humans share. It is an archetype, if you will. Everyone remembers being there but cannot remember how to get there; yet the hope of Shell Beach sustains them. The film's director, Alex Proyas, suggests that Shell Beach is "hope implanted in the humans" (Commentary). Once Murdoch creates a real rather than postcard Shell Beach, lighting there demonstrates a change from a constructed shadowy space where machines are hidden below to a more natural one so well-lit nothing can hide. Only at Shell Beach do we see a brightly lit day with intense colors that illuminate the shimmering waves of the new sea, the sparkling grain of the boardwalk, and the crystal sands that surround it.

Shell Beach sustains life and signifies hope, but without John Murdoch, who has climbed the evolutionary ladder and become more powerful than the Strangers, Shell Beach, and the ecosystem it houses, could not exist. Murdoch, with his powers to both create life and destroy the Strangers who would eradicate it, is the primary symbol of irrational nature and of a life unfettered by alien power. John Murdoch's search for identity and, consequently, salvation, is a search he can share, since its conclusion proves the salvation of all human and nonhuman life in Dark City.

Murdoch's role becomes evident when viewed in contrast with that of Mr. Hand (Richard O'Brien), the Stranger who is implanted with Murdoch's memories. Mr. Hand believes these memories will lead him to Murdoch, so the Strangers can use him as their source of life. According to Mr. Hand, Murdoch "follows clues" in the same way Mr. Hand "follows memories." Yet Mr. Hand admits from the start that the path he leads his fellow Strangers on toward Murdoch is based in instinct rather than fact, and "instincts are irrational," and hence uncontrollable.

Mr. Hand operates as Murdoch's foil, as an evil double also searching for identity. Only Murdoch and Mr. Hand see themselves in a mirror, highlighting this doubling. After Mr. Hand takes in the memories Murdoch was supposed to have, we first see Murdoch morph into Mr. Hand in the mirror that reflects a hotel room in which a prostitute has been murdered. Mr. Hand proclaims, "I have John Murdoch . . . in mind," and believes until the end that holding his memories is enough to possess him and his life force. The Strangers state it even more blatantly: "We need to be like you." The Strangers believe that if they duplicate John Murdoch's memories, they duplicate him and, consequently, possess him as a life force that can sustain them, as a young and powerful mind from which they can feed: They wish to "share [his] soul." To accomplish this, the Strangers want to implant their collective memories into Murdoch in order to survive. Mr. Hand follows Murdoch's memories first to Neptune's Kingdom, where Murdoch escapes with Emma's and the Inspector's help and finally to what Murdoch thinks is Shell Beach. Murdoch relies on Dr. Schreber's help; Mr. Hand follows Murdoch's implanted memories.

Yet the journey to "Shell Beach," the end of the city's limits, indicates an important difference between Murdoch and Mr. Hand. Murdoch, the inspector, and Dr. Schreber—who has been kidnapped from the water-filled pool—take a boat to "Shell Beach," floating on a canal that resembles the River Styx. Mr. Hand and his allies fly there above the water in a ghostly parade of trench-coated animated corpses. Mr. Hand, in spite of housing Murdoch's memories, is still a Stranger who cannot abide water and its damp life-giving properties.

Their journey to what should be Shell Beach, though, leads them literally to a brick wall—covered with a poster duplicate of Murdoch's Shell Beach postcard. Murdoch and the Inspector break down the wall revealing what Mr. Hand calls "the truth," that Dark City is actually a floating space station. According to Roger Ebert, this is "the first space station since *Star Wars* (1977) that is newly conceived—not a clone of that looming mechanical vision" (127).

When the Inspector falls through the hole he and Murdoch have created in a wild search for the real Shell Beach, he falls not into water but through Dark City's atmosphere into the space beyond. Another truth is revealed: Even though Dark City is a constructed experimental space, it too is an ecosystem, with a life-sustaining atmosphere, one we watch the Inspector shoot through to his death. Dark City floats in a natural, uncontrolled space lit by white and blue—signs of life, like water. Here nature and the constructed city are literally contrasted. And Murdoch and Mr. Hand are also contrasted. Unlike Mr. Hand, who killed women constructed as prostitutes when implanted with their memories (and would gladly kill Emma), Murdoch demonstrates his humanity by allowing himself to give up control and submit to Mr. Hand (at least temporarily), so Emma's life will be saved.

Murdoch's self-sacrifice conflicts with Mr. Hand's self-centered brutality, just as the mechanized Dark City contrasts with the natural space in which it floats. Instead of offering any self-sacrifice of his own, Mr. Hand takes Murdoch to the Strangers' underground lair to save his race. Murdoch is meant to serve the Strangers by becoming a recipient of their collective memories.

Conclusion

Realization of the life-giving properties of self-sacrifice illustrated by Murdoch's choice to help others, prepares us, and, perhaps, John Murdoch, for the battle that ensues in the underworld after Dr. Schreber rebels against the Strangers' commands and switches syringes. Instead of injecting Murdoch with the Strangers' collective memories, Dr. Schreber injects him with memories from a childhood at Shell Beach that include lessons about the Strangers and their machines. John Murdoch becomes both natural and godlike in the underworld because he defeats the Strangers without destroying their world. In fact, the squidlike strangers housed in the human corpses ultimately are defeated by the very force that sustains other life—water. Murdoch defeats the Strangers' leader, Mr. Book, by creating a water tower and then thrusting him through it. Once the Strangers' leader escapes his human house and dies, Murdoch chooses then "to fix things," to, in this case, make them more natural.

After Murdoch, godlike, completes his creation, Dark City is no longer dark; it is a city that has evolved and literally turned over, revealing a sunlit sky full of mazelike clouds all surrounded by water, now the sea that Shell Beach lines. The second to last scene of the film restates its message: "You wanted to know what it is about us that makes us human. . . . You're not going to find it in here," Murdoch explains to Mr. Hand, the last Stranger, as he points to his mind: "You went looking in the wrong place." Because humans are individuals with souls who thrive best in an interactive natural ecosystem Mr. Hand's conclusion comes as no surprise: "Your imprint is not agreeable with our kind." At least in the worlds of *Dark City* the most successful ecosystem is the most natural one—the one uncontrolled by the Strangers.

And this new ecosystem, although also constructed, is one in which nature can thrive because it is not completely controlled. When Murdoch creates a door to the sunlit boardwalk overlooking Shell Beach, he tells Mr. Hand: "I'm just making a few changes around here." Mr. Hand who, with the Strangers' collective mind, has controlled every change in Dark City, is appalled and asks, "Are you sure that's what you want?" But Murdoch, a human connected more with the irrational soul of nature than with the rational realm of the mind, is "prepared to take [his] chances," to create the possibility for nature, knowing such a possibility is beyond his control.

Figure 4.1. *Dark City*: No longer a dark city.

The success of this new ecosystem over those lifeless settings constructed by the Strangers, then, aligns with Dana Phillips's suggestion that we must "unmask history" in order to revise it and create the possibility of a future of nature and of ourselves. Phillips's reliance on Wendell Berry's assertion that "Nature is necessary" (220) provides the grounding for this suggestion. According to Berry, "Nature is necessary . . . in that it is necessity itself" (220).

Berry's later suggestion, however, may explain why the world John Murdoch creates is so much more successful than that of the Strangers. Berry argues that

> the use of nature as measure proposes an atonement between ourselves and our world, between economy and ecology, between the domestic and the wild . . . a conscious and careful recognition of the interdependence between ourselves and nature that in fact has always existed and, if we are to live, must always exist. (quoted in Phillips 221)

Murdoch chooses to sacrifice himself to save Emma, an example of humanist nature, and chooses to create a world in which both human and nonhuman nature can thrive.

In *Dark City*, then, history produced by the Strangers has been unmasked in order to revise it. Most importantly, Murdoch's choices demonstrate that he has not only thought through the past but has thought toward a future where, with hope, a dwelling—a home—can be shared. This sacrifice lines up with Dana Phillips's plea in "Is Nature Necessary?":

> If to imagine nature as something real, treat it accordingly, and understand why it is important to do so, is something new, then the revolutionary slogans for the future must abandon older formulas: if in smashing the multinational corporate state [read the Strangers], you have nothing to lose but your chainsaws [read implanted memories], the loss is nonetheless real and possibly quite painful, however necessary. (219)

John Murdoch has taken the tools of two genres—science fiction and horror—and rebuilt and brightened a third—noir—to reclaim life for humans imprisoned in the no-longer-dark city. With the life-giving elements of water and light, new life can emerge, just as John Murdoch rose from his bathtub like a newborn. Science fiction provides this new eco-system with a constructed space—a literal space ship on which to

Figure 4.2. *Dark City*: Anna/Emma and John smile at the light and water of life.

build a more natural home. Horror brings the dark tools of the Strangers (the tuning clock and—perhaps—Murdoch's will to live that is provided by struggling against the Strangers' parasitic nature). Science fiction and horror also combine to turn our noir hero—John Murdoch—into a superhero who can defeat the Strangers and choose to build a bright home for his fellow humans, complete with the hope of Shell Beach.

The noir world constructed by the Strangers is a world without light and without hope. John Murdoch transforms that darkness into light. And the filmic world Proyas constructs through technological innovations provides a space in which to explore these complex notions of home.

In the end, Murdoch's last conversation with Mr. Hand and his first with Anna clarify the differences between the two races, within the conflicting genres, and between a dead and a living ecosystem. Murdoch decides to "fix things" in Dark City, even though, as Mr. Hand argues, he may not be making the right choices. Murdoch, unlike Mr. Hand, is willing to "take chances," to correct the past and work toward a more organic, interconnected, and, therefore, less controllable, future—one in which nature, signified by the sun and sea, takes a predominant role.

And that willingness to take risks, to provide the possibility of a more interconnected future, applies to connections between human nature, as well, even if those risks are not completely controllable. In this new world, ecology, and home, John Murdoch is willing to take a chance with Anna—who had been his wife Emma before her memories were changed. Murdoch joins Anna on a pier overlooking the newly created Shell Beach and becomes himself, by naming himself in connection with another: "What's your name?" Anna asks him, and he finally knows. "John. John Murdoch."

5

Environmental Nostalgia and The Tragic Eco-Hero

The Case of *Soylent Green* and the 1970s Eco-Disaster Film

I N AN ARTICLE CELEBRATING THE thirty-year anniversary of Earth Day, Ronald Bailey argues that "Earth Day 1970 provoked a torrent of apocalyptic predictions" ("Earth Day, Then and Now"). For him, Earth Day and the environmental policies it represented were necessary in 1970. Yet, what he calls the "prophets of doom" were "*spectacularly* wrong" (emphasis Bailey's "Earth Day, Then and Now"). In fact, "many contemporary [2000] environmental alarmists are mistaken when they continue to insist that the Earth's future remains an eco-disaster that has already entered its final act" (Bailey "Earth Day, Then and Now"). To substantiate these assertions, Bailey delineates categories of predictions provided by these prophets of the 1970s that have since, in his mind, been proven wrong: "Soylent Greens," "Polluted Thinking," "Synthetic Arguments," and "Nonrenewable Anxiety" ("Earth Day, Then and Now").

Although Bailey, science correspondent for the online magazine *Reason*, attempts to debunk predictions from the 1970s in order to justify mass capitalism and consumption, his categories align with cinematic reactions to the environmental movement. And even though Bailey seeks to discredit what he calls doomsday prophets, his solution to environmental problems—wealth, another form of profit—would lead to a world where "forest growth . . . will increase" and "air and water quality will begin to improve." Bailey, like the prophets he critiques, harks back to a world where humans and nature coexist harmoniously. Even though he advocates development more than preservation, he believes (or at least asserts) that such development will result in a more ecologically sound Earth.

Like Bailey, films responding explicitly to Earth Day, the establishment of the EPA and other environmental programs of the 1970s look back nostalgically on Earth in its more natural state. In a direct reaction to the environmental movement, *Soylent Green* (1973) and, to a certain extent, *Silent Running* (1971) and *Omega Man* (1971) embrace the memory of an environment and ecology that no longer exists on their Earth—an eco-memory. At the same time, though, these films reflect a nostalgia for a world that does still exist for its viewers, both in the 1970s and today. These films represent the categories Bailey outlines in his article because they so clearly respond to the 1970s environmental movement (see articles by Gaylord Nelson and on the EPA Website, for example), with "prophets of doom" as tragic eco-heroes leading the charge for environmental causes. They also provide a way to exploit environmental ideas for commercial gain. Nostalgia, however, most directly connects the films to one another and to the ecology they all have lost.

As a reflection of the Green movement, class warfare, and a changing Hollywood in the 1970s, eco-disaster films like *Soylent Green* foreground environmental messages that focus on the creation of a tragic eco-hero who, like Bailey, remembers a green Earth with nostalgia. *Omega Man* includes two nostalgic looks at the environment—one from the perspective of the "infected" zombielike humans, and the other from those humans who are, or are trying to become, disease-free. In *Silent Running*, food serves as one manifestation of eco-memory, this time in terms of food Freeman grows but the other crewmen no longer wish to eat. Freeman also looks back nostalgically on an Earth covered in trees as in the bio-sphere-enclosed forest he presumably saves. *Soylent Green* foregrounds two different nostalgic visions of Earth's past—one from the intellectuals' (the Books') perspective, sometimes in relation to food, and the other from that of the corporations at the point of a human's termination.

All three of these films respond directly to the 1970s environmental movement. The films also highlight isolated eco-heroes who serve as doomsday prophets with messages similar to those to which the films appear to respond. *Soylent Green*'s narrative and the eco-hero that conveys it, however, most clearly parallel the rhetoric and rhetoricians of both "doomsday prophets" and their critics.

Few would dispute the idea that the American movie industry responds to contemporary cultural trends, presumably for economic gain, and filmic responses to the environmental movement of the 1970s were no exception. For example, when the *Soylent Green* DVD was released in 2003, reviews from distributors like "Home Theater" asserted that "Hollywood, never slow to jump on a trend, began to invest in ecological themed films [after the first Earth Day]. Perhaps one of the most famous is *Soylent Green*, released in 1973" (http://www.hometheaterinfo. com/soylent_green.htm).

Soylent Green even serves as one of Bailey's categories in his *Reason* article, since, according to Bailey, "Imminent global famine caused by the explosion of the 'population bomb' was *the* big issue on Earth Day 1970" ("Earth Day, Then and Now"). *Silent Running* aligns most closely with the "Polluted Thinking" category, since the only remaining forests were protected in outer-space biospheres. Images of dying forests on Earth reinforce the sense of loss destroying these domes will ensure. *Omega Man*, on the other hand, goes beyond Bailey's categories, amplifying Bailey's "Synthetic Arguments" with biological warfare.

Of these three films, *Soylent Green* falls most neatly into Bailey's discussion of the "apocalyptic predictions" he asserts Earth Day 1970 provoked. Although Peter Biskind describes Charlton Heston as one of the "Old Hollywood Right" (130) and disregards Richard Fleischer altogether, *Soylent Green* is clearly a film of the 1970s, a period in which the environmental movement gained mainstream approval. Unlike the antiwar movement, the civil rights movement, and the women's rights movement of the 1960s and 1970s, the environmental movement was supported by a cross-section of Americans, including those with right-leaning politics like those of Richard Nixon, under whose presidency the EPA was founded. So it comes as no surprise that a film like *Soylent Green* directed by an old-school director and starring an "Old Hollywood Right" actor embraces so strong an environmental message.

Soylent Green looks like a direct reaction to Earth Day and the establishment of the EPA. It also follows the same rhetorical strategies as do the doomsday predictions of contemporary environmental activists like Paul Ehrlich, whom *Life* magazine called "ecology's angry lobbyist." The film appears to agree with Ehrlich's predictions in his 1968 book *The Population Bomb* and illustrate them through the narration of its own prophet of doom—Thorn (Charleston Heston). From the film's opening montage shots of an increasingly overpopulated and polluted Earth to the film's 2022 urban New York City setting in which every inch is packed with people, the "population bomb" idea jumps off the screen.

In a world so overrun with humans, food sources for the masses come in the form of "soylents," including the infamous soylent green—people. *Soylent Green* provides a picture of what would happen on Earth if Paul Ehrlich's predictions came true: "Population will inevitably and completely outstrip whatever small increases in food supplies we make," he asserted in April 1970 (quoted in Bailey "Earth Day, Then and Now"). Thorn serves as a prophet revealing the most horrifying result—"Soylent Green is made out of people."

Tragic Ecological Heroes as Pioneers and Prophets of Doom

Constructing Thorn as a prophet also establishes him as a tragic eco-hero like that described by Joseph W. Meeker. According to Meeker:

> literary tragedy and environmental exploitation in Western culture share many of the same philosophical presuppositions. . . . Three such ideas will illustrate the point: the assumption that nature exists for the benefit of humanity; the belief that human morality transcends natural limitations; and humanism's insistence upon the supreme importance of the individual personality. (*The Comedy of Survival* 24)

In his earlier essay "The Comic Mode," Meeker defines the tragic hero in relation to biology: "Pioneer species are the loners of the natural world, the tragic heroes who sacrifice themselves in satisfaction of mysterious inner commands which they alone can hear" (161). Thorn more than fulfills Meeker's criteria for a tragic hero, gaining force as an eco-hero who both strives to save humanity and to remind them of their pristine past. Thorn is a pioneer, a tragic hero willing to speak up and resist homogenizing forces as an individual whose morality transcends all those around him. Even his name suggests that he is a prickly plant, one of the pioneering outsiders "whose life styles resemble behavior that men have admired most when they have seen it in other men. We celebrate the qualities in human pioneers that we despise in the pioneers of other plant and animal species" ("The Comic Mode" 161).

First as a rogue detective in a police state, and then (after his roommate's death) as the sole rational voice in the film, Thorn serves as an eco-hero, a human pioneer stamping out dehumanizing forces. Thorn proves the dreadful truth about Soylent Green for the intellectuals' Supreme Exchange, and he stands alone, morally superior to the corporate heads who control the food supply. For him, the crime is against humanity, not nature, since his biggest fear is that the company will raise humans "like cattle." "It's people," he says. "Soylent Green is made out of people." Thorn proclaims his message after fighting off bullets and punches from corporate thugs, first to his police captain and then to the scores of others sleeping in what is left of a church.

A suffering tragic eco-hero to the end, Thorn's words are the last we hear, and he passes the task of taking evidence to "the Exchange," the intellectual "Books' " haven, to his captain. Here the prophet, Thorn, reveals himself as a pioneer, a tragic eco-hero with a message that becomes his dying words. The film's cultural backdrop and its hero's role are obvious, but both serve as a direct response to the 1970s environmental movement and its prophets of doom.

Although *Silent Running* and *Omega Man* less directly connect to Bailey's categories and argument, they too are clearly products of the 1970s—both as responses to Earth Day and the environmental movement as well as the new Hollywood. *Omega Man* confronts both the dangers of technology and of biological warfare, clearly illustrating apocalyptic repercussions of exploitative human actions—a "plague-wasted city" after an "Armageddon, which battered the biosphere with . . . biological weapons" (Hladik). Its themes are like responses to the Vietnam war, the cold war, and the environmental movement.

Omega Man also illustrates changes occurring in Hollywood popular culture in the 1970s: It draws on the blaxploitation movement, incorporating a Black Panther Angela Davis look-alike character, Lisa (Rosalind Cash), and diegetic rhythm and blues music on Robert Neville's (Heston's) stereo into the film's mise-en-scène. It also pays tribute to the film *Woodstock* and its universal love theme, since both Matthias's (Anthony Zerbe) and Dutch's (Paul Koslo) respective "families" live communal lives based in ethnically diverse love.

In *Omega Man*, the youth culture of Woodstock and the Black Panthers meets "old school" when Lisa and Robert come together. Lisa, Dutch, and several children have gone "back to the land" from the plague-ridden city, returning only for supplies via motorcycle—more evidence of their youth. Robert Neville, on the other hand, stays in the city in his old apartment and is what Lisa calls an "exterminator." *Omega Man*, then, appears to be seeking out a young audience—as did other films of the 1970s. In fact, the Woodstock-type youth survive and drive off into the wilderness, while Heston's character ritually sacrifices himself for their future.

Silent Running responds to two cultures of the 1970s, a changing Hollywood and a shifting Washington atmosphere. The film's environmental message slaps viewers in the face: If we don't take care of our forests, they will die. As David Lichtneker puts it, "the eco message is a bit heavy handed (aided by the Joan Baez soundtrack)." Frederic

Brussat, however, suggests that the film "surpasses other ecology films in its ability to stir our awareness and imaginatively create concern for the consequences of ecological neglect." Brussat, one of the editors of the *Spirituality and Health* movie review section, even calls Freeman's character a hero whose "ecological conscience is a challenge to us all."

The dated Baez music and didactic message, however, are not the only qualities that connect the film to its 1970s context. Created for under a million dollars, Douglas Trumbull's *Silent Running* was one of the five movies with new directors authorized by Ned Tanen, producer in charge of Universal's and Lew Wasserman's youth division. It was Trumbull's directorial debut, although his special effects skills were well-respected (see *2001: A Space Odyssey* [1968]). Movie-making moved from the studio's to the director's hands under Tanen's plan, with the studio taking a hands-off approach to production, a big change in Hollywood, and one reason why Trumbull could direct such a confrontational film as *Silent Running* (Biskind 126). Most clearly, however, the film provides an apocalyptic message that calls contemporary humanity to action—save the forests now before they are eliminated.

As in *Soylent Green*, in both *Omega Man* and *Silent Running*, the films' heroes are tragic pioneers, willingly sacrificing themselves for the good of the species. Robert Neville is constructed as a Christ figure, sacrificing himself for humanity. When Dutch hears about Robert's immunity to the plague, he exclaims, "Christ, you could save us all," stating Robert's symbolic "name" and role. Bruce Dern's character, Freeman, not only kills his fellow crewmen to save the remaining forests. He sacrifices his own life, placing the last drone in charge of the last biosphere. As tragic eco-hero pioneers, both Robert and Freeman contrast with new more communal heroes—Dutch, Lisa, and the children in *Omega Man* and the last drone in *Silent Running*.

Environmental Nostalgia

This contrast between individual and communal visions of humanity also points to a rhetorical strategy that more effectively articulates all three films' environmental themes--the way each relies on ecological memory and nostalgia to make its point about the environment. A move toward communal living is a move back to a more natural state, in the context of these films, a state remembered and yearned for.

From its opening, *Soylent Green* harks back to better times. Here a series of old photographs from the nineteenth century until the 1970s demonstrates the burgeoning population growth that devastates the natural environment and leads to humans' reliance on Soylent Green for survival.

Photos from the nineteenth century show small groups of people sitting peacefully beside an ocean, perched on a hill, fishing on a bridge, lazing on a hay pile and then riding in street cars, then cars, and then airplanes. As the pictures reflect the turn into the twentieth century, automobiles and industry crowd out the pastoral scenes from the earlier photos.

The photographs pass by more and more quickly as Earth's population increases mathematically and the waste produced by industry and technology destroys more and more of the planet. A montage sequence showing increased numbers of machines and cars, devastating pollution, dying birds, smokestacks, nuclear explosions, humans wearing masks, and oil wells points to the painful repercussions of a population explosion. As the opening sequence nears the current time of the film, the photos slow down and reveal garbage dumps, more smokestacks, polluted water, overdeveloped urban centers, and cities covered in smoke. Then the title, *Soylent Green*, comes up, with a note about the setting—The year is 2022. This is New York City, and its population has now reached 40 million.

The passing photographs illustrate a progression toward the film's current setting, but they also demonstrate a nostalgic view of a past before overpopulation and environmental devastation destroyed sustainable communities and their values. The nineteenth-century photographs are yellow and faded, but the people they show us are happy, well-dressed, and relaxed. Later photographs show only the results of an overpopulated world—pollution, nuclear war, the death of nature. The first human enters the current setting only after the last montage shot of the polluted city. We hear a voice state something about "first stage removal." Then in Thorn's apartment we see and hear the governor on an old television talking about Soylent Green. Sol (Edward G. Robinson) and Thorn talk about what "books" can do to help solve a police case, but these people are cramped in their dark apartment, not lazing happily on the ocean's shore.

Sol serves as the reminder of better times—when "real" food was plentiful and the natural environment thrived. When Thorn offers Sol some soylent crackers, Sol exclaims, "Now, when I was a kid, food was food." But that was before people "poisoned the water, polluted the soil, [and destroyed] plant and animal life," according to Sol. Sol remembers and looks back nostalgically on a world before the "greenhouse effect." When Thorn leaves for work, the reason for such a dead world is clear: people, so many that Thorn must climb over or through hundreds sleeping on stairs and in the streets. What was once a world of plenty has turned into a corporate dictatorship where only the rich can afford fruits, vegetables, and meat—food other than the soylents corporations like Simonson's produce.

Figure 5.1. *Soylent Green*: Nostalgia for food.

Food symbolizes the nostalgic world of plenty in *Soylent Green*. When William Simonson, a corporate executive, is murdered, it is the food he leaves behind that gains Thorn and Sol's respect and attention—lettuce, tomatoes, apples, celery, onions, and even beef. Thorn takes the food—and some bourbon—as his reward from Simonson's apartment. When Sol sees the beef, he weeps. "How did we come to this?" he exclaims. "Nobody cares. Nobody tries, including me. I should have gone home long ago."

Since Sol remembers a better world, he creates a real meal for himself and Thorn and serves it on linen, giving Thorn the one set of authentic silverware with which to enjoy it. After feasting on beef stew and apple slices, Sol exclaims, "I haven't eaten like this in years." But Thorn doesn't remember more plentiful times: "I never ate like this." "Now you know what you've been missing," Sol tells him. "There was a world once, you punk." Sol provides the memories Thorn is missing—of beef stew and strawberries stolen on a spoon. But their real meal is juxtaposed with Sol's research on Simonson and Soylent Green.

Sol's research, too, brings up memories—of his previous life as a full professor, with as many books as he could read. Now the elite have air conditioning, showers, and space. The masses of impoverished humans sleep in piles and fight over genetically engineered food. With such a large population, "farms are like fortresses. Good land has got to be guarded, just like the waste disposal plants," so there's no place for Thorn and Shirl (Simonson's mistress, or "furniture girl") to go.

Intellectual property, too, must be guarded at what they call the Supreme Exchange. At the Exchange "books," former intellectuals including judges, perform research using the last real books, helping

Figure 5.2. *Soylent Green*: Sol's last eco-memory.

Sol solve Thorn's murder mystery but also making a much more devastating discovery about Soylent Green. Their discovery prompts Sol to seek the ultimate nostalgia—home, the place he believes God might be found.

Going home brings up both corporate and individual nostalgia for Sol. Going home means going to a corporate hospital for termination, but it also means enjoying twenty minutes of the Earth's past glory before his death. In a clean and spacious room where he is served by two attendants, Sol lies on a comfortable bed and enjoys his favorite color and music as they surround him.

But the memories of Earth—his home—are what he seeks here, eco-memories that are projected on the walls of Sol's room: deer in woods, trees and leaves, sunsets beside the sea, birds flying overhead, rolling streams, mountains, fish and coral, sheep and horses, and lots and lots of flowers—from daffodils to dogwoods. In the end, Thorn shares Sol's nostalgic moment, viewing it through a window and speaking with Sol on a microphone.

"Can you see it?" and "Isn't it beautiful?" asks Sol.

"Oh, yes," says Thorn, with tears in his eyes. "How could I know? How could I, how could I even imagine?" he gasps—now understanding what he and the rest of the world have lost. But in his last words, Sol also tells Thorn, out of viewers' hearing, the macabre source of Soylent Green—human flesh. And Thorn follows Sol's body to Simonson's soylent factory for proof.

With the knowledge of not only Earth's losses but also its tragic future, Thorn readily sacrifices himself to provide evidence that Soylent Green is people. Nostalgia and memories of nature give him enough incentive to want more, to want what the corporations provide the dying only in twenty-minute increments.

So the film's ending and its closing credits serve not only as a reminder, an eco-memory, but a road to hope. At the close of the film, then, when Hatcher, Thorn's superior officer, carries Thorn away, the corrupt political structures controlled by Soylent Green are beginning to break down. Even a cop-on-the-take like Hatcher responds to the powerful message Thorn tells him. But the closing credits that recreate Sol's last visions of "home" put a face on the eco-memory to which they now hark back. The film closes with the scenes Sol had seen on his literal death bed, but this time no death is connected to them. *Soylent Green* begins and ends with nostalgia, with scenes of what Sol calls home.

Soylent Green is a film of the 1970s and responds to the civil rights and environmental movements as it critiques contemporary (corrupt) political structures (see Vietnam, Nixon, and Watergate, for example). But it also looks back fondly from 2022 to a world very like that of 1973—especially after Earth Day and the EPA intervened—with nostalgia.

Nostalgia comes from both corporate and individual perspectives in *Soylent Green*. In *Silent Running* corporations seek to wipe out all remnants of ecology for economic gain, so nostalgia comes from a more personal viewpoint, that of Freeman Lowell. As in *Soylent Green*, the opening of *Silent Running* recalls a past where nature thrives, where plants and animals are sympathetically depicted as "children" under the care of a human "Holy Fool" or "St. Francis of Assisi." Opening shots show close-ups of snails, frogs, and fuzzy bunnies in a mossy forest, as well as a white-cloaked man (Bruce Dern's character, Freeman Lowell) caring for them and then interacting with nature by swimming in a calm natural pool. Only after Freeman climbs on shore do we realize that this ecosystem is constructed and protected within a bio-dome. As shots of the dome draw further back, the dome's location becomes clear—this dome is floating in space and surrounded by stars. In the world of *Silent Running*, technology is necessary to save "nature."

Nostalgia for the nature enclosed in the dome is shattered by a loud reality in which Freeman's colleagues drive over his plants in four-wheelers. Company logos cover the space station and even bins full of soil—Polaroid, AMF, Dow, American Airlines, NA Rockwell, and Coca Cola support this "natural" setting. Yet a voice-over claims these biosphere forests have been preserved as a way to re-foliate the Earth. The narration explains, "On this first day of a new century, we dedicate these last forests of a once beautiful nation in the hope that they will return and grace our foul earth. Until that day may God bless these forests and the great men that care for them." As David Ingram puts it, the film combines an "uneasy . . . nostalgia for a seemingly lost authentic relationship between human beings and nonhuman nature, before the despoliations of modernity, with a reliance on a technological fix to solve environmental problems" (180).

Despite these corporate claims, only Freeman Lowell shows any nostalgia for a once-green Earth. As in *Soylent Green*, eco-memory comes first in the form of food, fruits and vegetables that Lowell has grown in his forest garden. The other three crewmen on board have no use for Lowell's produce, even complaining, "Do you have to eat that stuff in here? It stinks!" Lowell's nostalgia for food he grows for himself makes it more palatable for him; it's "nature's greatest gift." But his fellow crewmen "can't see the difference" between his food and that produced by a machine. Lowell, however, associates the food with what he sees as better times on Earth. Not only does his food "have some taste." It also "calls back a time when there were flowers" and "valleys" and "things growing all over the place—not just in domed enclosures," Lowell explains.

Lowell recalls with nostalgia a time when Earth was green and ecologically diverse, and he laments the "dried synthetic crap" they now eat and the unchanging Earth they left behind: "On earth everywhere you go it's seventy-five degrees. Everything's the same. All the people are the same."

His fellow crewmen, however, celebrate Earth's sameness since there's "no more disease, no more poverty, [and] everyone has a job." In fact, earlier in the film when the other crewmen are playing poker, and Lowell talks about his dreams for reestablishing the Earth's parks and forests, one of the crewmen argues, "It's been too long. People have other things to do now." Lowell waxes nostalgically on a time when the Earth was green. The other crewmen—and everyone else, it seems—see nature as expendable. For them, a better Earth is as technologically controlled as their space station.

Unlike the proletariat in *Soylent Green*, everyone looks happy in the world of *Silent Running*—everyone but Lowell. When the crew hears about the corporation's plan to destroy their biospheres and put their ship back into commercial business, all but Lowell are overjoyed, since it means they'll go home to Earth. Lowell sees only the losses they'll all suffer: "no more beauty," "imagination," "frontiers." Children will "never . . . be able to see the simple wonder of a leaf in their hands," Lowell asserts.

Lowell's nostalgia is countered by his colleagues' apathy: "If people were interested, they would have done something about it a long time ago," one crewman argues. For Lowell, though, the domes and the forests they contain "are not replaceable."

Lowell sees nature as so necessary and irreplaceable that he willingly kills his colleagues to protect the last dome and save the last eco-memory of a natural Earth ecosystem. In *Silent Running* a binary between Lowell and everyone else has been established. But Lowell remembers his colleagues fondly and calls them friends, so he programs his drones to take on his friends' roles, even teaching them how to play poker with him. And he names the drones after his favorite cartoon characters, Huey, Louie, and Dewey. Memories of his friends and of the way he murdered them haunt Lowell as much or more than do memories of a charred Earth and once-thriving forests.

For Lowell, nature is necessary, but so are human companions, so he cannot bear the guilt his crime causes him through memories. Like a bottle thrown into an ocean, Lowell thrusts the last biosphere into space. Our last view of the dome shows us Dewey in charge of its (artificially) well-lit forest. But death is the only solution for Lowell, as a tragic hero who can't bear the memories he holds. Eco-memory and memories of human friendships merge in *Silent Running*, suggesting that Lowell's ultimate solution is only partially effective.

People take a front seat in *Soylent Green*; nature does in *Silent Running*. In *Omega Man*, supposed binaries become even more complicated but point to a merging of memories of nature and culture, especially from the perspective of Dutch's family and its escape to the "wilderness." Based loosely on Richard Matheson's novel, *I am Legend*, *Omega Man* updates the 1964 film version of *The Last Man on Earth* and replaces vampires with plague-ridden followers of Matthias. *Omega Man* also includes a prophetic "Christ-like" hero that is missing in *The Last Man on Earth*.

Figure 5.3. *Omega Man*: An isolated "pioneer."

Robert Neville's blood becomes a serum for the plague because he has injected himself with an effective vaccine he—as a scientist—has created. In *The Last Man on Earth*, Vincent Price (the hero) becomes immune to the vampire disease only because he, by accident, had been bitten by a vampire bat. *Omega Man* is definitely a product of the early 1970s and its environmental politics, since it asserts that humans' destruction may come as the result of a devastating biological war.

Like *Soylent Green*, much of *Omega Man* is set in the city—Los Angeles in 1977, two years after the Earth's population was annihilated by germ warfare. A cityscape opens the film and serves as a moment of nostalgia because the sole driver on the road looks like he is cruising for fun with music blowing out of his eight-track player. The overhead shot shows empty streets and the back of a woman seemingly sunning herself on a rooftop. The driver streams past green trees and tall buildings apparently carefree until he grabs a submachine gun and fires it at a black-hooded figure. As in *Silent Running*, a calm atmosphere is shattered, first by gunfire and then by a crash as the driver runs his red convertible Ford into a fence to avoid a barrier in the road. This time a calm cityscape only decorated by trees turns into a war zone.

The driver, Colonel Robert Neville, looks back with nostalgia on a world before war and before the plague had destroyed most of the Earth's population. His memories seem so real that he almost believes he hears phones ringing on the street. And when he goes into a dealership to find a new car after his tire goes flat, he reenacts a negotiation with a dead dealer—"How much? Can't say I'm crazy about the paint job. . . . Thanks a lot, you cheating bastard," he says, before driving away in a blue convertible Mustang. The calendar on the dealership wall reads March 1975, and Neville remembers the camaraderie haggling over the price of a car used to bring.

Memories continue with Neville's re-viewing of the movie *Woodstock* (1970), "held over for a third straight year." The clip from the film we see shows both the community Neville recalls and reenacts in the dealership and the peacefulness with which the film begins. During an interview, one of the Woodstock participants states the goals of the 1969 event—"Just to really live together and be happy." With such a world, people won't "be afraid to walk out in the streets" is the claim. This brief scene from *Woodstock*, though, sets up several ways in which nostalgia is treated in *Omega Man*.

The film *Woodstock* (and its accompanying event) embraces love and community with extended family connections. It also shows happy people interacting with one another in a natural setting, not the city where Neville lives. The film illustrates memories of family, friendship, and other social connections, as well as a more natural and pristine world. It also shows what is constructed as a better "family" than that of Matthias and a less destructive response to industry and technology run amok (even before the last global war).

Neville, though, sees *Woodstock* as a way to capture memories of movie-going itself: "They sure don't make pictures like that anymore," he quips. And when he finally gets into his apartment (through another blockade of black-hooded assailants) Neville's connection to technology and culture is reinforced. A generator provides electricity for the lights, appliances, and music—as well as for the surveillance cameras hooked into his big-screen television. Art fills the big living room, and a chess game is in motion on his table—between himself and a statue of a general. This glimpse of Neville's apartment is followed by shots of another form of nostalgia—this time for a world free of technology that is gained through violence and fire.

Matthias, former news anchor, leads what he calls The Family in their quest to cleanse the world of technology because he blames it for the plague they carry. A flashback shows Matthias's reactions as a news anchor during wartime: "Is this the end of technological man? . . . The age of the wheel? We were warned of judgment. . . . Well, here it is now," he proclaims. Matthias's attitudes have grown with his disease, so he rejects even weapons from the armory to fight Neville, the last human in the city who is untouched by the plague. Matthias and his family burn all remnants of culture—books, art—and try to kill Neville because he is seen as evil, but only with homemade weapons like catapults and spears.

Matthias and his family look back nostalgically on a world they never knew—before even the industrial revolution of the nineteenth century. Neville, the scientist and art lover, diametrically opposes Matthias's mission. That opposition becomes most clear during Neville's "trial" after he is captured by The Family. Since he represents science, medicine, weapons, and machinery—and has killed off members of The Family—Matthias finds Neville guilty of evil, so he is sentenced to suffer a sixteenth-century death by fire. Like a heretic convicted during the Inquisition, Neville wears a dunce cap and rides to the stadium for his execution on a wooden cart.

Somehow, however, the stadium lights go on and blast down on The Family. The plague has made them highly light sensitive, so they cower under the light and Neville escapes. His escape introduces the third reaction to the global war—Dutch, Lisa, and a "family" of children unharmed by the plague and living off the land away from the city, Neville, and Matthias. Dutch and his family provide an alternative response to plague—and embrace a different kind of memory, a nostalgia for a community much more like that depicted in *Woodstock*. Matthias wishes to destroy all remnants of the "new" world, including Neville. Neville wants to preserve what's left of it in his urban apartment—with paintings on the walls, books on shelves, technology running it all, and science in his working laboratory, but he wants all of Matthias's family members dead.

Dutch and his family, on the other hand, left the city to escape both Matthias and Neville—and their violent methods. Neville sees their countryside home when Dutch and Lisa free him from Matthias. In this pastoral setting, Neville also is introduced to humans who are resistant to the plague. The group has returned to a natural world outside the city and includes children scampering in from hilltop gun emplacements. Dutch and his family are far removed from both Neville, who is tied to the city as an exterminator, and Matthias, whose sole goal is the erasure of the past by a fire he claims will purify it.

Yet two of Dutch's group connect with both Neville and Matthias—Lisa and Richie (Eric Laneuville). Richie is saved by Neville's blood, which acts as a kind of serum. Because he's now plague-free, Richie offers his blood serum to Matthias and The Family. Although Neville willingly saves Richie, he does not want him to help Matthias. And Matthias not only rejects Richie's offer—he kills him because he, like Neville, is not one of the "chosen" (the plague victims).

Lisa bonds with Neville, as well—this time for love. But when she contracts the plague, she joins Matthias and helps them infiltrate Neville's apartment to kill him. Neville does die (and seemingly on a cross), but not before passing on a jar of serum to Dutch to save Lisa and the rest of Dutch's family. Dutch takes Neville's place, too, since he went to medical school before the war and now protects Neville's blood serum, this time not as a tragic eco-hero but as one attached to a more interdependent communal view of both humans and the natural world.

Matthias and what's left of The Family remain but are glued to the city they wish to purify. Matthias's apocalyptic message resounds for himself and his family, but not for Dutch and his, since they have hope. Unlike either *Soylent Green* or *Silent Running*, *Omega Man* shows a more positive future. Dutch drives away from the city and the plague—in a jeep that carries himself, Lisa, and the remaining children—into a green wilderness where Neville's serum can cure them all. The film not only warns of the dangers of germ warfare, it demonstrates its consequences, offering the only viable solution—an interconnected family.

Conclusion

Eco-disaster films from the 1970s (like *Soylent Green*, *Silent Running*, and *Omega Man*) provide overt environmental messages that serve as part of a public debate over "apocalyptic predictions." Right-wing politicians (including Nixon) supported Earth Day and the establishment of the EPA in the middle of the Vietnam war and diverse civil rights movements because environmental politics served a powerful cross section of the electorate—not just what politicians would call a fringe. All three films reflect this political change and the strategies of more radical elements of the environmental movement itself, in which a messenger, according to Bailey, acts as a prophet of doom. More importantly for our eco-reading, all of these films embrace nostalgia for a world like the one Bailey believes we can regain—if the world gets richer. Bailey talks about the "huge environmental gains made over the past 30 years" and insists that "increased wealth, population and technological innovation don't degrade and destroy the environment." Instead, "such developments preserve and enrich the environment" ("Earth Day, Then and Now").

Bailey, however, seeks to debunk apocalyptic predictions only by arguing that things have not become as bad as some thought they would—as soon as they said they would. Although he admits, for example, that "far too many people remain poor and hungry in the world" (from 800 million to 1.2 billion, according to Bailey "Earth Day Then and Now"), Bailey discounts their struggles because "we have not seen mass starvation around the world in the past three decades" ("Earth Day, Then and Now"). And Bailey suggests that because "the amount of land devoted to growing crops has barely increased over the past thirty years" that "millions of acres have been spared for nature," not recognizing that much of that land has been devoted to development of strip malls and subdivisions ("Earth Day, Then and Now"). He argues, too, that over-population (a category of predictions he names after the movie *Soylent Green*) is less likely because fertility rates have decreased.

Bailey also argues that because (as he sees it) air pollution has decreased, our main concern should be increasing other nations' wealth, since "once . . . income thresholds are crossed, societies start to purchase increased environmental amenities such as clean air and water" ("Earth Day, Then and Now"). He suggests that "similar trends can be found when it comes to water pollution" ("Earth Day, Then and Now"). Despite Rachel Carson's *Silent Spring*, Bailey also asserts that "there's a broad consensus that exposure to synthetic chemicals, even pesticides, does not seem to be a problem" ("Earth Day, Then and Now"). Until recently, Bailey also dismissed arguments about "depletion of nonrenewable resources, ostensibly disappearing biodiversity, and apparent global climate change due to human activity" ("Earth Day, Then and Now"). For Bailey, "a far greater threat for the next century comes from environmental activists" ("Earth Day, Then and Now"). Then Bailey makes his own predictions—about how the environment will improve over the next thirty years because countries (both developed and developing) will grow wealthier. And that improvement is based on a nostalgic look at our Earth as a cleaner place where nature can thrive ("Earth Day, Then and Now").

Although Bailey seeks to debunk the predictions made by what he calls apocalyptic prophets of doom, he, like these eco-disaster films from the 1970s and their tragic eco-heroes, responds to Earth Day and the environmental movement with his own predictions. He points out the relevance of both the political and popular culture repercussions of Earth Day, even paying tribute to *Soylent Green*. And the environmental movement's impact on popular culture continues (see for example *28 Days Later* [2002], *The Day After Tomorrow* [2004], and *Children of Men* [2006]. More intriguingly, films like these also contribute to environmental arguments by harking back to a more pristine past. *Soylent Green* and, to a certain extent, *Silent Running* and *Omega Man*, may reflect predictions whose timing was off, but the films' messages still resound and offer fair warnings. In these films, nostalgia for a present-day ecology serves the postapocalyptic message well.

6

The Comic Eco-Hero

Spoofing Eco-Disaster in *Eight Legged Freaks*

DEEP IN *EIGHT LEGGED FREAKS*, an ecological comedy from 2002, images from the 1954 film *Them!* appear briefly on a television screen, reinforcing the mutation of buglike creatures that serves as the catalyst for the action in both films—ants in the earlier *Them!* and spiders in *Eight Legged Freaks*. The homage is direct and loving, but it is 2002, and mutation is now a source of comedy as well as fear. This juxtaposition of the 1950s film footage from *Them!* with its more recent version, *Eight Legged Freaks*, also points out the mutation of an older genre—the science fiction warning film—to its comic and, perhaps, less heroic form, from the late 1980s until today.

Films dealing with eco-disasters in the 1950s through the 1970s and early 1980s were a serious affair: See in addition to *Them!* (1954), *Godzilla* (1956), *On the Beach* (1959), *The Birds* (1963), *Silent Running* (1971), *Omega Man* (1971), *Frogs* (1972), *Soylent Green* (1973), *The Swarm* (1978), *Piranha* (1978), *The China Syndrome* (1979), *Humanoids from the Deep* (1980), and *Silkwood* (1983). But later films highlighting similar eco-disasters—beginning with the late 1980s *Toxic Avenger* series (1985 and 1989) and *Class of Nuke 'Em High* and its sequels (1986–1989), and including *Who Framed Roger Rabbit* (1988) and *Naked Gun 2½* (1990)—look at toxic waste dumping, energy overconsumption, and radiation poisoning from a more comic perspective. *Eight Legged Freaks* continues this move toward comedic eco-disaster.

To get to the bottom of this change in the eco-disaster genre, we explore eco-comedies like these in relation to three main questions: How can the same environmental message be presented at least as effectively in a comedy in 1985 or today as it was in a serious science fiction film in 1954? What are the consequences of such a genre change? And, more importantly, what made such a dramatic genre shift possible? Our answers: First, the eco-disaster genre has come of age and can now be satirized through comic versions. Another change relates to a movement from rugged individualism to a more communal approach to solving ecological problems, at least in relation to the 1970s eco-disaster films. And even more importantly, these films all exploit historical and current events, either explicitly or implicitly, making us laugh within different contexts and with different intentions and results.

This shift from serious disaster films to parody aligns with the shift made in eco-disaster films from the 1950s to the present. According to Maurice Yacowar, "A genre comes of age when its conventions are well enough known to be played for laughs in a parody" (267). Eco-disaster films have come of age, so their themes are now played for laughs, but this shift from serious to comic explorations of environmental issues also changes expected genre conventions. An example of this shift is *Eight Legged Freaks*, where allusions are made to serious eco-disaster films from *Them!* to *Skeeter* (1992), but a toxic waste disaster is played for laughs here, with giant spiders even personified as dirt bike racers in sun glasses. Ultimately spiders are defeated, and the desert town in which the battle is set grows rich on gold garnered from the mine that once stored toxic waste—one eco-disaster, then, is replaced by an eco-tragedy, pit mining, in an ironic twist that parodies resolutions sought in serious eco-disaster films.

Stephen Keane builds on Yacowar's historical and structural analysis of the disaster genre, providing both an overview of the history of the genre and an analysis of the social and cultural influences behind the genre's changes and fluctuating popularity. According to Keane, "disaster films are born out of times of impending crises" (7–8). Keane also foregrounds technological innovations as key to the spectacular events driving most disaster films from 1898 forward. He argues, for example, that these technologies

> can also be drawn through the 1930s historical disaster cycle, again with the qualification that what might be so much engineering was fundamental to the resulting spectacle and subsequent commercial draw of these films. From Melies's trick shots and stock footage of Vesuvius blowing its top to

the full-size sets built and destroyed by Griffith and DeMille, the 1930s would see the full scope of earth, fire, wind, and water effects. (11)

See John Ford's *The Hurricane* (1937) as representative of this period. Keane's work most closely examines what he calls "disaster dramas" (121) from the 1970s through 2000.

For Keane, disaster films are serious. Yacowar, however, ends his list of disaster genre types with an extensive discussion of comic disaster films in which he delineates three subcategories of disaster comedies: films with "happy endings," films in which "the destruction can be extended into exuberant absurdity," and "parody" (266, 67). This shift from serious disaster films to parody aligns with the shift we see made in eco-disaster films from the 1950s to the present, a shift that moves eco-disaster films into the comic realm and (as we read it) away from a "nature attacks" vision to one in which humans attack the natural world.

Eight Legged Freaks serves as an eco-disaster comedy that illustrates both of these shifts. Ecological disaster—in the form of toxic waste dumping and its consequences—and a comic plot and characters meld well in the film and serve as a call to dispose of toxic waste in environmentally safe ways. Geoff King explains how satire is comedy with a "political edge" (18). Parody, on the other hand, shifts comic motivation from "the social-political arena to that of film forms and conventions, although this distinction is far from always entirely clear" (King 18). *Eight Legged Freaks* as comedy includes elements grounded in both satire and parody, since it couches a political message in comedy, while also responding to particular film forms and conventions.

Eight Legged Freaks responds to the heroic motifs of tragedy by comically constructing the characters of drama to serve both a comic purpose and a satirical premise and plot. In an eco-comedy, heroes with more than one tragic flaw are fore-grounded, according to Joseph W. Meeker's *The Comedy of Survival*. Heroes in comedies tend to bumble and require a community of allies to succeed, as they do in *Eight Legged Freaks*, demonstrating the move from tragedy to comedy in an eco-disaster film.

Meeting a disaster as a community separates eco-comedies from tragedies. Only in 1950s science fiction classics like *Them!* do we see a matching of communal elements in both the human and "ant" worlds—as is reflected by *Eight Legged Freaks*. But *Them!* highlights no single hero, not even a bumbling one. Instead, the community of scientists, politicians, police, and a well-prepared military work together to eliminate the foe their radiation has created. In serious dramatic and/or tragic eco-disaster films where a hero stands at the center, that hero takes on the characteristics of Meeker's tragic hero. *Omega Man* and *Soylent Green*, for example, foreground a tragic hero.

As a way to define differences between the serious and the comic, Meeker begins with the premise that "literature is essentially an imitation of the actions of men" (155) but distinguishes between tragic and comic perspectives on these actions, concluding that the comic is "universal" because it "grows from the biological circumstances of life" (158). Tragedies like *Oedipus the King*, on the other hand, depend "upon particular ideologies or metaphysical circumstances" where the hero "takes his conflict [with nature, the gods, moral law, passionate love] seriously, and feels compelled to affirm his mastery and his greatness in the face of his own destruction" (157). See, for example, 1971's *Silent Running*. In contrast, the comic hero may be weak, stupid, and undignified" but he "survives without [ideals]" (158).

According to Meeker, comedy reflects mature nature and its actors—it "depicts the loss of equilibrium and its recovery" (159), demonstrating that humans "muddle through" without concern for "progress or perfection" (160). Once ecosystems mature, heroic solitary pioneers, the tragic heroes represented by *Soylent Green*, *Silent Running*, and *Omega Man*, become not only unnecessary but also subordinate to the group. In a mature or climax ecosystem, "it is the community itself that really matters, and it is likely to be an extremely durable community so long as balance is maintained among its many elements" (Meeker 163).

Literary and film comedies offer a space in which to explore how humans might survive in a mature, climax ecosystem where the goal is survival of the community rather than "survival through the destruction of all our competitors and [. . .] achieving effective dominance over other forms of life" (162). According to Meeker, "civilization, at least in the West, has developed as a tragedy does, through the actions of pioneering leaders who break new ground and surmount huge obstacles" (162–63)—overcoming and/or subjugating other humans on the basis of religious and philosophical differences and destroying or exploiting other species for the good of their own.

Not only classic literature like *Oedipus the King*, but also mainstream and pulp science fiction novels by authors like Carl Hiaasen and Sheri Tepper take on environmental issues from a tragic perspective in which heroes take on their destructive enemy no matter how horrific the results (see Tepper's *The Gate to Women's Country*, for example). And Realist and Naturalist fiction takes a serious look at nature, sometimes with natural elements serving as characters more powerful than their human contenders—as in the fiction of Jack London and Stephen Crane. Edward Abbey's *The Monkey Wrench Gang* asserts an outlaw approach to overcoming environmental issues—what is now called eco-terrorism.

Comedy, on the other hand, pokes fun at heroic intentions, demonstrating our heroes' flaws. Meeker mentions a revisionist look at *Oedipus*, but few literary and/or filmic works take a comic view of nature and environmentalism, except perhaps in fantasy and science fiction films so campy they become humorous, like *The Time Machine* (1960) or *The Day of the Triffids* (1963). Eco-film comedies, however, burgeoned from the late 1980s through the present, perhaps because they poke fun at extremists and provide a space where heroes so flawed they become nearly ineffective can show us the positive consequences of placing the good of community—a climax ecosystem—above the individual.

Ellory Elkayem's *Eight Legged Freaks* begs the question, what's so funny about environmental disasters? But it also points out a change of strategy—laughing about the environment and its degradation may not only stimulate awareness; that laughter might also point out a path toward change. In spite of its sometimes overpowering campy humor, *Eight Legged Freaks* shows the consequences of disturbing a pristine ecosystem and offers a viable solution to greedy humans' exploitation of the natural world. Although clearly what Derek Armstrong calls a "horror comedy," at least on the surface, *Eight Legged Freaks* goes beyond *Them!*, where ants are mutated by atomic testing, the film it most closely parallels, since the goal is not only to destroy giant buglike creatures (in this case spiders), but also to counter the cause of their mutation—toxic waste.

Eight Legged Freaks offers a space in which to apply eco-critical approaches in relation to film studies and the eco-disaster spoof. The film responds to a variety of theories of comedy, humor, and laughter: those gleaned from cultural studies, from anthropology and psychoanalytic theory, and from eco-critics such as Joseph Meeker. It also complicates genre analyses of both comic and disaster films, especially when read through multifaceted lenses. From another perspective, the film provides a space in which ecological problems audience members now know about can be examined and scrutinized through campy humor that intensifies an environmental message while minimizing didactic and pedantic proselytizing that a more serious approach might foster. Michael S. Keane argues that "camp involves the ironic appreciation of low, failed culture, and the parody of taste codes that rank cultural works as 'high' or 'low' " (xiv). Keane suggests that "disaster movies are especially prone to unintentional camp for the way they juxtapose low, trivial pop culture sensationalism with the high and important fight for group survival and, in many cases, the endurance of the United States" (xiv). Because that camp is intentional in *Eight Legged Freaks*, it becomes part of the comic view of the environment both characters and audience members share.

A comic approach works because of this awareness, and the shared knowledge helps build community as spiders outside the human group become ridiculous as well as frightening. The communal, sometimes comic, attack reflects both an anthropological view of evolution like that Mahadev Apte describes in *Humor and Laughter: An Anthropological Approach*, and a more literary view focusing on climax ecosystems and flawed heroes such as those Meeker asserts emulate mature communities in the natural world.

The power of comedy to do more than induce laughter and look at issues with a sense of humor is clear, especially within the context of *Eight Legged Freaks*, where an environmental message is heightened by the film's absurd camp. Comedic films are a complex form of cultural expression, which have a history of both perpetuating the social order and attempting to subvert it. Comedies are a way to demonstrate the absurdity of society's problems and hypocrisies.

From the 1980s forward, eco-disasters have served as fodder for comedy because audiences know enough about the issue to laugh about it. Comic films make fun of issues audiences understand, and those issues change as times and audiences change. By the late 1980s, problems associated with environmental disasters seemed old hat. Gas was unleaded, catalytic converters on cars were mandatory, recycling was on the rise around the country, and new EPA controls were firmly in place. Film audiences, then, didn't need to be warned or taught about environmental problems. And they already had institutions in place that took the issue seriously. Some films highlighting environmental problems took a comic turn.

Viewing the eco-comic film in relation to crises of the period serves to situate our reading of *Eight-Legged Freaks* as a comic disaster film. The later 1980s were a time when modern American industrial values were being questioned, as they are in *Roger and Me* (1989), since more workers were moving away from now-vacant factories into technology-driven and service-sector employment. Audiences, however, might not respond well to serious (and didactic) appraisals of, say, New Jersey. Instead, for example, Troma Studios took a comic approach to the toxic waste dumping and nuclear radiation spilling that came to be seen as inevitable in urban industrial centers. The result was the *Toxic Avenger* and *Class of Nuke 'Em High* series. Troma's films marked a new way of looking at ecological disasters, especially those caused by human overuse or exploitation of natural resources. Films like *Men at Work* (1990) meekly draw on the Troma phenomenon. The eco-disaster film, like the species it sometimes documents, is an ever mutating genre.

What these eco-comedies show us—especially *Eight Legged Freaks*—is a change in cultural context, a change in audience expectations, and a change in genre focus for presenting significant ecological problems and possible solutions to them. An overview of previously broached psychoanalytic readings of humor and laughter provides another context for our reading of *Eight Legged Freaks*. The power of laughter as a coping and teaching tool increases as awareness, and the apathy it sometimes causes, intensifies. John Cleese suggests, in a conversation with psychoanalyst Jennifer Johns, that comedy "frees people up to have new thoughts." At the same time, however, Freud argues that jokes are part of a "social process" (171), in which audience members must comprehend the joke's context. According to Freud, "jokes are the most social of mental functions with a requisite condition of intelligibility" (179). Jokes are meant for an audience that understands the punch line, so they build community (and are built on it) and don't work without awareness—understanding.

Comedy can be seen as a cultural force. Film comedies can also be an effective way of commenting on aspects of society, examining hypocrisies and how absurd they are. Some may seek to deal with the painful aspects of life in such a way that the humor not readily apparent in such things as Nazism or racism is used to diffuse the horror surrounding it. Kaminsky notes that in *To Be or Not to Be* (1983), for example, Mel Brooks "has attempted to retain the comic persona against the serious background of a social issue, fascism" (168) because "the vision of struggle might not be accepted by audiences without the performer's comic persona" (168).

We apply Mahadev L. Apte's perspective specifically to our reading of *Eight Legged Freaks*. As Apte argues, the reasons why humans laugh at comedy depend on biology, sociocultural perspectives, and, of most interest for our reading of *Eight Legged Freaks*, evolutionary change. According to Apte, "facial expressions acquired communicative functions during the evolutionary process" (242). Since laughter is chiefly a human expression of joy, it is said to come later in infants than smiling (Apte 248). Humans smile innately, but "the question of whether laughter is innate has not been satisfactorily answered" (Apte 249). Apte concludes with several theoretical propositions.

The following anthropological theories inform our reading of *Eight Legged Freaks*: "Smiling among humans probably evolved from an expression of fear among primates. Laughter and smiling are evoked by different stimuli both across and within cultures" (259). Humans gained the ability to laugh through evolutionary changes. "The innate, involuntary smiling that occurs in infants right from birth becomes social smiling as a result of interaction with adults. . . . Laughter is generally more susceptible than smiling to restraint in accordance with sociocultural norms of propriety because laughter has more apparent derogatory and aggressive connotations" (259–60). Smiling and laughter in humans, then, have become social acts performed in conjunction with acceptable stimuli and sociocultural contexts.

Eight Legged Freaks provides a space in which ecological problems audience members now know about (as part of their own current sociocultural contexts) can be examined and scrutinized. These problems can be laughed at—as a community—when illustrated through campy humor that intensifies an environmental message while minimizing didactic and pedantic proselytizing that a more serious approach might foster. A comic approach works because of this awareness, and the shared knowledge helps build community, even as the film's spiders, alien from the film's human group, become ridiculous rather than frightening. When the audience sees these attacks as comic, and the film's community fights back as a collective, two theories are on display: both an anthropological view of evolution like that Apte describes and a more literary view focusing on climax ecosystems and flawed heroes like those Meeker asserts emulate mature communities in the natural world.

The environmental message and the call for interconnected relationships between humans and the natural world in *Eight Legged Freaks* look superficial and rest on spaces and species constructed by humans—all of which come from somewhere else. But ultimately, the film's environmental message resonates in spite of itself. The worlds of both the spiders and the humans are artificial constructs. Joshua (Tom Noonan), the town's eccentric, builds a spider farm housing arachnids from all over the world—not native to Arizona, where the film is set. Wade (Leon Rippy), the "businessman," builds a mall in the middle of a desert, attempting to destroy downtown shopping and disturbing the pristine desert milieu. And Chris (David Arquette), the "prodigal son," comes back to rejuvenate the mines beneath the town, excavations that, again, alter the natural environment.

Chris, Joshua, Wade and the rest of the townspeople—like the spiders—are outsiders. None of them are Native Americans and, thus, native to the Arizona desert. All the characters in this film are alien to the natural environment and change the ecosystem as soon as they enter it and begin consuming its resources for survival.

Within this constructed space, however, *Eight Legged Freaks* highlights toxic waste and its devastating effects on the natural environment from beginning to end. The film first juxtaposes the sound of Harlan

Figure 6.1. *Eight Legged Freaks* (2002): Toxic waste dumping into a stream near the spider farm.

Griffith's (Doug E. Doug) conspiracy theories blasting over his radio station, KFRD, with shots of a truck flying past the sign for the film's setting, Prosperity, Arizona, introducing the film's campy tone. We see and hear Harlan ask his audience, "Do you know what it's like to feel your heart beating in your chest so intensely that you can't even breathe? This is a story of monsters, creatures, hideous nightmares that crawl . . . I've seen them. I've seen them in visions. And you will too."

But instead of foreshadowing the giant spiders to come, Harlan is warning his audience about space aliens with probes—comic relief highlighted by Harlan's laughter. As the truck drives by a diner, Harlan admonishes his audience, "If you still believe that Neil Armstrong walked on the moon, Oswald killed Kennedy, and a black man's vote in Florida still counts," you need to "wake up people, look to the skies—unless of course, you're driving."

The comedy Harlan's conspiracy theories set up is aligned with serious shots of a truck from the Viroanol Corporation, driven by a radio audience member having a hard time staying awake. When the truck veers to avoid a rabbit, a barrel of toxic waste rolls off its tailgate into a clear pond and creates the catalyst for the horror to come. The sound of Harlan's radio broadcast claiming outrageous governmental conspiracies sets up the comic genre, but the toxic waste barrel accident suggests that this comedy will be grappling with a serious issue—ecological disaster.

Even the message on the side of the truck mixes these genres. It reads, "Modern Chemicals for Enhanced Living," a message that sounds good but, with the toxic waste sign on the barrels it carries, becomes ironic. Toxic waste doesn't align well with the idea of enhanced living in most viewers' minds. What is missing, however, is a clear distinction between what is natural and what is constructed. Both Harlan and his radio station and the Viroanol driver and his truck full of toxic waste look out of place in this desert environment.

The next scene introduces the repercussions of the accident. The toxic waste has entered the ecosystem, infecting the crickets the patron of a commercial spider farm (Joshua) feeds to his spiders. When Mike (Scott Terra), Sheriff Samantha Parker's (Kari Wuhrer) son, visits the farm, the spiders have grown astronomically. Joshua even calls the crickets "spider steroids" as he introduces the many species of spiders on his farm, including the queen to whom smaller males take gifts of living prey. Joshua's parrot caws, "I see dead people," an allusion to the film, *The Sixth Sense*, which Joshua says his parrot loves, and a line that foreshadows dangers to come.

But neither Joshua nor Mike knows the cause of these spiders' rapid growth, so Mike leaves with only a bit of excitement over the change. And Joshua senses no danger when one of his spiders lands on him and poisons him to his death. It's not until another week later, when the spiders have grown even larger, that any suspicions concerning the cause of their growth arise—and then only because when Mike returns he discovers one of Joshua's boots in the middle of the now-ransacked spider farm.

The main elements of this "eco-comedy" have been introduced. First, this is a comedy where outrageous conspiracy theories on the radio are replaced by a toxic waste "accident" that has devastating environmental consequences. Second, *Eight Legged Freaks* highlights problems associ-

Figure 6.2. *Eight Legged Freaks*: Spider farm.

ated with disrupting ecosystems with artificial (toxic) waste. Third, with the introduction of a comic hero and a community to support him, the film offers a communal solution to an eco-disaster, all in the context of a campy representation of B-horror movie spider monster attacks like those in *Tarantula* (1955) and the eco-comedy *Arachnophobia* (1990). What's intriguing about *Eight Legged Freaks* is how it demonstrates the continuing shift from serious film representations of eco-disasters to spoofs and playful, sometimes anarchic, comic depictions of ecological toxic tragedies begun in the 1980s.

American film comedies highlighting environmental problems have been around since at least 1952, when Robert Wise directed *Something for the Birds*, a satire targeting lobbyists—one working on behalf of preservation of the California condor (Patricia Neal), and the other for oil interests threatening the birds' sanctuary (Victor Mature). But up until 1985, when Michael Herz and Lloyd Kaufman directed *The Toxic Avenger* for Troma Studios, few films took a comic look at ecological disasters with a human cause. *Eight Legged Freaks* serves as one of the latest in a series of eco-comedies addressing toxic waste disposal that began with *The Toxic Avenger* and its sequels in the 1980s and continued into the 1990s with *Men at Work*. In spite of what Derek Armstrong calls a "rigid enslavement to formula," however, *Eight Legged Freaks* takes the eco-comedy beyond issue-raising and into the realm of sustainable development and mature ecosystems where humans and the natural world are interconnected.

As a stand-alone environmental comedy, however, Elkayem's *Eight Legged Freaks* first illustrates what happens when the good of community is placed before that of an individual hero, the bumbling Chris Mc-Cormack, or his corrupt contender, Wade. Both the spider and human communities have been disrupted by an individual seeking personal gain no matter what the consequences, a pioneer overcoming other citizens in the town with no regard for other species or for the water and earth that sustain them.

But, drawing loosely on Joseph Meeker's theory of comedy and the environment, this is a comedy where tragic heroes become absurd because the spider and human communities live in balance with one another until disrupted by both Joshua's spider farm and Wade's toxic waste dumping. This scenario appears in *Arachnophobia*, but in *Eight Legged Freaks* the theme of disturbing "pristine ecosystems" and stirring up disastrous "new diseases" in the form of spiders on steroids takes a capitalist turn, since Joshua buys the spiders for profit.

In fact, the spider and human communities parallel one another as well as counter one another in an ultimate conflict. Before the disruption

Wade provides both species, the two interact in a multispecies ecosystem. But Wade bankrupts the town of Prosperity through his various schemes, including the toxic waste dumping—for profit—that leads to Joshua's spiders' miraculous growth and a loss of ecological balance for the town. Joshua raises and observes the mutating spiders on his farm, also for profit. Chris returns to his hometown of Prosperity to determine what closed his father's mine and killed the town, as well as to renew a romance.

But because of Wade's greed, a stray barrel falls from a truck into the water source for Joshua's spiders' feed—crickets. The town believes its former source of employment, The Aqua Mesa Mine, is played out, so Wade plans to use it all for a toxic waste dumping ground, after buying out the other townspeople's shares in the mine. Only Wade has reconstructed nature for economic gain when in fact the town had profited from exploitation of natural resources from its beginning, earning their living from the mine. Joshua, too, has created an aberrant ecosystem in his spider farm; yet the artificiality of both spider and human environments before Wade's intervention goes unnoticed.

Wade's disruption destroys ecological balance and undermines two "climax communities" so much so that the two must fight one another to survive. The two outsider groups compete for control of the town and its mine and mall. But both spiders and humans occupy similar interconnected ecosystems from the beginning of the film when we know that these exotic spiders come from outside the region. Even though Joshua oversees an exotic spider farm where he—and Mike, the sheriff's son—watch spiders of different types living in harmony, on a steady diet of crickets from a nearby pond, these are spiders brought into the region from all over the world, outsiders co-existing because of Joshua's careful manipulations. At the farm, when Joshua introduces Mike to the diverse species of spiders living there, he shows him how they dwell and perambulate—from inhabiting burrows beneath trap doors to jumping from food source to food source in a powerful sidewise fashion.

Joshua and Mike act as observers, disrupting the spiders' ecosystem first by moving them from their native environments to an indoor setting like their own and then feeding them crickets they collect instead of allowing the spiders to hunt for their food. Joshua hopes to earn even more of a profit from these quickly growing spiders. "I'm going to make a fortune!" he exclaims before letting Mike know he had to "bribe every customs agent from San Diego to Tucson" to get the pair of exotic orb weavers into the United States. Wade's plan to earn a fortune by loading the mines with toxic waste appears to more drastically disturb the equilibrium, since the feed crickets are now soaked in a toxic chemical that leads to rapid mutation—not evolution. Both Joshua and Wade, however, disturb and exploit nature for profit, constructing an artificial ecosystem teeming with mutated species of spiders.

The human community, too, had thrived before residents lost their jobs and moved away after the mines closed, in what appears to be a "natural" prosperity for Prosperity. The town's disintegration looks "unnatural," so when Chris returns on a Greyhound bus, he is shocked to see his Aunt Gladys (Eileen Ryan) working alone in a dusty mine office above now-vacant mines. As the town's name suggests, it was prospering when Chris left it years before. The photographs on the office wall of miners outside shafts illustrating the town's former affluence are in black and white and reflect a time gone by. Gladys even mutters, "We're not hiring. We're laying off. We're three days off from a going out of business sale," to Chris, before she recognizes him.

But this is a comedy, so Chris had left to escape the pain of a lost love, not economic failure, and he returns because his father has died, not because he feels compelled to save the town. To heighten comic effect, Gladys fails to recognize her nephew at first, and her dog bites Chris's leg as if he were a stranger. Yet Chris's return to the once-booming town does highlight the extent of its deterioration, and only he and a few other miners believe in the vein of gold his father may have found before his death from ingesting methane gas.

The area is economically depressed, but the blame rests on the shoulders of Wade, the town's mayor and corrupt entrepreneur, more than on the community's failure to diversify its economy, according to the film's narrative. The film introduces Wade's failed business attempts—the ostrich farm, since ostrich meat just never caught on, and the empty Prosperity Mall—to show his lack of business sense. But as mayor, he is exploiting the town's property, its mines, to profit from toxic waste disposal, nearly causing the environmental destruction of Prosperity, a town already in decay. Wade's intervention—his investment in Viroanol and its illegal toxic waste dumping—interrupts what looks like an equilibrium established in both the human and arachnid communities. Yet both communities are highly artificial and unnatural, especially since neither the humans nor the spiders are native to this desert environment.

The disturbance in this supposed natural balance is quickly manifested in the human world, first with Joshua's death by spider attack. Sheriff Parker ironically tells her son, Mike, "Those spiders are dangerous," and within a week spiders have entered a human home and set up housekeeping in new drywall where they attack a prowling cat in a battle in which cat and spider shapes of comically equal size appear in relief on the wall. The sheriff's son, Mike, can tell by now—from an analysis of a piece of exoskeleton, that the spiders are now five times their original size, and still growing. Spiders' connection with the human world and with Wade's intervention is reinforced by the mine opening near Joshua's spider farm where the spiders have set up a new home. Wade's plans become more explicit at the town's mall—the site of the final showdown between humans and spiders—where Wade attempts to buy out the rest of the town for the Viroanol Corporation and expand the area for the toxic waste dumping.

The human community has its first explicit encounter with these monster spiders when they return to the mines to find the last vein of gold, while determining the extent of decay and the amount of methane gas in its tunnels. One miner swallows spiders by accident from a hose he's trying to unclog. What look like hundreds of baby spiders climb out of his mouth, but it's not the babies but a huge mother spider that kills him, leaving what is left of his flesh for her brood. This monstrous act, so comically orchestrated, is juxtaposed with glimpses of a monster movie marathon on Mike's television. According to Mike's mother, Sheriff Sam Parker, watching films like *Them!* will cause "media-induced paranoid neurotic nightmares," an irony in light of the brutal and real killing we have just witnessed.

The film's next two spider attacks are even more comic, with flying ostrich feathers on Wade's ostrich farm signaling the birds being dragged into trap door spiders' lairs and, the next morning, racing spiders chasing after dirt bike riders. The racing spiders resemble the motorcycle racers they chase, so anthropomorphized that they look like they're wearing sunglasses when light is reflected in their eyes. Parallels between the spider and human communities are clear—all because Wade had disrupted both ecosystems. It comes as no surprise, then, that spiders find their way to the human community through the mines beneath the town that house the toxic waste because the human community, too, had traversed there. Bret (Matt Czuchry), the last surviving dirt biker, races through the mines, as well. In spite of the horror, however, the film remains comic. For example, jumping spiders chasing Brett smash into a tanker truck with a squishing sound and a spray of green ooze.

To add to the comedy, Aunt Gladys is captured (and wrapped in web) by a spider from a mine shaft opening in her basement, but the male spiders capturing Gladys for their queen spin her from the mine shaft ceiling like a top, all while absurd music resounds in the background. Still, a new spider leg Mike examines shows that spiders have become so large now that humans serve as their only adversary and most available source of food.

The spiders are clearly attacking as a group, so the humans cannot defend themselves without teaming up in a "safe" artificial environment where they can act as a community—The Prosperity Mall. After fighting off spiders attacking her daughter, Ashley (Scarlett Johansson), and friend, Chris McCormack, Sheriff Parker realizes that she can reach the townspeople best through Harlan's (the conspiracy theorist's) radio station. Her broadcasted message encourages the townspeople to get to the mall for safety and survival, in a takeoff from films like *Dawn of the Dead* (1978). Like the spiders, who are attacking together, regardless of their subspecies, humans of all types must gather together to defend themselves and their community. The spider attacks faced on the way to the mall demonstrate spiders' communal aggression and humans' need to form alliances for survival. The competition between these two outsider groups, however, is more artificial than natural because they are fighting over constructed spaces—the mines, the mall, and the town.

Together the human community fends off the mutated spiders. Harlan and Chris attempt to send a cell phone message across the mountains from the top of the mall's antenna. Ultimately Sheriff Parker and Chris, with the help of other townspeople, blow up the mine shaft and destroy the last wave of attacking spiders—with Chris on one end of the methane blast and Sheriff Parker on the other. Only after the blast does the Tucson Police and Fire Department arrive. In the process, Wade, who had tried to escape with no concern for his fellow townspeople, is captured by a spider; but, still alive, he is discovered and released, muttering about his worries over insurance. Gladys is found wrapped in webs but still alive, and the Aqua Mesa lode Chris's father had spoken about is rediscovered.

Humans ward off the spiders, surviving only because they act as a community. But this cooperative town has been constructed on mines dug for profits from gold. Even though the town's wealth appears to be shared, since the last shot we see of Harlan shows him smiling wide enough to reveal his new gold fillings, it is gained only at the expense of the natural world. The film's final song, "The Itsy Bitsy Spider," makes clear that this is a comedy, not only with a happy ending but with a communal spirit restoring equilibrium among humans, with mutant spiders destroyed and a natural environment to exploit. The mutant spiders, outsiders from other milieus in the first place, have no place in this ecosystem. The only remnant of the toxic waste dumping that we see is Deputy Pete's new hair growth. But humans can only exist in this desert because they have constructed an artificial world to sustain themselves.

The film highlights a contrast between exploiting the environment by using it for toxic waste disposal—as does the "businessman," Wade, and developing it in ways that sustain both humans and (presumably) the natural world—as does Chris. In *Eight Legged Freaks*, the town of Prosperity regains economic strength because gold is found in a mine. Mining clearly exploits the natural (if not living) world. But the film also asserts that mining disrupts the natural world much less than does toxic waste dumping—dumping that is sure to kill human and nonhuman nature. The narrative of *Eight Legged Freaks* follows a comic formula where conflict is overcome (sometimes in humorous ways), and happiness is restored to the surviving townspeople of Prosperity. Here too, equilibrium between the human and "natural" world looks like it has been restored.

This artificial balance and the binary on which it is built break down under scrutiny, especially since neither settlers nor spiders are indigenous to the Arizona ecosystem. Harlan tells his radio audience that he stays in Prosperity because "This is the only place where I can tell you the truth and they can't get me." Sheriff Sam Parker stays, as her daughter explains, because she got pregnant at sixteen and became a "trailer trash sheriff." Chris McCormick has been gone for ten years and returns only for the dream of love and money. The town has been (literally) built on the gold mines that served as their source of income. None of the characters, no matter how well they have adapted the environment to serve their needs, could be called "native" to the Arizona desert. Joshua's spiders, too, come from elsewhere, just like Wade's ostriches. No matter how aligned to a "sustainable development philosophy" the characters look, they all also exploit their environment for financial gain.

But Chris is seen as less exploitative than Wade because he opposes toxic waste dumping and works for the whole human community. Wade, on the other hand, seeks wealth only for himself. Wade's greed is amplified by the phone conversation he has with Viroanol, all while ignoring his son. Wade asks them, "Do you know what the people of this town would do if they knew we were storing toxic waste without their consent?" Wade is more concerned about losing money than losing lives or destroying the environment. Chris and the rest of the townspeople, on the other hand, seek to live a more equitable life built on community ideals that serve a collective humanity that seeks to at least preserve the natural world, a comic narrative that provides more harmonious (and comic) results.

Eight Legged Freaks does more than tell an environmentally conscious story. It also deliberately draws on B-horror and comedy films from the 1950s through the 1990s, showing how representations of eco-disasters have changed over the last five decades, while reinforcing the environmental message on display. Elkayem's direct response to horror films, spoofs and playful (sometimes anarchic) comic representations of ecological disasters not only pays tribute to these earlier films, it also strengthens *Eight Legged Freaks'* environmental message. The homage to *Them!* has been noted.

Them! came out at the height of the Cold War, when fear of the effects of atomic testing was real and based in fact. The impact of radiation on the environment—especially on ants in *Them!*—is compared to the negative effects of toxic waste on ecosystems in *Eight Legged Freaks*. When Rebecca Murray asks Ellory Elkayem what "the mutant bugs [were] a metaphor for now," he replies, "If you want to take anything away from [the film], it would be don't pollute the environment and be careful with toxic waste." Elkayem also talks about the B-movies from the 1950s he most responds to in his work: *Tarantula*, *Them!*, *The Incredible Shrinking Man* (1957), and *Creature from the Black Lagoon* (1954). For Elkayem, the tribute he plays to these films in *Eight Legged Freaks* is meant to tell viewers, "Okay, we know what kind of movie we're in for. Just go with it and have fun and escape for a couple of hours." The homages tell viewers not only what to expect stylistically but also thematically and ideologically. Like 1950s B-horror films, *Eight Legged Freaks* argues against human exploitation of the natural world, this time not from radiation but from toxic waste, all in a world already constructed by human hands.

Eight Legged Freaks includes tributes to other film genres, as well, and each adds to the film's comedic effect. Horror and comedy mix with the Western genre in two parallel scenes. First, when Sheriff Parker asks Pete to "get together weapons" and meet at her house, he throws belted rounds of ammunition around his shoulders and carries piles of rifles to his car. From there the film moves to a shot of one of the town's barbers watching a Western on television. As a fistfight ensues on the screen, a spider attacks and spins him like a top, covering him with a webbed cocoon. The Western theme of both scenes meets spider horror so over the top and campy it becomes ridiculous—and funny. Later, too, the mall becomes the fort, and spiders the Indians.

Shots of the town's diner, too, bring earlier films to mind—especially Hitchcock's *The Birds*. As in *The Birds*, townspeople in the diner first are incredulous about the natural attack. But when they see giant spiders attacking and killing outside the restaurant's windows, the diners panic and run for their cars, just as they did in *The Birds*. Spiders of different species form alliances, just as did Hitchcock's attacking birds. Like the "natural attack" disaster films Maurice Yacowar describes, *Eight Legged Freaks* "pits a human community against a destructive form of nature," (761) as in *The Birds*, *Frogs*, *Them!*, *Tarantula*, *Skeeter*, and *Arachnophobia*. But this is comedy, so when the spiders break through the restaurant window and attack, one of them tries to attack a mounted deer head, fails, and spits out sawdust.

Even the mall scenes, which also resemble shots from George Romero's *Dawn of the Dead*, take on a comedic vein. After showing panicking townspeople escaping, the film moves us to the nearly empty mall food court, where Wade sits alone, eating the ostrich burger the lone cook has prepared. "It's always slow here," she says, not realizing the irony of her statement. The battle between the town and arachnids behind the mall's concrete walls and steel doors breaks the silence. Horror meets comedy; natural disaster film meets comedy; Western meets comedy; science fiction meets comedy—all within the framework of *Eight Legged Freaks*. The anti-toxic waste message of the film is couched in comedy, but presenting it within a film that references eco-genres in which that message is taken more seriously adds force to its rhetoric.

To foreground the multigenre base for the campy natural disaster on display, *Eight Legged Freaks* draws on technologies that may counter the environmental messages of the film. But relying on animation rather than large sculpted models makes the film's production more eco-friendly. The film's production notes explain, "The limited special effects offered by the genre movies that had inspired the filmmakers have little resemblance to today's computer generated visual effects." Instead, during this film's production, Karen E. Goulekas, Thomas Dadras, and Drew McKeen worked with a staff of seventy animation specialists to create "a virtual world inside the computer, consisting of digital cameras, lights, actor models and spider models" and "combined . . . 3-D spider imagery with the [live film footage] and created a new original negative with spiders on it" (http://eightleggedfreaks.warnerbros.com/frameset.html?btscenes. html *Eight Legged Freaks* Production Notes). Goulekas asserts that "more than 2,000 animated arachnids were created" for the film, minimizing the need to recycle or dispose of full-scale models. These images combined with sound effects and mechanical models of giant spiders and cocoons to demonstrate the technological innovations available today to produce an eco-comic disaster film, this time with an ecological message that resonates in part because of the technology driving it.

Eight Legged Freaks, then, makes us laugh at the environment because it not only fits comic theories about humor, it also intertwines genres in which we expect serious issues to be tackled. Even though the film's director argues that toxic waste dumping in the film serves only as a plot device, the film leaves spectators with the impression that the success of humanity depends on interdependence with the natural world and stewardship toward nature in a communal environment. But, more than anything, *Eight Legged Freaks* provides a space in which we can laugh at eco-disasters, look at environmental catastrophe with a sense of humor, and, perhaps, make changes that will serve both humans and the natural world best.

7

Eco-Terrorism in Film

Pale Rider and the Revenge Cycle

They just literally mow the mountains away, you know, the trees
and everything . . . all that was outlawed in California some years
ago, and they still do it in Montana and a few places.

—Clint Eastwood quoted on turnerclassicmovies.com

It was outlawed way back, even before ecological concerns were as
prevalent as they are today. So we play on that in the film. It's kind
of an ecological statement.

—Eastwood quoted in "Eastwood on Eastwood"
by Christopher Frayling

I NSTEAD OF FOCUSING ONLY ON the classic western conflicts of earlier
Westerns—the battle between cattlemen and farmers, or between
free range and fenced ranchers—Clint Eastwood's remake of *Shane*
(1953), *Pale Rider* (1985), highlights and critiques the consequences of
1850s–1880s' corporate mining and its continued repercussions into the
1980s, hydraulic mining that must be destroyed through eco-terrorist

means, according to the film's blatant rhetoric. Unlike any other East-wood Western, *Pale Rider* provides its audience with a clear vision of the environmental horrors hydraulic mining causes, even including detailed descriptions of the technique, while showing the devastating results of this great engineering feat.

As a way to foreground the horrors of this technique, deep into the film, Josh LaHood, the corporate miner's son (Christopher Penn), explains how he and his men are able to thrust two hundred pounds of pressure per square inch of water at the side of a mountain, a process called hydraulic mining that was engineered around 1850 to extract as much gold as possible from mountain crevices. Josh describes the process to fourteen-year-old Megan Wheeler (Sydney Penny), a prospector's daughter, and his detailed description is juxtaposed with images of falling trees and soil devastated by pressurized water shooting out of monitors, the water cannons used to strip the hills of topsoil and growth to make the gold beneath easier to find, all more powerfully presented through Bruce Surtees' camerawork. Josh LaHood narrates:

> About three quarters of a mile upstream we diverted half of Cobalt Creek. See, it flows through a ditch along the contours of the slope and ends up about a hundred yards up yonder. . . . It flows into . . . a three-foot pipe and then flows down slope real steep. And then that narrows to a two-foot pipe. And then a one-foot pipe. You see all the time that water's flowing downstream, it picks up speed. And it picks up force by going into the thinner pipes. . . . By the time the water reaches the monitor, I've got about two hundred pounds of pressure per square inch. I can blast that gravel out of that cliff and then it washes into the bed and then it travels right through the sluice.

While looking at the land around her, Megan comments, "It looks like hell." But Josh is only interested in the product of the degradation: "You know I can get twenty tons of gravel a day in this river," he says. Seconds later, while the audience watches hydraulic monitors shooting water at the cliffs above the Yuba River, Josh attempts to rape Megan, in an obvious parallel to what is happening to the landscape. Josh fails only because Preacher (Clint Eastwood) saves her.

This scene from *Pale Rider* introduces one of its most important themes: the violent exploitation of the environment and of those most connected to it. Although this theme is prevalent in mining films like *North Country* (2006) and *Silver City* (2004), it is missing in any other

Eastwood Western. In fact, *Pale Rider* is the only film directed by East-wood that focuses blatantly on such an environmentally packed issue. *Pale Rider* not only examines how the environment can be exploited, it also takes the time to demonstrate a better way, an alternative to the absolute destruction of large-scale corporate mining centered around the fact of hydraulic mining. Just as Preacher saves Megan, the individual miners the LaHoods oppose ("tin pans") can save the land from the mining baron, LaHood, and halt his environmentally devastating methods using violent eco-terrorist means.

But *Pale Rider* not only problematizes corporate mining techniques, suggesting that the corporation should be obliterated; it also provides a viable alternative to the consequences of hydraulic mining—individual tin panning in a cooperative community seeking to plant roots and raise families, an alternative that is attainable with the help of eco-terrorism. In contrast with LaHood and his greed for gold, individual miners like Hull Barret (Michael Moriarty) and Spider Conway (Doug McGrath), say "gold ain't what [they're] about" (*Pale Rider*). *Pale Rider*, then, offers a politically charged solution to the environmental destruction threatened by hydraulic mining interests.

This solution in *Pale Rider* has not received any detailed examina-tion. Extreme eco-terrorist violence drives the ultimate solution offered in *Pale Rider*, and while it is couched in mythological terms similar to *High Plains Drifter* (1973), the inclusion of Hull Barret in the mayhem and killing keeps the environmental argument grounded in the here and now and provides for an alternative to the individualist "progressive" model of the Western, as defined by Richard Slotkin in *Gunfighter Nation* and *Regeneration Through Violence*. Since Preacher and Hull take a collaborative approach to eco-terrorism, they promote communal sustainable develop-ment rather than individual progress like that Slotkin describes.

Instead, the resolution of *Pale Rider* harks back to *The Outlaw Josie Wales* (1976) where, according to Slotkin, Josie forgives his enemy with the statement, "All of us died a little in that damn war" (633). It also prefigures the antirevenge themes in Eastwood's critically acclaimed *Un-forgiven* (1992) and *Mystic River* (2003). Although violence does provide "regeneration" (Slotkin's word) in *Pale Rider*, it ultimately serves both a working-class community and the natural world that sustains it.

A Brief History of Hydraulic Mining

Violence is used to thwart a corporate mining company that is destroying lands with hydraulic mining techniques implemented in California gold mines from the mid-nineteenth century until later in the twentieth century.

According to Ken Huie, a park ranger in Malakoff Diggins State Historic Park, "Hydraulic mining was born and raised here in California. . . . And no matter what you think of the result, it was a tremendous engineering feat" (Kiester). Huie oversees a park in the Sierra Nevada mountain range where the topography wears the mark of hydraulic mining from the 1850s to the 1880s, a mining technique so effective it was used all over the western United States.

According to Edwin Kiester, Jr., "Hydraulic mining applied a simple method familiar to all who've used a garden hose. Direct a forceful stream of water at the earth, and it will carve a ditch and carry away loosened soil." To create a large-scale mining system, "Engineers built a network of reservoirs, lakes, ditches and flumes extending as far as 40 miles to catch every precious drop of rain or Sierra snowmelt. Propelled by gravity along a vertical drop of up to 500 feet, the captured waters converged into a single, powerful stream. Then they were fed into water cannons trained on the gold-bearing hillside" (Kiester).

In Malakoff Diggins State Historic Park, these cannons are on display. Huie explains, "A single monitor [water cannon] with an eight-inch nozzle like this could direct 16,000 gallons of water a minute. . . . It could tear away 4,000 cubic yards of earth from the hillside every day" (quoted in Kiester). And debris resulting from such destructive mining was dumped into the Yuba River, so tainted water flowed into the Feather River, the Sacramento and even San Francisco Bay (Kiester). The Yuba River became so contaminated that "The mine's operator, North Bloomfield Gravel Mining, lost a lawsuit in Jan 1884 for polluting the Yuba River with tailings that caused massive floods in previous years" (Kiester).

According to these reports, hydraulic mining hurt not only the environment—the mountains made bare by pressurized water—but also the economic welfare of those flooded out by the dammed-up rivers and streams. Reports from the period, however, highlight the benefits rather than negative consequences of hydraulic mining.

In 1850, Edward G. Buffum, a member of the Seventh Regiment of the New York State Volunteers who spent six months in the gold mines, saw hydraulic mining as a way to facilitate rather than damage economic development, just as do the LaHoods in *Pale Rider*. Buffum explains that hydraulic mining was a way "to offer to the oppressed and downtrodden of the whole world an asylum, and a place whereby honest industry, which will contribute as much to our wealth as their prosperity; they can build themselves happy homes and live like freemen" (138). According to Buffum, hydraulic mining offered "an immense field for the investment of capital throughout the world, and for the employment of a large portion of its labouring [sic] population" (141). Buffum's view, like that of the LaHoods, however, was short-term and driven only by capital.

A Frequent Binary: "The Big Guys Against the Little Guys" in *Pale Rider*

Such an attitude about nature, and about the environmental costs of mining, is also reflected by films of the Western genre where mining, especially mining by individuals, is romanticized and corporate mining like hydraulic mining is denigrated only if it interferes with the economic progress of the individual miner. Westerns like *The Badlanders* (1958), *The Far Country* (1955) and *Bend of the River* (1952), however, fail to examine environmental degradation accompanying corporate mining. Only the corporate barons' impact on the individual is called into question in these films. *Pale Rider* places environmental concerns at the forefront, with a corporate baron seemingly agreeing with Buffum's argument about hydraulic mining's potential and an avenging angel apparently agreeing with the park ranger's. The binary is established between the evil La-Hood and the good Preacher, but Hull Barret and his community of small miners deconstruct the binary established between LaHood and Preacher because they negotiate a resolution to the conflict by offering an alternative to both.

The opening to *Pale Rider* immediately establishes a classic binary between good and evil found in Westerns like *Shane*, where cattle barons resist the inclusion of small farmers and fenced ranchers into their open range. The film opens with juxtaposed shots that contrast the pristine forested Sawtooth Mountains with thunderous riders, who disrupt the

Figure 7.1. *Pale Rider* (1985): Preacher as Avenging Angel.

peace represented by the natural world. Lennie Niehaus's score heightens the threatening effect of what we discover are Coy LaHood's (Richard Dysart) men on horseback, who aim to invade the small miners' village and drive them out, so LaHood can steal their gold. The pounding of these riders is also contrasted with the laughter of the families in the village where small miners carefully pan for gold in the clear water of a stream. LaHood's riders disturb the tranquility of the village, destroying homes as they tear through, even going so far as to kill a cow and Megan's pet dog.

LaHood's riders clash with the small miners and the natural world represented by the mountains, the stream and the village animals, but nature also serves as the space in which the avenging Preacher is summoned, when Megan Wheeler prays for a miracle over her dog's grave. The first few minutes of the film, then, set up good and evil elements in the film: the good stewards of nature—Preacher and the small miners—stand out against nature's destroyers—LaHood and his men.

Images of the clear stream nurturing the small miners are reinforced by the quiet tranquility, both visual and aural, of Carbon Canyon where the small miners pan for gold, and by Hull Barret's attitude toward a large rock in the creek bed that he believes holds gold. According to Barret, "If I could split that rock there, there'd be gold underneath," but in spite of his faith in the rock's holdings, Barret chooses not to blow up the rock because of the degradation it would cause to the stream: "Well, I thought of drilling and blasting the son of a gun, but you know, uh, that would . . . ," Barret begins. And Preacher finishes his thought "That would wreck the stream, wouldn't it." Barret agrees, saying, "yeah, the stream would be dammed up. . . . be the end of everything."

Even though these small miners dig for gold, they refuse to destroy the stream in order to obtain the gold beneath it, choosing instead to sustain nature, so it can sustain them. In fact, the small miners continue gold panning instead of evolving to more "productive" but destructive techniques common in the 1850s like the two-man rocker, the two-man Long Tom, or the sluice box (Crouch). According to Richard Schickel, "These peaceful souls are presented in the film almost as a hippie commune" (403).

Coy LaHood and his men, on the other hand, strip the earth of all of its wealth. Juxtaposed with scenes of Barret and Preacher hammering communally on the rock are images of a train bringing LaHood back from Sacramento, where he had sought to obtain control of the small miners' claims. The discussion Coy LaHood has with his son, Josh, and one of his gunmen, McGill (Charles Hallahan), emphasizes their destructive mining techniques and their greed for gold at any cost. The corporate miners led by LaHood "play out" vein after vein of gold, in the "number five shaft" and "down in Cobalt Canyon" (*Pale Rider*). According to Josh LaHood, they also "went another twenty foot down twelve shaft and pulled out nothin' but magnetite and shut her down." After excavating almost all of the gold on his property, LaHood only wants more.

In a desperate search for more gold, wealth, and complete control, LaHood not only sends riders to intimidate the small miners and take over Carbon Canyon; he also tries (and fails) to intimidate legislators in Sacramento to sign over the small miners' claims. According to Coy LaHood, "Sacramento ain't worth moose piss" because legislators there "didn't sign the writ." The scene does not stop with this blow to "the big guys"; it also makes a blatant environmental statement when Coy LaHood exclaims, "some of those bastard politicians want to do away with hydraulic mining altogether. Raping the land, they call it." Annette Kolodny's *The Lay of the Land* provides further literary references to "raping the land" for its resources, references that have made the metaphor part of popular culture.

Even though LaHood realizes the consequences of governmental intervention in his mining business, he responds from his own avaricious perspective: "We've gotta move on Carbon and move fast," he exclaims, "'cause the way the wind's blowin', another couple of years, we may be out of business."

LaHood's greedy proclamations are contrasted with the small miners' cooperative stewardship of nature. After Preacher runs off Josh LaHood and his oversized lackey, Club (Richard Kiel), Barret and Preacher, with the help of other community members, finish splitting the big boulder on which they had been hammering, and later on Barret discovers a large gold nugget beneath it. Such a scene in most Westerns would provide the motivation for at least a spark of greed in the other miners, so they would invade Barret's rock in search of more gold. Instead, Barret shows his nugget to Preacher, to Sarah (Carrie Snodgrass), Barret's fiancée, and to Megan, her daughter, and the four go to town to pay the community's debts. The other miners go on with their own mining efforts without much comment. Only Spider's sons respond, chasing the wagon and wishing they too could go to town.

The four-ounce gold nugget inspires a family outing, communal responsibility in the form of debt paying, and continued work, not greedy arguments and bloodshed. When, later in the film, Spider finds a gold-filled stone as big as his head, the community again shows no real emotional response, maintaining their labors but demonstrating no feelings of greed. As Sarah puts it, it is "his turn." Spider and his sons, just like Barret, celebrate by going to town, even though their nugget appears after LaHood dynamited the river and dammed up the communal stream, points that would certainly anger a community in other Western films.

The communal trust the small miners have established becomes most evident when they begin discussing the purchase price of $1,000 a claim Coy LaHood offers them after Coy attempts (and fails) to negotiate with Preacher, offering him a bribe, as well. As a last effort to legally seize Carbon Canyon before bringing in a gun-slinging mercenary and his deputies to kill Preacher and run the small miners out, Coy offers to buy each miner's claim. Hull Barret intervenes when it sounds like the rest of the small miners wish to take the offer and avoid trouble:

> Startin' fresh sounds good when you're in trouble. But before we, uh, vote, uh, and pack up and leave, I think we oughta ask ourselves why we're here. 'Cause if it's no more than money, then we're no better than LaHood himself. . . . If any of us turned up $1000.00 of nuggets, would he quit? Hell no. He'd build his family a better house and, uh, buy his kids better clothes. They'd build a school or a church. If we were farmers we'd be planting crops. If we raised cattle, we'd be tending them, but we're miners, so we dig and pan, and break our backs for gold, but gold ain't what we're about. . . . I came out here to raise a family. This is my home. This is my dream. I sunk roots here.

Barret and the other small miners have built a community in Canyon Creek that they wish to maintain, so they need to sustain the creek and canyon that nourish it. Hull Barret sees small mining as a means to an end—building a family and a community with schools and churches—not as a quest for gold, money, and the power it represents.

Coy LaHood, on the other hand, hauls out as much gold as possible as quickly as he can for the money and power it provides. After failing to bribe Preacher with the town church and a full collection plate, LaHood defines his own mission, owning and controlling everything rather than joining a community of individuals with agency: "I opened this country. I made this town what it is. I brought jobs and industry. I built an empire with my own hands, and I've never asked help from anyone. Those squatters, Reverend, are standing in the way of progress." For LaHood, the land is meant to own and exploit, not to sustain for future family members: "What's mine's mine," he exclaims, "and if you make me fight for it, I will."

Coy LaHood sees himself as representing progress, but it is a destructive kind of progress meant only for LaHood and his followers. The small community of miners, which sustains the environment, is standing in the way of such progress. These miners are squatters who should be "run out" or paid off, so the canyon can be stripped of all of its wealth without delay. In fact, they must be destroyed, as Marshal Stockburn (John Russell) and his deputies destroy Spider and his gold stone when Spider and his sons come to town to celebrate their good luck.

Barret and the small miners, then, are clearly established as law-abiding, ethical, and community-minded (good) "little guys," and Coy LaHood and his followers counter them as evil corporate "big guys," who take what they want at any cost. This story, as Eastwood suggests, is nothing new for Westerns. The environmental message the film nearly shouts out, however, sets *Pale Rider* apart from all other Eastwood-directed films.

The film, then, endorses both community values associated with the small miners and sustainable development illustrated by their less invasive mining techniques. To do this, it first argues strongly against extreme mining techniques associated with a "fair use" philosophy that justifies exploiting all natural resources on one's own property (even when stolen). LaHood and his men follow a fair use philosophy, taking extreme measures to extract minerals quickly and without thought to maintaining the land for future generations. As a testament against extreme environmental exploitation, the film highlights the degradation caused by LaHood's hydraulic mining techniques with three focused scenes and two explanations of the process and its results: one from Hull Barret and one already mentioned from Josh LaHood, the mining baron's son.

Images of Hydraulic Mining: A Contemporary Environmental Message

The film's introduction to LaHood's mining camp provides the first demonstration of the consequences of hydraulic mining techniques. This scene shows viewers the procedure without explanation, emphasizing the power of water pressure coming from the hydraulic cannons (monitors). The scene begins with a long shot of these powerful streams of water and then, a few shots later, shows these torrents stripping the hillside of all life, with the blare of the rushing water reverberating everywhere. The scene establishes a new setting—LaHood's camp—but it also illustrates both the amount of water pressure the procedure creates and the environmental devastation this shooting water produces, images recreated

Figure 7.2. *Pale Rider*: Hydraulic mining tools.

in California's Columbia State Historic Park, an historic gold mining town where hydraulic mining was prevalent from the 1850s through the 1870s.

The visual introduction to hydraulic mining is followed by the film's first explanation of the process, this time from the perspective of a small miner, Hull Barret, in a discussion with Preacher. According to Barret, "Coy LaHood came up here in '54 or '55 . . . [and was] the first man to strike it rich." Barret has no objection to LaHood's luck, but Barret's tone changes when he talks about LaHood's current methods: "Last couple of years he's been using them hydraulic monitors. . . . blasts the place to hell." Barret's description of the results of hydraulic mining are juxtaposed with images of the clear stream where the small miners work less intrusively, a stark contrast to the lifeless shots of the stripped hills in the previous scene.

Barret's conversation with Preacher also reveals the small miners' legal right to Carbon Canyon, not LaHood's. Barret makes clear that "the only way he can take this land legally is if we leave it." The destruction caused by LaHood's mining methods is introduced and explained thoroughly enough to reveal the film's not-so-subtle environmental message against extreme environmental exploitation, a message heightened by LaHood's greed for more land to exploit, and thus for ownership of, Carbon Canyon.

The second scene showing viewers the effects of hydraulic mining occurs after the small miners have voted to reject LaHood's offer of $1,000 per claim. When Preacher rides into the hydraulic mining camp to pass the vote results on to LaHood, the film shows even more of the destruction caused by pressurized water shooting out of monitors. Instead of showing only soil streaming down the hillsides, after a long shot of the water-shooting cannons similar to those in the introductory scene, the film shows trees being ripped from the hillside along with the eroding earth.

The scene also reveals the first clear sign LaHood receives from the small miners that his methods are failing—their rejection of his offer. Environmental degradation in LaHood's camp parallels the destruction he causes after he learns about the small miners' vote and blasts the creek, damming it up. The film here shows us immediately how devastating one blast can be, as the rippling creek dries up and narrows to one small stream of water.

Figurative and Literal Rape

The third and arguably most powerful scene set in LaHood's hydraulic mining camp provides us with images of the shooting monitors and their devastating consequences as well as a detailed explanation of the process, an engineering feat highlighted by the noise of the pressurized water in the background, a noise so loud Megan declares, "It hurts my ears." Here the audience watches the monitors from Megan's point of view, since she has ridden into camp and toward Josh LaHood to defy Preacher (who has rejected her love) and her mother. Megan's gaze aligns with her words: "It looks like hell." We have already recorded Josh's description of the hydraulic mining process, a description that highlights only the wealth it provides him and his father.

But "raping the land," as they called it in Sacramento, is lined up with raping a woman—Megan—in this scene. The parallels between the two "rapes" are underlined because LaHood's men leave their water cannons to watch the rape and cheer it on, just as they watched the rape of the landscape caused by those same cannons. So when Preacher rescues Megan by shooting first Josh's gun and then his hand, the film shows us what methods are needed to stop both the literal and the figurative rapes.

Solution to "Fair Use":
Sustainable Development and Eco-terrorist Violence

Preacher's intervention also demonstrates that the small miners' community and the environment it sustains cannot survive unless Preacher and the small miners resort to force. These scenes, then, demonstrate the film's first environmental argument—that extreme methods like hydraulic mining are too devastating to the environment and should be replaced by the more gentle methods of the small miners, who seek to sustain their canyon for future generations. But the film highlights the

Figure 7.3. *Pale Rider*: Hull Barrett as eco-terrorist.

strength of the myth of sustainable development as an alternative to fair use techniques like hydraulic mining not only by illustrating the more positive results of panning in an un-dammed stream; the film also offers a viable (if violent) way to eliminate corporate mining and the greedy baron controlling it.

Here the film complicates the simple binary between good and evil prevalent in contemporary Westerns, since in order to save the land and their community, Preacher and the small miners' representative, Hull Barret, must visit on LaHood's corporation the same destruction that LaHood inflicted on the small miners and the environment—a difference from *Shane*, where Shane eliminates Joe's participation in a fistfight. After LaHood's marshal and his deputies mutilate Spider (who had gone to town only with his sons), Preacher clarifies the small miners' mission: "A man alone is easy prey," he explains, so "only by standing together will you beat the LaHoods of the world."

The next morning when Preacher rides off to take on LaHood and his men alone, it seems that he's negating his claim about the need for community, but Barret accompanies him, representing the communal spirit Preacher had forged. As stewards, the small miners learn that they must protect themselves, their families, and the environment using any means possible, including violence. Preacher is loaded down with dynamite, so he and Barret are able to blow up LaHood's mining camp, the hydraulic mine's cannons, and its infrastructure, returning water to its source.

This last scene of LaHood's camp occurs at sunrise, before the workers have risen, so the cannons lie dormant, and the remaining hillside is uninjured. In this scene, no men are killed; they all escape

Figure 7.4. *Pale Rider*: Preacher and Barrett blow up the camp.

from the blasted tents and outbuildings, but the mining operation is destroyed when Preacher and Barret finish their work. Since Preacher does not work alone, the small miners and Preacher stand together to beat LaHood until Barret picks up a stick of dynamite Preacher drops, and Preacher chases Barret's horse away. "You're a good man, Barret," Preacher explains. "You take care of Sarah and the girl."

The suggestion here is that Preacher will destroy the marshal, his deputies, and LaHood without assistance, exacting the personal revenge to which the film has alluded since Preacher's arrival. Preacher has prepared for his confrontation with Marshal Stockburn. When Preacher arrives in town, his image is superimposed on that of LaHood, since he is reflected in the window out of which LaHood peers. And the marshal looks stunned when he first recognizes Preacher and exclaims, "you!" It seems, then, that Preacher will kill off LaHood and his men as a sole gunman, an avenging angel seeking retribution for the wrongs Marshal Stockburn had committed.

Preacher easily kills Stockburn's deputies one by one in ghost style, able to appear and disappear at will—demonstrating his seemingly supernatural status. And he faces Marshal Stockburn in the street, in a showdown scene as old as western films. It appears, then, that Preacher has taken on LaHood and his gang without Barret and the community he represents. But after Preacher shoots the marshal in the same six places in which he'd been shot—and then one more time in the head—La-Hood appears by his office window, this time with a Winchester rifle in hand, and we see him from Barret's point of view just before Barret shoots LaHood down.

Barret has arrived on foot instead of wings, and he has killed La-Hood, so LaHood is killed by a human agent, Barret. Barret serves, then, as the nominal leader of the sustainable community and represents its values: The community can't wait for the law to stop something this destructive. Preacher, who is now on his horse and looking at Barret, simply says, with a smile, perhaps of thanks, "long walk." Barret replies with his own smile and a laconic "yep." Such an ending makes a final connection between Preacher and Barret, illustrating that they have won this battle together.

Conclusion

Pale Rider, then, argues for sustainable development as an alternative to extreme fair use methods like hydraulic mining in several ways. It demonstrates that hydraulic mining is wrong, moving beyond mere historical accuracy. It even shows us that the government in Sacramento is against hydraulic mining because it dams up rivers, so that when Coy LaHood tries to sway legislators and fails, he recognizes that he'll have to shut down his corporate mines in a couple of years.

But when LaHood's reaction is to extract as much wealth as possible before he's put out of business, without thought to the environmental consequences, the film combines the elements of Eastwood's other Westerns with an environmental message: A Preacher, called from nature, must implement vigilante justice—a communal eco-terrorism—to stop LaHood's desperate devastation of the environment. Such a clear and strong environmental message deserves serious examination, especially since Eastwood "made a point of discussing the environmental subtext of *Pale Rider* with Todd McCarthy of *Variety* (McGilligan 377) at the Cannes Film Festival where it was screened in 1985.

Thus like other Western films, *Pale Rider* deals with a contemporary set of political problems by placing it into a particular past. In this case, Eastwood interrogates ecological devastation caused by fair use politics by placing a symbol of the problem, hydraulic mining, in its contemporary setting, the mid-1800s. And the film feeds off the Man With No Name persona and employs the revenge theme from other Eastwood Westerns. A gun is also the best way to deal with political problems. Since the environment will be destroyed before the government can legally stop it—there is no functioning legal system in the town—it must be dealt with extralegally through an avenging spirit who comes literally from nature to protect the community and the environment while gaining revenge on his murderers.

Ultimately, *Pale Rider* makes a contemporary environmental argument against fair use and for sustainable development, an argument with continuing relevance in light of lawsuits in Montana over open-pit mining and the aftereffects of hydraulic mining and other destructive mining techniques like those using cyanide and arsenic to better extract minerals. Jared Diamond's *Collapse* offers three examples of the consequences of such mining methods: toxic waste, sediment, and cyanide (35–41).

The end of *Pale Rider* reinforces this argument. After Preacher and Barret destroy the corporate mining camp and kill off all its leaders, unlike *High Plains Drifter* or *Unforgiven*, the Eastwood films to which *Pale Rider* is most often compared, the focus is placed not only on Eastwood's Man With No Name—Preacher—but also on the representatives of the small miners' community—Barret and Megan. Preacher does not ride off into a desolate desert after looking back on a town he had destroyed, as does Eastwood's character in *High Plains Drifter*. Instead, Preacher, a representative of the natural world, rides off into the Sawtooth Mountains on his pale horse and disappears into the snow, a sign that he has returned to the natural world from which he had been summoned. Barret and Megan, on the other hand, ride back to their village, presumably prepared to build the school and church for which they strive.

The last message of the film centers on love and community, with Megan's declaration of love for Preacher and her proclamation that the whole community loves him, too. The revenge cycle has been completed, and vigilante justice has been achieved. Yet something new emerges in *Pale Rider*: a call to action that serves not only violent ends but also environmental conservation. When Barret kills LaHood, he also eradicates LaHood's fair use politics that destroy the environment that Barret and his community wish to sustain.

8

Car Culture and the Transformation of the American Landscape in *The Fast and the Furious*

As a kid growing up in Vietnam and meeting the (American) military personnel, we all grew up wanting an American car—and the Mustang was *it*. . . . The Mustang really stood for everything that's about America. It's big and bold and powerful and it's accessible. It's available to everyone.

—Tang Thai, "The Mustang Was It,"
St. Louis Dispatch, 7 January 2004

ROM AN ECO-CRITICAL PERSPECTIVE, Rob Cohen's *The Fast and the Furious* (2001) and its sequels, John Singleton's *2 Fast 2 Furious* (2003) and Justin Lin's *The Fast and the Furious: Tokyo Drift* (2006), like the 1954 John Ireland film *The Fast and the Furious* that inspired them, not only illustrate the devotion to souped-up high-speed cars and the stylish culture they represent; they also take environmental degradation to hyperbolic levels. These films go beyond merely highlighting the car as an American icon and valorizing a concrete highway built for racing. Despite the more liberal class and race politics in the later films that serve to critique human exploitation, all these *Fast and Furious* films advocate a heightened abuse of nature and ecosystems. They rest on transformed natural and man-made environments and on the environmental impact that is inherently a part of car culture.

In the contemporary *Fast and Furious* films, the situation is the same as it was in 1954—car culture celebrates speed and control, as well as the transformation of the natural landscape into a man-made landscape that is, in turn, itself transformed without questioning the environmental expense. These films demonstrate that the environmental impact of cars and the car culture in America has been treated as natural and desirable, as a given. Drivers in all the films appear to rebel against a conformist suburban culture that uses roadways for commuting and garages for parking instead of racing; however, they also conform to this same culture through their acceptance of environmental degradation in the form of both a transformation of natural and man-made landscapes, and reliance on nonrenewable fuels that contribute to global warming.

Drivers in all four films not only use artificial landscapes built on ecosystems, they also further exploit this artificial landscape, transforming its former utility into a roadway for speed, thrills, and status. The 2001, 2003, and 2006 films merely mask their attitude toward the landscape by including one inconsequential difference, from an environmental standpoint: an updated race and class politics rooted in post–World War II Southern car culture that responds to *The Dukes of Hazzard* (1979–1985), a television series with similar roots. While racial and class hierarchies may have been deconstructed in the later films, exploitation of the environment is not only accepted but is presented as a way to even the class and race stakes. Even though hierarchies appear to have changed from 1954 to 2006, when it comes to the natural world, environmental degradation is not only a given but a goal. An eco-critical reading of these films suggests that little changed between 1954 and 2006 in an ideology that worships speed and advocates the conquest of the natural world as a transformative development aligned with progress and democracy.

The thematic and plot parallels between the films spanning half a century are striking. They highlight a car culture that juxtaposes elements of consumption and consumerism, as well as food and fast cars, with sex and power. Linking sex with food is a staple of cinema, since both work together to elicit desire and stimulate our appetites. In these films, viewers are encouraged to stimulate our appetites for consuming the environment and to think of that consumption as empowering and pleasurable.

Food links all of these *Fast and Furious* films. Produced by Roger Corman and directed by Edward Sampson and John Ireland, the 1954 car culture film, *The Fast and the Furious*, begins with a truck crash that is juxtaposed with a shot of high-end foreign cars racing down a two-lane road. The plot then focuses on Connie (Dorothy Malone) driving into a diner (The Paddle Creek Lodge) in her two-seat Jaguar for a sandwich. This low-key scene escalates to a kidnapping and car hijacking when Frank Webster (John Ireland) grabs Connie and escapes the diner in her Jaguar. Webster has broken out of jail after being wrongly accused of murder—as seen in the film's opening truck crash—and now seeks to prove his innocence and redeem his life. The film's thin plot line is meant to showcase the high-end sports cars at the road rally and race that make up much of the film, as well as the constructed all-asphalt landscape further transformed into a racetrack.

Like the 1954 film after which it is named, Rob Cohen's *The Fast and the Furious* begins with a shot of a truck on a highway in an acrobatic high-speed hijacking. Cohen's film also introduces its main characters over food, in a discussion about tuna fish sandwiches that ends with a jealous fight in the street outside. Food, sex, and speed serve to foreground the social construction of cars and the car culture as desirable items of consumption. In the sequel, *2 Fast 2 Furious*, sandwiches are replaced by lunch on a mansion patio, Brian O'Connor's (Paul Walker) and Roman's (Tyrese Gibson) reward for winning a race to retrieve a Cuban cigar. In 1954's *The Fast and the Furious*, Dorothy Malone's character (Connie) must ride off in her two-seat Jaguar as Frank Webster's hostage (before eating her sandwich). And in *The Fast and the Furious: Tokyo Drift*, Sean Boswell (Lucas Black) makes connections with Tokyo-bound Americans in a high school cafeteria before meeting them and other teenage "drifters" in a parking garage.

All of these films also foreground an existing landscape that is already man-made, thus making it easier to forget that it is an already transformed landscape. The real natural landscape that serves as the basis of this transformation is not even evoked anymore. In Baudrillard's term, it is all a simulacrum already. The receding natural landscape that is the basis of these films becomes further erased by the multiple transformations of the man-made landscape. It is not so much the landscape that is transformed—as the frontier closed in 1890—but the use that is made of this landscape. The only available frontier left is the new use one can make of what is there, following, of course, a similar ideology as the one that informed the transformation in the first place—a particular version of landscape and power.

As important as food, romance, and sex are, the cars, asphalt, and transformed landscape are the centerpieces of the films. In the 2001 *The Fast and the Furious*, kicked-up Japanese compacts are driven on Los

Angeles pavement by an assorted group of multiracial young male hellions. With an ethnically ambiguous leader—Vin Diesel's Dominic—and street racers of Asian, African American, and Hispanic descent, the film shows us a globalized car-crazy, hip-hop–driven subculture where urban youth in their twenties invest thousands of dollars to soup up lightweight Toyotas, Mitsubishis, and Hondas for inner-city ultra-speed. Two big races and three car chases make up most of the movie, providing speed-driven highs to drivers, passengers, and (if box office numbers speak the truth) audience members. This loud and fast underworld thumbs its nose at the establishment—in this case represented by the FBI and, at first, its undercover agent, Brian. They even appear to reject the utilitarian reasons behind the construction of the asphalt and concrete landscapes they exploit, even as they reappropriate it for their own use in a semblance of rejecting all that is bourgeois.

The Original *Fast and Furious* Film in its Cultural Context

The 1954 *Fast and Furious* embodies an ideology that erupted after World War II, when returning veterans flocked to the newly developed suburbs where they gained access to home ownership under the Veterans Administration acts. Eisenhower's goal to build an interstate highway system made movement between city jobs and suburban homes not only a possibility but increasingly a reality. But since Frederick Jackson Turner's 1890 argument about the significance of the American frontier in the formation of the American character, at a time when the frontier seemed to no longer exist, images of American culture's vision of an open road—a frontier to conquer—seem to have changed.

The image of an existing frontier—while there are no geographical frontiers left—remains an important image to maintain in an American consciousness shaped by mythical frontier ideals like independence, self-reliance, and ingenuity. The automobile creates a symbolic space in which dreams of freedom and conquering frontiers can be kept alive. The automobile helps us maintain the illusion that we are still conquering space/place, that there is still a frontier we can explore, every day, as we drive long distances on these highways. For the disenfranchised—by middle-class standards—that is, those relegated to the inner city rather than the suburbs, the need to create their own illusion of a frontier is played out in parking garages and urban streets. These ethnically diverse films sell the American frontier dream to all cultures. This American dream and American identity depend on the transformation of the landscape, as they always have—whether the open space of the West or the closed space of the inner city.

Much has been written about the roots and reasons behind America's love affair with the automobile. An "automotive ideology," partly driven by advertisements meant to sell those automobiles, defines Americans' attitudes toward their cars. According to Thomas Detwyler in "Selling the Car Culture through Advertising," car ads suggest that cars can give Americans "excitement," "success," "power," "status," "speed," "sex," "style," "bravery," "seclusion and coddling," "toughness," "romance," and "adventure." This ideology has become so engrained in the American mind and culture that by 1963, and after the inception of the federal interstate system, Lewis Mumford explained, "the current American way of life is founded not just on motor transportation but on the religion of the motorcar, and the sacrifices that people are prepared to make for this religion stand outside the realm of rational criticism" (234).

Alexander Wilson asserts in *The Culture of Nature* that since 1956, when the Eisenhower administration began constructing the U.S. Interstate Highway System, "the speeding car along the open road has become a metaphor for progress in the U.S. and for the cultural taming of the American wilderness" (34). In *America*, Jean Baudrillard describes a post–World War II America of "empty, absolute freedom of the freeways [. . .] the America of desert speed, of motels and mineral surfaces" (5).

According to John Urry, these landscapes "stand for modernity and the rejection of the complex histories of European societies. This emptiness is a metaphor of the American dream" (5). But landscapes also stand for the promise of speed. Baudrillard asserts that "speed creates pure objects [. . .] Its only rule is to leave no trace behind [. . .] Driving like this produces a kind of invisibility, transparency, or transversality in things, simply by emptying them out" (7). Such invisibility enhances the emptiness and helps facilitate the sense of freedom and progress associated with the American dream. The present passed by the vehicle and the past the vehicle leaves behind are seemingly erased, in favor of a future that signifies progress. Wilson argues that in the 1950s, "What we saw out the window of a speeding car [. . .] was the future itself" (34).

Landscapes seen through a speeding car window further evoke the freedom found only on the open road. Concrete and asphalt roadways have come to represent progress, the future sought in the Old West. This is another way in which we rapidly consume landscapes, in both a symbolic and literal sense, as we move through them rapidly in a car. We metaphorically consume the landscape as we race over and past it. Yet, we literally consume natural resources and use them to transform natural landscapes so as to create a space for cars and their culture. Car culture films laud and validate this ideology of consumption.

Numerous films from the 1950s and '60s have extolled this car culture suburban landscape, a landscape against which the *Fast and Furious* films rebel. For example, in the closing scenes of the 1962 Cinerama, *How the West Was Won*, we hear Spencer Tracy's voice-over rhapsodizing over transforming the desert into a garden while we see panoramic images from a bird's-eye view of a megadam, an open-pit mine, farms, and a massive logging operation that dissolves into the megahighway systems of Southern California; this is a landscape of concrete ribbons and cars replacing desert sands and stone, demonstrating that the highway is another sign of progress. Like the building of dams, the mine, and the logging camp, highway construction involves the extraction of resources, the transformation of the environment, and ultimately its replacement with something else.

These series of transformations present a vision of triumph of a suburban culture that is, according to the film's soundtrack, "bound for the promised land." Aerial images of cloverleaf highways show countless cars merging onto superhighways from ramps leading to and from the suburban American dream. It is a landscape that is willingly welcomed by the new and powerful—and conformist—American suburban order, but it is also a landscape made possible only because of ultra-cheap oil and inexpensive automobiles.

Figure 8.1. Original *Fast and the Furious* (1954): Race to Mexico.

In this context, the 1950s represent the heyday of car culture and of car culture films. With the beginning of the interstate system in 1956, cars and their drivers are poised to head out on the ultramodern four-lane open roads. Car culture films in the 1950s highlight unique class and regional reactions to the automobile.

The 1954 B movie *The Fast and the Furious* is a product of this era. The film illustrates upper-class California car culture and showcases high-end foreign two-seat racers. It revolves around a romance, camaraderie, and mutual respect among car racers, as do the later *Fast and Furious* films, while resting on similar ideas regarding landscape. In its cross-country race, the first *Fast and Furious* film speaks to issues of freedom and the open road, reflecting the 1950s ethos. During the race, we see the landscape from Frank Webster's perspective, as he speeds toward Mexico and freedom—both literally from prosecution and figuratively from a present and a past that inhibit progress. The more recent *Fast and Furious* films draw on this nostalgia for wide-open spaces associated with the Old West and the progress it promises. Speeding down an open road at least temporarily recaptures this sense of freedom.

Only in one way does the earlier film deviate from visions of individual freedom—in terms of the race/class dimensions found in the later films. Despite similar settings, plot, and thematic elements, the 1954 film does not embrace the progressive class and race values found in the later films. But these seemingly progressive values are limited and, from an eco-critical standpoint, rely on the same ideology of the 1950s highway system, an ideology built on individuals' rights to consume and on freedom of mobility.

Even though Frank Webster represents the working class—he is an independent truck owner and driver—Connie Adair's group embodies the wealthy leisure class who can afford to buy and race Italian and British sports cars for recreation. In the film, Webster has been accused of the murder of a rival truck driver. Because he does not trust authority—this time the police—Webster breaks out of jail and takes Connie along as his hostage. Although Webster eventually is cleared of the murder and gains the respect of the jet-setters he races, his working-class status is not valorized. Instead, Connie, a member of the upper class, heroically races to stop Webster from getting arrested by the border police, demonstrating how effectively the status quo and its class politics can be perpetuated.

Cars, then, are the real focus in the film, not rebellion or challenge to the class status quo. Instead, the film draws on an ideology of progress that burgeoned under a politics of consumption meant to spur the economy and provide a reward for ending a world war. Such an ideology might be forgivable in this 1954 context; yet, it served as the foundation for a globalized car culture with dire consequences for us and our environment.

Car Culture as Nostalgia

Few would dispute the impact the car has had on the environment, especially in the United States where, by the mid-1990s, Americans owned 34% of the world's motor vehicles (some 201 million) even though Americans comprised less than 5% of the world's population. With so many motor vehicles, Americans burn 143 billion gallons of fuel a year. Motor vehicles in the United States cause more than 50% of air pollution and produce heaping solid waste (millions of cars and tires) and leaking oil and gasoline (250 million gallons of motor oil and countless gallons of gasoline leaking from at least 500,000 underground tanks) (Detwyler "U.S. Auto Culture and the Environment").

Cars also account for the paving of America: In Los Angeles, two-thirds "of the ground space is reserved for the sole purpose of moving and storing cars" (Goff). Constructing the car as a source and symbol of freedom, pleasure, and identity, while drawing on images of an open road built on our drive to move west toward progress, is counter to any truly progressive ecological vision for the future.

One would expect the 2001, 2003, and 2006 *Fast and Furious* films to embody a more enlightened view of the consequences of speeding down an open road, since they respond to contemporary popular culture, a culture now universally aware of the reality of environmental degradation and its causes. In the context of recent documentary films like *The End of Suburbia: Oil Depletion and the Collapse of the American Dream* (2004), *An Inconvenient Truth*, and *Who Killed the Electric Car?* (2006), these *Fast and Furious* films appear irresponsible and archaic despite having updated their politics by effectively blurring racial boundaries. *An Inconvenient Truth*, for example, provides clear visual evidence of changes in the environment due to increased levels of carbon dioxide and greenhouse gasses in the atmosphere by juxtaposing images from the 1970s with similar images taken recently—we see Mount Kilimanjaro's snows receding with the passage of time.

The recent *Fast and Furious* films draw on collective historical memories harking back nostalgically to mid-century car culture's association with the freedom of the open road, rather than highlighting the real environmental damage this culture promulgates. These films consciously evoke a landscape already transcended by concrete and speeding cars, as when in the 2001 film Dominic hijacks a truck from a speeding car with no natural landscape in view in the frame. In a long line of car culture films, the recent *Fast and the Furious* films reinforce the ideology associated with the car culture as they elicit in viewers a longing for the mythical freedom cars provide, especially American "muscle cars."

Muscle cars, in particular, are associated with the thrill of speed rather than with utilitarian transportation purposes. From Junior Johnson to Smokey and the Bandit, high-horsepower autos are built to race. They draw on strategies found in advertising since companies started selling cars, still using images of Steve McQueen (*Bullitt*) to sell Ford Mustangs. But the 2001 *The Fast and the Furious* and its sequels, *2 Fast 2 Furious* and *Tokyo Drift*, go beyond the white-American-male images presented in both car ads and earlier (white-bread) films foregrounding cars, car racing, and car culture. Unlike the 1954 *The Fast and the Furious*, the recent sequels move cars into a racially progressive era of car racing where men and women of diverse races mingle amicably, and cars represent a new global economy in which foreign products are far superior to their white American competitors.

While the recent *Fast and the Furious* films present an ideologically progressive portrayal of race and class politics, they perpetuate a policy of overconsumption and exploitation of environmental resources, displaying cars that run on both gasoline and nitrous oxide. We may not be shown drivers refueling their cars, but we do see them switch from gasoline to nitrous oxide almost instantly during races. The films also exacerbate

Figure 8.2. *The Fast and the Furious*: Racing on Los Angeles streets.

our acceptance of an already-reconstructed landscape in which nature is paved over to accommodate cars, by erasing traces of the original natural environment on which these concrete and asphalt roads were built. By further transforming an already-transformed landscape of inner-city roadways and parking garages into race tracks, the films treat pavement as natural, essential, and original.

Although the 1954 *Fast and Furious* film celebrates the transformation of the landscape to accommodate the car and make movement and exploration of the new suburban "frontiers" possible, the remakes assume an acceptance of an already-altered landscape, with no visible vestiges of what predated the cities. In the later films, the same sense of power and freedom gained from exploring new frontiers is now achieved by reappropriating this man-made landscape of highways and parking garages. But the impetus and motives to transform the landscape are the same as in the 1954 film.

While the return to the inner city appears progressive and challenging of middle-class values represented by the flight to the suburbs, it is modeled on similar aspirations. These films perpetuate the same attitudes

Figure 8.3. Original *Fast and the Furious*. Food and romance as tropes in the fast and furious films.

toward society and the environment, their visions relying on notions of progress and consumption to justify the exploitation of the land and its resources. The films exploit cars, culture, and the environment to draw in audiences who like fast cars and thumb their nose at the conformist attitudes embraced by middle-class suburbanites, as when the characters run from the police and shut down streets for racing. Their transformation of the paved landscape also "shuts down" more conventional drivers who rely on the automobile to commute to jobs and choose reliability, utility, and luxurious ride over speed.

Americans' love affair with the car has been widely documented. Cars serve utilitarian purposes, promise freedom on the open road, and connect different regions of the United States. While the racing culture in the *Fast and Furious* films purports to be in opposition to suburban car culture, their goals are the same. Even though all the *Fast and Furious* films highlight foreign cars, the culture they represent, according to Andrew O'Hehir, supports the view "that freedom and friendship are more important than order," a point particularly clear when Brian protects Dom and his gang from the FBI in 2001's *The Fast and the Furious*.

This view emphasizes the youth culture underpinning these car culture films, as well. O'Hehir argues that one of the film's real issues is that "Americans really believe that driving a kickass machine down an open road, with your past receding in the rearview mirror, will make you live forever." Since colonists first arrived on the shores of North America, the American dream has emphasized new opportunities and the freedom to pursue progress at any cost, not just opportunities for self-actualization, ideals associated with youth culture. Drivers in all the films reflect this obsession with youth, with the most recent installment—*Tokyo Drift*—highlighting the youngest protagonist.

On the surface, the *Fast and Furious* films aim to transcend a suburban American ideal, since the freedom offered by the open road must be altered to accommodate urban car racing. Here, the car itself, independently of the landscape through which it moves, represents the American dream of freedom (especially from authority) and camaraderie. Authority in this case represents a limit to one's actions, limits that should be eliminated to gain the freedom of action an open road provides. Driving the car even through an urban landscape provides the exhilaration an open road suggests. Emphasizing freedom of action, however, conflicts with goals to address dwindling resources and the environmental consequences of insistent refusal to accept ecological limits.

Focusing on the car itself, instead of on the open road, also aligns with American car culture ideology. According to Blackburn and Mann, "Driving a car can be a source of intense pleasure: of flexibility, skill, possession and excitement" (quoted in Urry 6). But, as John Urry argues, studies in sociology have limited their focus to "the ways that car ownership in general or the ownership of particular models does or does not enhance people's status position" (3). Urry goes on to assert that "sociology has regarded cars as a neutral technology, permitting social patterns of life that would have more or less occurred anyway" (3), a regard unshared in our belief systems even when reality conflicts with this image.

Critiques of car culture and its valorization demonstrate the effects cars have had on popular culture and mainstream American society. Sociological studies of car advertising suggest that manufacturers not only construct consumers of automobiles but also stimulate changed perceptions of cars, of commutes from suburbia, and of suburban and urban development built around cars (see Flink and Detwyler "Selling the Car Culture through Advertising"). Even though Urry examines environmental resource use and Phillip Goff equates car culture with "the landscape of subtraction," overviews of percentages of resources consumed by car manufacturers and pollutants emitted into the air and water do not change Americans' attitudes toward their cars. The same can be said for drivers in the *Fast and Furious* films.

In fact, environmentalists studying urban spaces focus attention on economic development, even if this means bringing industry to the inner city or paving over the landscape as long as it accommodates the poor. Most Americans embrace development in urban and suburban areas because it symbolizes progress and booming economic markets, that is, jobs and economic security. Environmental writers like Michael Bennett and Andrew Ross argue against anti-urban white flight to the suburbs, not because it thrives on and encourages further "subtraction" of the landscape through suburban sprawl, but because it parallels "capital flight" (Bennett 176). Andrew Ross asserts "that anti-urbanism and back-to-nature movements 'can be tied directly to the economic cycles of investment and disinvestment in city centers'" (Ross 100, quoted in Bennett 173). Urban environmental movements seek to improve the infrastructure of inner-city poor rather than increase green spaces or encourage a more interdependent relationship with the natural world.

Bennett suggests that the solution to the ghettos such white flight has constructed in inner cities is not "gentrification," that is, a redevelopment of inner-city space to accommodate only the rich, generally white home buyer, but to provide employment and better schools to the urban, mostly African American population already in place. White flight meant capital flight—loss of industry and other employment sources in cities like Los Angeles: "In Los Angeles [. . .] an investigating committee

of the California Legislature found that the South-central neighbor-
hoods in which the city's African American population is concentrated
experienced a fifty percent increase in unemployment between the early
1970s and mid 1980s, while community purchasing power declined by
a third" (Bennett 179). So, urban environmentalists are faced with a
dilemma. If "one of every six U.S. jobs supports the auto" ("U.S. Auto
Culture and the Environment"), and the solution to inner city ghettos
is employment and the better support services they might provide, then
how can environmental degradation such development would bring be
recognized and curbed?

Ironically, car culture films like *The Fast and the Furious, 2 Fast 2
Furious*, and *The Fast and the Furious: Tokyo Drift* offer the car as a viable
solution to the alienation and poverty that seem inevitable in decaying
cities like Los Angeles, Miami, and (to a certain extent) Tokyo—the three
films' respective settings. These films endorse the views of contemporary
environmentalists, like Bennett and Ross, to provide the inner city's racially diverse populations with capital and a means of both production
and support. The films, like liberal urban environmentalists, support
progressive attitudes toward racial diversity and inner-city reclamation
by native populations. But they perpetuate the implicit and explicit as-
sumptions that the adverse consequences of burning fossil fuel are an
inescapable by-product of class and racial progress, and that asphalt and
concrete landscapes represent development, sustaining not only car culture
but human lives in the inner city.

Looking at the 1954 *The Fast and the Furious* in relation to the 2001
remake and its 2003 and 2006 sequels demonstrates that the politics of car
culture films has progressed in relation to social and urban environmental
concerns. But such a comparison also illustrates the limits of an urban
environmentalism based on capital and racial and class politics. Even
though the later films update race and class politics, they still valorize
exploitation of the natural world.

Remakes or Revisions:
The Limits of Race and Class Politics

While the *Fast and Furious* films rewrite class and racial politics, con-
doning multiethnic interactions among inner-city (poor) youth, they also
embrace the traditionalist values of progress at any cost. They promote
exploitation of the natural world and advocate a consumer-driven su-
perficiality that undermines any progress but that represented by speed.
The misogyny in the films serves only as another signifier of the goal
of the car races—freedom from any limits on actions. These films are

much more class-conscious than the 1954 version because they respond to both the 1954 film and to Southern car culture and its media offspring, *The Dukes of Hazzard*.

Southern car culture highlights less affluent drivers driving less expensive cars. It is manifested today in NASCAR races where drivers earning millions of dollars still mingle with the masses. NASCAR racers drive American cars in stock-car races, listen to country music, and maintain a working-class persona. Founded by William H. G. France in 1947, NASCAR made its home in Daytona Beach, Florida—not California—near the site of the first auto racing time trial at Ormond Beach in 1903 (Korth). France owned a gas station and witnessed drag races on Daytona Beach in the 1930s. In 1965, when Tom Wolfe wrote for *Esquire* magazine about Junior Johnson—winner of fifty NASCAR Winston Cup Series races—stock-car racing earned drivers big bucks, "grossing [Johnson] $100,000, in 1963" (Wolfe 211). Johnson embodies the working-class image NASCAR still preserves. According to Wolfe's epigraph, Junior Johnson "is a coon hunter, a rich man, an ex-whiskey runner, a good old boy who hard-charges stock cars at 175 mph. Mother dog! He is the lead-footed chicken farmer from Ronda, the true vision of the New South" (211). Southern, working-class, good old boy values that make class barriers more than permeable still prevail in the NASCAR circuit.

The *Fast and Furious* films embrace the same values exemplified by Southern car culture, but with an updated hip-hop multiracial twist. In the cars, drivers are masked and anonymous; in the 2001 film, the cut to characters at the luncheonette reveals a class structure and racial diversity missing in the 1954 *Fast and Furious*. The film's protagonist, Brian, is what Hector calls "typical white bread," down to his name, and stands out as the only white blond in the film. The fight over the "girl" overseeing the luncheonette reveals the racial diversity embraced by urban car culture. Vince—a dark ethnic, perhaps Italian—fights Brian over Dominic's (Vin Diesel) sister, Mia (Jordana Brewster). Even though Dom's and Mia's last name is Toretto, the two have the perfected look of the new "ethnically ambiguous." The drag race Brian enters the evening after the fight highlights this racial difference from earlier car culture movies with mostly, if not all, white casts. The four drivers in the race exemplify this diversity, with an African American and a Hispanic male, and Dominic and Brian racing for money and group status. Brian's white-bread difference to this racially diverse gang is emphasized by his role as an outsider, an FBI agent investigating this inner-city car-racing subculture.

As the only blond, blue-eyed male in the film, Brian has been compared to Steve McQueen—an earlier car movie icon in films like *Bullitt*

(1968) and *Le Mans* (1971). His love interest, Mia, who resembles Ali McGraw, is of mixed-race descent. As do the car races, romance highlights racial diversity in the film, not only between Brian and Mia, but also between Mia's brother, Dom, and Letty (Michelle Rodriguez). Letty is of Hispanic descent and Dom has an Italian name, but they both sport the ethnically ambiguous look. After the 2000 census in which individuals could check more than one race to define themselves, it comes as no surprise that racial lines have become so permeable. With the exception of Brian, characters in Dom's gang look multiracial and remain loyal to a racially diverse gang. Even the FBI includes racially diverse detectives and agents. Diversity is celebrated in the film—and serves a broad audience well. Only the Asian gang members Brian first suspects as responsible for the truck-jackings look racially "pure," in this case Chinese.

Not only are racial lines blurred in *The Fast and the Furious*, so too are class boundaries. Class differences are represented by cars, especially when Brian and Dom's compact "blows away" a Ferrari, whose older, upper-class driver tells them they "can't afford" his car. A compact Japanese car beating a Ferrari makes a clear statement about class, both social and economic, that is reiterated in the contrast between the FBI and the car-racing gangs. Brian represents the establishment—the FBI—along with Sergeant Tanner (Ted Levine) and Agent Bilkins (Thom Barry). The car racers represent opposing inner-city Los Angeles gangs, with Dom leading his mixed-race group and Johnny Tran (Rick Yune) heading up the Asian gang. This gang subculture is part of an underclass where money for hot cars, fashion, music, and girls comes from street racing and criminal hijackings.

Figure 8.4. *2 Fast, 2 Furious* (2003): Winning a cigar and diversifying race.

Brian acts as a link between the two groups, choosing the anti-authority gang and its members over the FBI. Driving fast cars in the spirit of a gang, a loyal family, appeals to Brian so much so that he defies the FBI, lets Dom escape, and—as we learn in the film's sequel—runs away from the establishment (FBI) to Miami, where he embraces street-racing culture and a new last name. When Brian helps Dom escape, he reinforces the concept that freedom and friendship are more important than order in American (car) culture. Brian, then, blurs boundaries between cultures and classes in the film by choosing the anarchy of inner-city car culture over the conformity of the FBI. Within this framework, however, the rebellion Brian embraces maintains similar (conformist) hierarchies, especially those that allow for the degradation of nature. The film takes destruction of nature to hyperbolic levels since it advocates the destruction of resources and landscapes. The race and class politics merely mask the environmentally destructive nature of car culture.

The film's sequel, *2 Fast 2 Furious*, also blurs racial barriers while taking a conservative approach toward the establishment. Beginning with a street race, this time in the polyglot car gang subculture of Miami, complete with a Rastafarian, the film color codes cars and their drivers to foreground racial diversity and capture an audience obsessed not only with cars but with videogames. As in the 2001 film, Brian (Paul Walker) is featured as the only white male blond, blue-eyed driver, having remained outside the law, never returning to the FBI he fled in the previous film. Brian, then, starts out as a white member of the underclass, the car gang subculture.

The race itself, however, shows how extensively car racing gangs adapt the urban auto-friendly landscape to their racing needs. Unlike in the first film's drag race, *2 Fast 2 Furious* brings us a race on a closed city course, altering the concrete landscape for speeding cars. Car gang members block off city streets with orange cones, self-assured that they will keep traffic clear for their race—in inner-city Miami. Racers line up four across and run a street course empty of other cars at speeds reaching 160 mph, when nitrous oxide is activated.

Control over a landscape already transformed for the automobile is clearly portrayed near the end of the race, when the race coordinator orders gang members to break into the controls of a draw bridge and open it just wide enough so each side of the bridge is angled like a ramp. Racing cars fly up the ramp and jump across the bridge in an ultimate challenge. Making the jump (and ultimately winning the race) provides both thrills and status for drivers. Running from police in a high-speed chase scene after the race foregrounds these gang members' rejection of the establishment and of the utilitarian reasons behind the construction of the auto-friendly landscape they have transformed. Yet, the anti-establishment ethos of the film presupposes an acceptance of the transformation of the landscape by car culture; that is, an acceptance of the establishment values they seem to reject. In this respect, the gang culture subscribes to the same set of values as those they defy; they simply appropriate what the culture has already established and defined as desirable.

Racial lines are blurred, and empowered females take a driver's seat in the progressive politics highlighted in *2 Fast 2 Furious*, but in the end, traditional hierarchies are perpetuated. For example, Brian's class loyalty switches back to the establishment, when he is captured by the FBI after the opening race. Brian comes back to the fold but will only comply with the FBI if he can choose his own partner, his good friend Roman, an African American. In exchange for clean records, he and Roman work with another undercover agent, the sexy Hispanic Monica (Eva Mendes), to close down a huge drug trafficking operation headed up by the Hispanic Carter Verone (Cole Hauser). With a more traditional plotline and videogame aesthetics that point to the total erasure of nature and the construction of a completely artificial environment, *2 Fast 2 Furious* provides few surprises: Brian and Monica hook up; Brian and Roman foil Carter's operation; the establishment overcomes the drug underworld. Brian's former allegiance to car culture comes through only when he enlists Tej (Ludacris) to confuse both the FBI and Carter's gang in a sea of vehicles in which his and Roman's cars can hide.

All in all, *2 Fast 2 Furious* adheres even more tightly to racial and gender pigeonholing than its 2001 predecessor, undermining the progressive politics of the film. Brian and Roman's relationship plays into the black–white antagonism laid out in films like *48 Hours* (1982)

Figure 8.5. *The Fast and the Furious: Tokyo Drift*: American diversity in Tokyo.

Figure 8.6. *The Fast and the Furious: Tokyo Drift*: Parking garage drifting transforms concrete for speed.

and *The Defiant Ones* (1958). Verone's drug-running Hispanic character builds on the Colombian drug lords found in films like *Traffic* (2000). Michael Hasting's review of the film asserts that "Singleton doesn't try to downplay the various ethnicities of his cast the way Rob Cohen did with the first film," but Singleton's choice reduces the color coding of cars and the playing up of hip-hop culture to the level of stereotype. As Hastings points out so well, the film is "attempting to be the big-screen equivalent of Grand Theft Auto: Vice City," a Playstation game with "a keen awareness of its own clichés" (Hastings), an element missing from Singleton's conventional plot and stock characters. *The Fast and the Furious* has inspired its own video game, and the *2 Fast 2 Furious* DVD actually includes a game where players can race in the film characters' cars. Playing into consumer culture so blatantly cements the conformist ideology preached by the film.

The same can be said of the most recent *The Fast and the Furious: Tokyo Drift* (2006), in which an American, Sean Boswell (Lucas Black), is sent to Japan to live with his military father because of his rebellious car-racing activities at home. He befriends both Japanese and multiracial American expatriates, ultimately winning the heart of an ethnically ambiguous girl with ties to a yakuza gang. The nostalgia for American muscle cars is strongest here, since ultimately Sean and his father trick up a 1970s American Mustang to enter a race to the death against a mobster's son. The film introduces a new racing style called "drifting," necessary in the cramped racing locations of Tokyo, especially the large, multilevel parking garages.

This new international setting offers even more concrete environments and shows us new ways to adapt already transformed natural environments for racing. The final outdoor "drifting" race Sean wins with his Mustang takes place on a parking-garage–style mountain road with numerous hairpin curves. The race might have provided glimpses of the natural world, but since the mountain setting is always filmed at night, darkness veils the green landscape. And the mountain, a natural landscape, is associated merely with death when cars fall from its cliffs. So again, racial politics are transcended, and gender and ecological politics conform to those of the 1950s. In *Tokyo Drift*, nature is erased both literally and figuratively: races in hyper-artificial tight garages are juxtaposed with outdoor races that deliberately prevent any awareness of the natural world by masking it in darkness.

Environmental Degradation as Necessary Consequence

As progressive as the *Fast and Furious* films purport to be in relation to class and race, their endorsement of the urban auto-friendly landscape echoes that in every other car culture movie. The environmental impact of burning fossil fuel and the altering of the landscape go unquestioned. There are few, if any, explicit mentions of the need for fuel in any of the films. The only acknowledgment that cars need gasoline to race occurs in the 1954 film when Webster stops at a gas station to fill up the hijacked Jaguar. In the later films, there are no gas stations in sight.

The transformation of the landscape is blatantly displayed in all of the later films while natural settings are erased, even in scenes shot on highways that have not been altered by the drivers. Even the open highway where Dom and his gang rob trucks in *The Fast and the Furious* (2001) runs through a barren landscape, with no trace of the natural world except when cars crash onto grassy shoulders. In *2 Fast 2 Furious*, Miami's ocean waters and shorelines are viewed only through racing cars or boats. And in *Tokyo Drift*, scenes outside the city are filmed only at night.

All these films offer tricked-up Japanese cars as a solution to economic and racial injustices, as well as to the alienation caused by the lifeless inner-city concrete world in which characters live. They create consumers for car products and accessories, for the films and video games featuring them, and for the products and ads embedded in the films. The *2 Fast 2 Furious* DVD contains a game that allows players to "build" cars of their own to "race" in a completely artificial game space. Most importantly, they create car-worshiping consumers for whom concrete landscapes, fuel overconsumption, and carbon emissions are not only acceptable but appropriate signs of progress, of inner-city rebuilding, and of an urban environmentalism that purports to overcome ecological racism. As Andrew Ross argues, city centers suffered at least partially because of anti-urban back-to-nature movements. Bringing capital back to the inner city may help revitalize inner-city ghettos. But the development necessary to bolster the economy may also contribute to environmental degradation, making conflicts between environmental justice and environmental racism more difficult to resolve.

The creation of consumers for car products is aided by psychologists, like Jungian archetype specialist Dr. Clothaire Rapaille, whom Chrysler hired to sell the new PT Cruiser model. According to Dr. Rapaille, "Freedom in America means something different here than it does anywhere else [. . .] It is tied in to this notion of wilderness. [. . .] [P]eople are looking for something that offers protection on the outside, and comfort on the inside" (quoted in Johnson). Dr. Rapaille's words suggest that the selling of cars is still tied to the idea of the American frontier and American ethos of conquest of space, the same motives that drive the gang members in the films to transform their concrete landscapes. With this ethos drawing us to the car, we can more easily overlook the depletion of resources necessary for driving and racing. As Johnson explains, "The power of intuition and psychology has more influence over our car culture than we think. [T]he Environmental Protection Agency and others' warnings haven't deterred many of us from making an average 15 car trips per day, or from buying gas-guzzling vehicles."

In the *Fast and Furious* films, drivers race tricked-up compacts on urban streets and in parking garages instead of commuting at the speed limit, but this practice still rests on the belief in the democratic potential of the automobile. Both mainstream and "progressive" drivers express themselves through their use of the car and through their consumption of natural resources. Democracy, here, is equated with freedom to consume without reservation.

The 2001 *The Fast and the Furious* was inspired not only by the 1954 film of the same name, but by an article in *Vibe* Magazine about car-racing gangs, as is documented in all reviews and on the *Internet Movie Data Base* (imbd.com). The article's description and analysis of car racing gang life—especially through its portrait of Rafael Estevez—explains much about car culture and the attitude toward the environment and the consumption of resources it encourages. Estevez raced a Nissan 300ZX on streets and parkways in New York, but the "urban polyglot" racing here looks similar to that portrayed in both films' settings—Los Angeles and Miami. Like Dom, Brian, and the other racers in the *Fast and Furious* films, Estevez tricked out his Nissan in three ways—"by stroking the engine, adding a supercharger, and hitting the 'juice' (nitrous oxide: a gaseous liquid once used to boost bomber planes in WWII)" (Li).

Drivers quoted in the article illuminate the psychology behind the race culture presented there and in the films: "It's about power. It's about the control of power," asserts one driver. "The excitement of going fast is like nothing else," says another, who also argues that "another group gets excitement from doing drugs or whatever. Speed excites us." Estevez himself asserts, "Drag racing is war. If you bring a knife, and I bring a machine gun, you're dead. That's it." Drag racing, then, provides both thrills and power, especially if a driver wins by conquering his prospective enemy at the wheel. And, as Estevez's biggest rival explains, "Half of the race is psychology, [and] mentally [Estevez has] got it." This same sense of power comes from drifting, as defined in the video *Drift Society Volume I* (2004), a feeling of power linked with desire and libido—represented by food and sex in the films. Overcoming enemies in cars serves as another sign that drivers have the power to conquer their own frontiers.

The Dukes of Hazzard, Estevez's inspiration for joining the urban car gang culture, calls attention to another key element in urban car culture—defying authority. Like the Dukes, drivers like Estevez skirt the law in cat-and-mouse games that move races from street to street. What sets current street racers apart from their counterparts in films like *Rebel Without a Cause* (1955) is the racial diversity of car racers and the absence of American muscle cars. Estevez's story echoes that of Junior Johnson, Tom Wolfe's whiskey-running NASCAR champ. Estevez defied the law just like Junior, but now races legally in the East Coast drag race circuit. He quit school to work in garages, where he perfected his skills as a mechanic and earned money to purchase accessories for his own Japanese car. He then earned money by winning illegal races, finally entering legal races—again like Junior—where he set records and gained enough product endorsements to pay for more of his expensive car parts.

Current urban drag-racing enthusiasts seek thrills and power through speed and defiance of the law, just as Junior Johnson did in the 1950s and '60s. Even though contemporary films like *The Fast and the Furious*, *2 Fast 2 Furious*, and *Tokyo Drift* provide a progressive portrait of the ethnically ambiguous urban polyglot, through the windshield of a tricked-up Japanese compact or a 1970s Mustang, the values behind car racing and the culture they represent remain the same as those in car culture films from the beginning of film history. Speed represents power for the disenfranchised youth, so consideration of the fuel consumption and paved landscape that make speed possible are portrayed as irrelevant, if not ludicrous. In addition, environmentalists tend to be white, male, liberal intellectuals; they look more like the police and the suburbanites these drivers are trying to defy than like the radical street racers they aspire to be with their anti-establishment values.

These radicals, however, are not as radical and anti-establishment as they think they are since they are oblivious to the environmental degradation to which they contribute. Instead, these so-called radicals hark back to an illusory time when nature seemed to offer an inexhaustible flow of resources; the myth of the American frontier further fuels the pursuit of freedom and individuality in the name of progress, a powerful mainstream and "establishment" ideology on which to build transformed concrete landscapes.

No one can deny that *The Fast and the Furious* (2001), *2 Fast 2 Furious*, and *Tokyo Drift* highlight a racially diverse cast that appeals to a broader demographic and makes a seemingly progressive point about race and class politics, especially in terms of the new ethnically ambiguous look. But the films also show what can happen to an urban landscape already altered—paved over—to accommodate the car and its driver. These films use the concrete landscape to assert individuality and a refusal to bend to authority. With the exception of Brian and perhaps Roman, these inner-city car racers don't want to be reintegrated into society. They race cars to gain status and money, to impress sexy women, and to defy the police—just like Junior Johnson and the Dukes of Hazzard. But, like the conformists and suburbanites they reject, they act like everything in nature exists to be consumed and exploited. To them, the concrete paved landscapes of inner-city Los Angeles, Miami, and Tokyo are natural. Only their exploitative transformation of them provides them with what they see as a radical edge. When concrete landscapes go unquestioned, so do their transformations.

9

Film Ecology

Simulated Construction and Destruction in *Hooper*

THE IDEA OF FILM ECOLOGY RAISES issues related to environmentally friendly approaches to filmmaking like carbon-neutral production, as with *The Day After Tomorrow*, or set recycling, as with *The Matrix 2* and *3*. Yet films and filmmaking have impacted on the environment since at least 1896 when *Oil Wells of Baku* was shot. Deliberate manipulation of the environment during the filmmaking process has also been a part of film history since the inception of the film industry, as in *The Life of an American Fireman* (1903), directed by Edwin S. Porter, in which a fireman, played by Arthur White, battles flames and saves a girl from a burning building. The fury of fires on-screen entertains audiences in films from *San Francisco* (1936) and *In Old Chicago* (1938) to *City on Fire* (1979), *Daylight* (1996), and *Wild Hogs* (2007).

Such spectacular effects have their own impact on the screen, but they also damage the ecology involved in each film's production, causing environmental destruction with spectacular effects that is sometimes used to publicize the film. *Gone With the Wind* (1939), for example, was promoted before and during its production before the epic spectacle made it to the screen. The success of the novel, *Gone With the Wind*, a highly publicized talent search for the film's stars, and the burning of the Atlanta Depot as the first scene shot in the film, were meant to impress potential audiences. The film gained notoriety in part because

165

it resulted in so much actual ecological destruction, destruction used as part of the promotion package for the film. *The Atlanta Constitution*, for example, states, "Ranking with the greatest spectacle scenes in motion picture history is the burning of the ammunition trains" (quoted in Haver 303). *The New York Times* asserts that "the siege of Atlanta was splendid and the fire that followed magnificently pyrotechnic" (quoted in Haver 305).

The destruction was massive, with the burning of the Atlanta Depot standing out as the most integral and damaging scene in the film. This was the first scene to be shot, a scene in which scores of old sets on the studio backlot were burned, including the "Great Gate" from *King Kong* (1933). For this scene, 113 minutes of footage were shot, with costs of less than $25,000 accumulated, "just $323 more than the allotted budget" according to *David Selznick's Hollywood* (Haver 258). During filming of the scene, all seven of the Technicolor cameras in Hollywood were used to capture flames that shot up 500 feet from a set that covered forty acres. To protect the studio and its stars, production manager Raymond Klune made sure the area was ringed with fire trucks from both the Culver City Fire Department and the Los Angeles Fire Department (Haver 254).

Yet, according to Haver, the fire was seen as a real eco-disaster by the residents in the area: "As the inferno raged, the low-hanging clouds spread the reflection of the flames over most of Culver City, and for the hour and a half that the fire continued, the phone lines in Los Angeles were jammed with anxious callers, all of whom seemed convinced that MGM was on fire" (258). To one witness, "it was just suddenly the holocaust . . . it scared all of us . . . it was like a whole town suddenly going up in flames. . . . Just as this ferocious thing happened, up comes Myron with these two people . . . all three seemed to be a few sheets to the wind and Myron said something to Mr. Selznick but he just shook him off, he was so engrossed in the fire" (257–58).

Such destruction was meant to heighten audience interest, but its potential for damage to the film's stars meant that stunt men and women doubled for the stars. Scarlett O'Hara (Vivien Leigh) was doubled by Aileen Goodwin, Dorothy Fargo, and Lila Finn, and Rhett Butler (Clark Gable) was doubled by Yakima Canutt (arguably the greatest stuntman that ever lived) and Jay Wilsey. Canutt (one of Butler's doubles) led the wagon carrying Dorothy Fargo (one of O'Hara's doubles) through the fire, for example. Construction and destruction of both the stunt men and women, who serve as "doubles" to the star, and of the environment provide spectacle on the screen and in the tabloids of the time.

Such construction and destruction also highlights how Hollywood represents stunt artists and ecology as expendable, an attitude most evident in films like *Hooper* (1978). In *Hooper*, the impact of stunts on the stunt artists who perform them is both made transparent and critiqued. The film also shows us the environmental impact of the special effects that accompany each of those stunts, occasionally commenting on their negative effects on ecology. *Hooper* interrogates the consequences of attitudes that construct human life and the environment as expendable, even as it climaxes with a spectacular and awe-inspiring scene meant to capture audiences: a representation of the destruction of Los Angeles that is parallel to the Atlanta fire scene and residents' reactions to it in the production of *Gone With the Wind*. With this special effects–driven scene and others, *Hooper* shows us how complicated critiques of film production practices become in an industry where entertainment is the goal. Yet, despite this conflict between spectacle and critique, *Hooper* stands out as a film that exposes how dangerous film productions can be to both stunt artists and the environment.

Construction and Destruction of Human and Nonhuman Nature in *Hooper*

Hooper opens with an extreme close-up of a shoe and crew sock accompanied by a thunder of brass instruments leading what sounds like a march. We watch as hands wrap an elastic bandage around the leg, stretching the band around the knee before pulling on football padding. A trumpet sounds, turning the march into a mariachi dance. The credits come up as more padding is tied around the figure's waist, and then a pad with the name "Hooper" written on it in black marker, is tied into the waistband. More and more "Hooper" pads are pulled over arms and elbows before pants and boots are pulled on, to the beat of the brass band. The figure changes his watch and pours himself a drink of whiskey. We still have not seen his face, and his torso remains shirtless. He drinks off-camera and puts on a leather jacket, showing us a deep and broad scar on his shoulder before reaching for a motorcycle helmet on a table. He puts on the helmet and walks off, leather gloves in hand, and the face mask is so dark, we still cannot see his face.

We assume the figure is Hooper (Burt Reynolds), but we cannot be sure. He jumps on a motorcycle and races out to the road with someone off-screen yelling, "good job, Hooper" before doing a wheelie down the road for a few yards. But this is not the stunt. The director, Roger (Robert Klein) arrives and launches himself up on a crane with the cameraman, as Hooper revs his motorcycle engine. The clapper starts the action for "The Spy Who Laughed at Danger," and Hooper motors down the road toward a jackknifed truck, slides himself under it, and comes out still on the motorcycle, just in time to jump over a car into a bed of flowers. The director yells "cut," and the stunt ends.

This long opening introduces us to the dehumanizing effects of stunt work, showing us a human part by part, whose body is seen as expendable, but also shown as constructed by the padding and masking of the character on display. It also foreshadows the film's suggestion that the environment is expendable, whether natural or constructed, when the motorcycle not only blasts smoke but crashes into a flower bed, smashing both stuntman and flowers beneath it. With Hal Needham, a well-respected stuntman, as its director, *Hooper* makes the stunt work involved in the filmmaking process transparent and, consequently, reveals some of the negative consequences of stunt "gags" for both the stuntmen and the environment their stunts destroy.

The fallibility of Hooper—and of stuntmen he represents—is on display soon after the motorcycle crash. Publicly, Hooper hides his suffering, looking free-of-pain as he walks side by side with Adam West, the star of "The Spy Who Laughed at Danger." Hooper is portrayed as indestructible in these early scenes. No crash can harm him.

But privately, Hooper recovers only after taking Percodan provided by his friend and fellow stuntman, Cully (James Best). He is obviously suffering from multiple injuries. Yet Hooper seems to buy into the image of indestructibility he presents to the studio, the film's director, and its star. Even after multiple injuries, Hooper will not retire and competes fervently with a young rival, Ski Chinski (Jan-Michael Vincent), who challenges him at a stunt contest fundraiser.

Hooper's attitude toward his body and toward his rival comes as no surprise, since the studio—both director and producer—treat him like both an animal and an immortal. In fact, the studio protects animals more than it does its stuntmen—a representative from the Humane Society must be on set if animals are used in a shot. This representative refuses to allow a dog to take a fall, for example, and the studio acts as if it complies with his ruling. But here, too, entertainment values takes precedence over safety, so when they take the shot, they replace a stuffed dog with the real one on the rooftop. Sonny protects the dog's life with his body and falls harder than he should have, coming close to permanent back damage after the fall into an air bag.

Sonny's fallibility becomes increasingly apparent between stunt gags and fight scenes. After the fall with the dog, Cully gives Sonny a shot of Zylocaine, a stronger painkiller, since he hit the bag harder than expected. And even though, after the charity stunt show, Sonny and Ski lead a bar fight in which Hooper smashes a jukebox with his head, once at home, Sonny watches a film of his past stunt work, looking as if he mourns the loss of physical abilities. Ski looks on and stares longingly at Hooper's trophy case, all from past competitions. These signs of Hooper's past glory are exacerbated when he and Jocko (Brian Keith) talk about Jocko's own past stunt glory, and Hooper's rivalry with him. Ski is now Hooper's rival, just as Hooper had been Jocko's, so Hooper's fading glory is a sign of his loss of indestructibility. His fight against this loss plays a large role in his competition with Ski.

As Hooper's glory fades, his fight to retain it grows, so the stunts he and Ski perform become increasingly more dangerous both to themselves and to the environment. The level of danger increases with each stunt Ski and Hooper attempt. They race around a town square with a fountain in the center in a car chase that nearly ends in a violent crash, but the director is unsatisfied, saying they "missed by a mile." Ski's youth and competitive edge contrast with Hooper's complacency here when Ski proposes changes to the stunt to increase its entertainment value. To exaggerate the spectacle of a car chase, Ski suggests that they shoot at night and turn the chase into a fire scene.

The stunt Ski suggests intensifies levels of risk for the stunt artists and levels of destruction for the environment. In this scene, Ski and Hooper stand in front of a church in monk's robes watching a gasoline truck cover the street with gas. Hooper lights the street, and the two "monks" run through the fire into a car to save the heroine. After the shot, Tony (Alfie West), the assistant, asks, "are you waiting for an invitation to put that fire out? L.A. has enough smog," pointing out one of the environmental repercussions of the fire. The environmental issue involved with the stunt is treated as an aside and is not broached again in the film. In fact, Roger, the director, is so impressed with Ski's idea that he wants him to do a stunt "gag" the next day. Human life is less important than the spectacle created in the work of these stuntmen. And environmental consequences of special effects carry just as little weight as did the Humane Society representative in the earlier jump gag.

Ski, on the other hand, has usurped Hooper's role as indestructible stunt artist. Because Ski has proven his worth as a stuntman, Roger hires him to run over rooftops like a cat burglar, dodging bullets, and sliding down a glass skyscraper with only a rope to break his fall. James Bond–like music accompanies his run to enhance its effect. Hooper sees the run as a challenge, since he recognizes that Ski is taking his place as the superhuman and infallible leading stuntman. To compete with Ski and all he represents, Hooper jumps 224 feet from a helicopter into an air bag to both break a record and one-up his new rival.

The jump is a success, but Hooper's fragility is even more apparent when he struggles up from the air bag. After putting on a show for Ski,

Hooper begs Cully to take him to the doctor. Hooper's vulnerability is literally on display in the doctor's office, on an X-ray showing two areas of instability in Hooper's spine. The doctor exclaims, "If you were a horse, I'd shoot you," after explaining that one good impact at the neck would paralyze Hooper from the neck down.

Hooper highlights the impact stunt work has on the stuntmen's bodies while foregrounding the insensitivity of directors willing to sacrifice human lives for spectacular effects in most of the "gags" on display in the film. But the last "gag" in *Hooper* (and "The Spy Who Laughed at Danger") most powerfully illustrates how both human lives and ecology are seen as expendable in this filmic world, as long as movies make enough money. Ski's ideas have inspired the director, according to the film's producer, Max Burns (John Marley), so he rewrites the script's ending and adds lots of stunts culminating in the destruction of Los Angeles on screen.

The stunts Roger constructs to end the film seem outlandishly impossible in a 1978 film without access to computer-generated graphics. When Roger explains the new ending to Hooper and Ski, it sounds like a nightmare on screen. According to Roger, Hooper and Ski will drive through "the biggest earthquake ever," but a bridge will blow up, so Hooper and Ski will need to rappel down the mountain to escape—and Roger will capture this stunt in one shot. The ending stunt sounds spectacular enough, but Ski, the young "immortal," wants more and suggests, "Why not jump a car across the gorge." After speculating

Figure 9.1. *Hooper*: Blowing up "Los Angeles" in the film's last stunt.

about the distance a rocket car might jump, even Max thinks this stunt is too risky. But Hooper sees the stunt as a way out of the stunt business: They can do this last stunt for $50,000 each, and then quit.

The film complicates Hooper's choice by focusing on the vulnerability of a friend and older rival, Jocko. Jocko had competed with Hooper years before in the stunt world, just as Hooper now competes with Ski. Complicating the situation even further, Jocko is also the father of Hooper's girlfriend Gwen (Sally Field). Jocko has a stroke and falls in the shower and is rushed to the hospital. But Jocko, like Hooper, will not admit his own infallibility, at least publicly. Hooper, however, sees his own future in Jocko, so with some coaxing from Gwen and Cully, Hooper agrees to quit instead of jumping the gorge, eventually quitting the film altogether. But this interlude merely builds suspense, since Max Burns, the producer, has a change of heart and convinces Hooper to do the jump to protect Ski.

The big stunt goes as planned: Roger watches from a helicopter and yells, "Action." Then we hear and see an explosion, and a building collapses. Crashing cars are everywhere. Hooper and Ski keep driving past exploding gas stations and a series of explosions on the road. Cars overturn and collide with one another. Then another series of explosions pours out spectacular fumes of fire and smoke. A tanker goes through a building and another set of explosions cracks open the other side of the road. Hooper and Ski continue driving their rocket car, now racing through a line of collapsing smokestacks that nearly hit their car. They're almost to the bridge and watch as a truck full of explosives blows it "to shit." The pressure in their nitrous-powered rocket car seems too low for the jump, but Hooper demands they continue, and they fly across the ravine, landing safely on the other side.

This spectacular filmic event destroys the set and looks like it destroys the city of Los Angeles. It nearly kills two stunt men, who barely make it across a ravine in a car built to jump half the distance. Max fires Tony, the assistant. And Ski and Hooper look at the fallen bridge at the bottom of the ravine in awe. Yet Roger, the director, merely exclaims, "Spectacular, wonderful. I knew you could do it!" As Roger sees it, they have captured a "tiny piece of time" on film, so the stunt, no matter how dangerous or destructive, was worth that strip of film.

Hooper seems to scoff at this attitude, since Hooper gets the last shot, a punch to Roger's chin before the credits. Yet the spectacle on screen does capture both viewers of and characters in the film. Hooper thrives on the risks both stunt work and a life driven by bar fights and car chases provide. His transformation after Jocko's stroke and, especially, the big jump seems contrived and unresolved. He and Ski have their

Figure 9.2. *Hooper*: Blasting the bridge before the ravine jump.

money and, presumably, Hooper will walk off the set forever, purchase his ranch, and raise horses with Gwen. But the film leaves us yearning for the explosions and punches with which it ends rather than a pat ending consisting of a union between Hooper and Gwen.

Hooper at least marginally critiques the exploitation of human flesh for effect, since it shows us the injuries and chronic physical damage Hooper and Jocko endure after performing risky stunt work. The film's narrative sets up Roger as a villain willing to sacrifice stuntmen for a good show and the film industry as an economy where greed runs rampant. The film gives a nod to both nonhuman nature (a dog with a Humane Society advocate is saved by Hooper) and to the environment (Tony mentions pollution and smog in Los Angeles as a reason to quickly extinguish a fire). But ultimately, the stunts themselves capture our attention, just as Roger suggests when ruminating on the power of film as a medium that can capture time. In the context of the film, the last, most dangerous, and (consequently) most spectacular stunt also "saves" Hooper, since it provides him with the funds he needs to buy his ranch.

The effects in *Hooper* are not only critiqued in the film's construction of "The Spy Who Laughed at Danger" but also valorized in their own right. *Hooper* was nominated for an Academy Award in the sound category. Walter Frith calls the movie "action on laughing gas." In "Excessive Disclosure in Burt Reynolds' Star Image," Jacob Smith sees drunk scenes as "prolonged excuse[s]" for laughter (29). Smith highlights the promotional image for *Hooper*, an "iconic cowboy with mustache, squinting eyes, and cowboy hat, but with mouth obscured by a pink balloon of bubble gum," (30) to support his claims about Reynolds's image as an actor seeking fun, not work, in both film and life.

But the image also showcases the stuntman's roots in Western lore—cowboys willing to take risks and live isolated lives on the range just like stunt artists sacrificing themselves for spectacular effects on the screen. The film seems to validate that individualist image rather than a communal one connecting humans and nature. Smith asserts that *Hooper* "ridicules environmental activist and humane society representatives," those advocates working for nonhuman nature. The film praises the work of individual stuntmen willing to take risks, overcome obstacles, and provide awe-inspiring spectacle on the screen. *Hooper* critiques "the conceited dramatic actor and pretentious director," according to Smith. It does not seem to critique the work of stunt men. Instead, it valorizes the spectacular results of their stunts.

Still *Hooper* examines the filmmaking process in a unique way, since it highlights stuntmen and their work, showing us a behind-the-scenes view of the effects these stunts have on both the stunt artists and the environment. By making the consequences of stunt "gags" transparent, *Hooper* provides a critical reading of the filmmaking process and its negative effects on its stuntmen and the environment their stunts destroy. Even though the critique is couched in the film's own rhetoric about the entertainment value of spectacle, it provides a space in which we can begin to discuss the impact of filmmaking on both human and nonhuman nature.

The Stunt Man and Human and Nonhuman Nature

These same conflicting messages are apparent in *The Stunt Man* (1980), a dark comedy blatantly critiquing the exploitation of stunt artists. Here, as in *Hooper*, the entertainment value of the stunts themselves, rather than real repercussions of the risks involved, takes center stage in spite of its hyperbolic critique of such exploitation. In *The Stunt Man* we, like its star stunt artist, wonder when the movie world begins and ends. The film's opening begins this blurring of boundaries between filmic and "real" that continues even to the film's ending.

The film opens with a high-action scene that appears to be part of a production being filmed from a helicopter: A vulture flies off a telephone pole. Then the scene cuts to a golden retriever on the ground panting near a police station. The opening credits begin with a clapper slamming down for "action," that exposes this as a film, and the dog licks himself in front of a police car.

After a series of interconnected shots, a police officer arrests a man (Steve Railsback) who is playing pinball in a cafe because of a tattoo on his arm. The man runs away wearing handcuffs, racing by telephone repair workers in the woods. After an altercation the tattooed man knocks out a worker with his tool bag and then runs away with the bag, stopping to free himself from his cuffs. He keeps running.

Then the camera cuts to a vintage car driving across a wooden suspension bridge. The car seems to stop to pick up the tattooed man, but the driver pushes him out once he opens the car door. The car turns around and tries to run over the tattooed man, but the man throws a wrench from the tool bag, and the car crashes through the bridge cables into the river below. A helicopter with a cameraman photographing the fall appears from under the bridge, with what looks like a director looking on.

The tattooed man runs on toward a crowded boardwalk. A helicopter and a biplane float in the distance, but a crowd looks down on a beach, where a scene from a World War I drama is being shot, a scene that shows some of the possible environmental consequences of film production. Explosions are applauded by the crowd until they see what appears to be real loss of life and limb on the beach. Soldiers lose eyes and legs with each explosion. The crowd and the tattooed man scream for help. Then we hear, "Cut. That's a print." The "dead" and "wounded" soldiers climb out of the sand alive and well, pick up various prosthetic devices (the arms and legs destroyed in the fight) and walk away. The tattooed man saves the lead actress, Nina (Barbara Hershey), from the World War I movie when she falls into the water, and he exclaims, "This is just like being in the movies," as she takes off an old lady mask. "I am the movie," she replies, reinforcing filmmaking as the focus on *The Stunt Man*.

Various levels of action are revealed in this opening of *The Stunt Man*: The World War I film within the "action/fugitive on-the-run" film meet head on and combine when the tattooed man joins the film production as a stuntman and falls in love with Nina. We learn the tattooed man's name (Cameron) and that he is a fugitive ex-Marine on the run from the police. To hide his identity from the law, he is hired as a stuntman for the production at $600 per stunt and disguised as Burt, a stuntman who drowned in a car crash on the bridge.

With a stuntman dying during the film's opening, *The Stunt Man*, as in *Hooper*, constructs these workers as expendable. But *The Stunt Man* takes this dehumanization one step further, since Burt's drowning, although caught on film, is covered up, and Cameron is asked to do a similar stunt and replace the film footage Burt "ruined" through his death.

The director, Eli Cross (Peter O'Toole), is constructed as even more despicable than Roger in *Hooper*, since he chooses not to explain the stunts to Cameron, so that they look more realistic. Cameron seems to run for his life in some stunts, since he is unaware of the "assassins" involved in chase scenes. Before the last surprise stunt, Cameron attempts to drive away from the set with, he thinks, Nina in the trunk of the car. But Eli has set him up and forces him to do the stunt that killed Burt. When, during his "escape," Cameron drives onto the bridge from the opening scene, Eli orders his crew to blow it up, and Cameron falls through the bridge rail into the river below.

Cameron is able to perform the stunt despite such a surprise. Even though the equipment in the car meant to save him does not work, Cameron is able to swim out the window, out of the river, and onto the shore. Soldiers are waiting for him on the shore and capture him. Then Eli yells "cut" and "good job," so Cameron knows it's a stunt. He laughs when Nina waves at him from the trees, and he argues with Eli over his payment for the stunt. The film ends with Cameron yelling at Eli in his helicopter and over a walkie-talkie. The helicopter disappears as the credits roll, leaving Cameron on the shore of a now quiet river.

Figure 9.3. *The Stunt Man*: Cameron's crash from the bridge.

In *The Stunt Man*, Cameron has become so dehumanized that he is not only exploited but duped. He is not even informed about how that exploitation will occur. At least Hooper knew how each "gag" would develop. Cameron, on the other hand, is cut out of the planning to enforce more "realistic" reactions from him during each stunt. In *The Stunt Man*, the filmmaking process is critiqued through hyperbolic shots of explosive war scenes and unreasonable expectations from a pretentious and self-centered director without thought to the consequences of his demands. But like *Hooper*, *The Stunt Man* is a comedy, so the elements of the filmmaking process being ridiculed are exaggerated in such laughable ways that they may not be taken seriously. Cameron begins to believe Eli is trying to kill him, since the stunts are unexplained and seem so real. Cameron's life is on the line as he, like the viewer, is unaware of when "reality" begins and ends. This is a "situation the film repeats, over and over, scene after scene, all the way to the end," according to Roger Ebert.

Ebert explains:

> That's what bothered me. I caught on right away (it didn't take much deep thought) that the method of the movie was to deceive and mislead me. Because the ability to do that is completely within the director's ability—because I can know only what he chooses to tell me—I found the movie's approach more frustrating than challenging. *The Stunt Man* is like magic tricks done by a magician in a movie: It doesn't matter how well they're done, or even if they're really done, because cinematic special effects make it all trickery, anyway. ("*The Stunt Man* Review")

Ebert sees *The Stunt Man* as flawed because the deceptions become so hyperbolic they seem impossible:

> The stunts were also sneaky. At one moment in particular, Railsback's on a tower that's blown up in flames. We think there's no way he could have escaped alive—and the movie merely cuts to another shot of him, without explaining his escape. A film that depends on deceiving us has got to play by its own rules. If we are going to be deceived in general, fine, but then we can't be cheated on particulars. (Ebert "*The Stunt Man* Review")

These flaws make the critique of filmmaking, and of stunt work in particular, much less effective in *The Stunt Man* because they are buried beneath the "trickery." The film's multiple layers become equally incredible, so the consequences of the outrageous stunts Cameron performs lose their credibility, as well.

Yet there are real, sometimes deadly, consequences for stuntmen and other labor involved in film productions. In a 2002 *Cinema Journal* article, for example, Charles S. Tashiro reminds us of an accident on the set of *Twilight Zone: The Movie* (1982), when a shot of a helicopter hovering over the film's star, Vic Morrow, and two child extras went wrong. According to Tashiro, a hut was set to explode when the helicopter approached it, but, "after photographing the shot, the force of the explosion grew too great for the pilot to handle, sending the helicopter careening out of control. As it crashed to the ground, its rotors decapitated Morrow and the two children. The pilot survived the crash" (27).

The child extras killed during this "accident" were exploited in at least two ways during the filming of *Twilight Zone*. They were working illegally under California labor regulations because "the shoot took place later than the children were allowed to work" (Tashiro 27). More importantly, these child extras' lives were taken because they were too close to both a helicopter and an explosion, risks stunt artists take every day on film sets. Tashiro uses this accident as a way to examine labor and production policies of contemporary Hollywood to encourage an informed criticism of production practices, a critique both *Hooper* and *The Stunt Man* attempt, and that criticism includes the impact these production practices have on the environment.

Environmental Impact of the Filmmaking Process

Despite their flaws, *Hooper* and *The Stunt Man* reveal not only the filmmaking process—as do more recent films like *Bowfinger* (1999), *Adaptation* (2002), *V for Vendetta* (2005), and *Kiss, Kiss, Bang, Bang* (2005)—but also show us some of the hazards of the filmmaking process, both for human and nonhuman nature. These hazards are well-documented in the *UCLA Institute of the Environment Report* from Charles Corbett and Richard Turco. The report demonstrates that the film and television industry produces almost as much pollution and greenhouse gas emissions as do oil refineries in California.

Spectacular effects on-screen clearly contribute to these large amounts of emissions and pollution. In an action film like *Terminator 2*, for example, one scene stands out as a disaster as great as the Atlanta Depot fire in *Gone With the Wind*. Instead of using scale models to emulate an explosion as they did in an atomic bomb dream sequence earlier in the film, the filmmakers created a more realistic effect when blowing up the Cyberdyne Building: They actually blew up an abandoned factory in Fremont, California, shooting the blast from different angles using eleven cameras. Within the context of the film, obliterating the Cyberdyne Building meant that the computer data that would produce the terminator robots built to annihilate the human race would also be destroyed. But, in reality, exploding a factory to replicate the destruction of the building also contributed in blatant and obvious ways to pollution, toxic chemical, and greenhouse gas emissions.

The parallel with *Gone With the Wind* is even greater in *Jarhead* where creating oil well fires was the most challenging effect produced for the film. The visual effects supervisor from Industrial Light & Magic, Pablo Helman, explains, "In this 'third act' of the film, every shot was a visual effects shot. We thought that we would shoot a bunch of fires on set, but the fires of Kuwait were so huge that actually we only got one fire on set" (*Jarhead* Production Notes). According to the production notes, "Helman had his own effects crew filming fire and smoke footage, and from that ILM would later cull the photographic elements that could be manipulated and composited into DP Roger Deakins' plate photography." Helman continues, "We created a library of fires shot at different distances under different lighting conditions and under different weather and wind conditions. It was really important to Sam that the scale of the fire was right, so we never shot miniature elements" (*Jarhead* Production Notes).

The one fire shot on set was a single flaming oil well that shot burning crude oil 400 feet into the air. This shot, along with other fire shots taken at different locations, "were then turned into a library of fires from varying points of view, which were then used to create three separate types of oil fires," according to the production notes. When discussing the final compositing, Helman explains, "It was a very complex compositing environment" that was accomplished without having to add 3-D computer-animated elements. The fires were real and, according to Helman, "We were shooting about 170 ft. from many of them, and my eyebrows are still growing back!" (Production Notes). The ignited oil well fire and smoke look like they produced even more toxic chemical and greenhouse gas emissions than the explosion in *Terminator 2*.

In *Hooper* and *The Stunt Man* the stunts and their repercussions under critique also clearly damage the environment. The final stunt sequence in Hooper was referred to as "Damnation Alley" and destroyed its location, a World War II military hospital in Alabama that had been used as married housing by the University of Alabama.

In *The Stunt Man* cars are destroyed on-screen, crashing into the river. Buildings blow up in flames. Artillery shells explode. Planes strafe the ground with machine gun fire. Smudge pots create billowing black streams of smoke.

Spectacular effects like these appear in countless Hollywood movies, and the costs to the environment are recorded in blatant and obvious ways in both the films and their production notes. Other environmental costs are less evident. Set materials after production consist of tons of waste materials, if not recycled. The amount of material recycled after productions of *The Matrix Reloaded* and *The Matrix Revolutions*, for example, added up to 11,000 tons of concrete, steel, and lumber. The steel was recycled, and thirty-seven truckloads of lumber were used to build low-income housing in Mexico (Corbett and Turco 10).

The film and television industry also emits high amounts of air pollution and greenhouse gases both directly and indirectly. According to Corbett and Turco, "electricity consumption generates pollutant emissions at remote power stations. On the other hand, the use of vehicles for local transportation results in direct emissions in the area of operations" (8).

The driving force behind the industry and its impact on the environment is profit. The industry seeks to make the most money from its movies with the least financial outlay. The *Matrix* movies' set-recycling program shows how important money and outside influence become when groups attempt to "green" the film industry. According to Ted Reiff, president of the nonprofit group hired to recycle the sets, "the county and city of Alameda, where the films were made, 'were really leaning on Warner Brothers to step up and do the right thing.' Alameda officials were concerned that the tonnage of the sets represented about ten percent of Alameda's annual solid waste stream." The cost to dismantle and reuse the sets was also cheaper than it would have been to demolish the sets. Based on these experiences, Reiff argues that the film and television industry is "not green at all except when they're forced to be" ("Study: Television, Filmmaking Industries are Big Polluters").

Sam Staley, the director of Urban Growth and Land Use Policy at Reason Foundation, responds to this *UCLA Report* with a similar conclusion about the film and television industry's lack of motivation to "go green." He concludes his brief commentary with a call to action: "Instead of imploring us to do something, Hollywood should focus on its own pollution. Moviemakers should pioneer new technologies and strategies for protecting the environment and reducing greenhouse gases that are both practical and cost effective." Staley seems to suggest that Hollywood is doing nothing to offset the pollution it creates, even when making films with environmental messages.

In fact, one company, NativeEnergy, is pairing with film production companies to create carbon-neutral productions, including *Syriana* and *An Inconvenient Truth*. These films both "implore us to do something" and seek to reduce greenhouse gases in "both practical and cost effective" ways. Although *The Day After Tomorrow* was, arguably, the first publicly carbon-neutral production, its carbon emissions were offset with funds from the film's director, Roland Emmerich. Paramount paired with NativeEnergy to ensure that *An Inconvenient Truth* was carbon-neutral. Warner Brothers teamed with NativeEnergy when producing a carbon-neutral *Syriana*. NativeEnergy is a Native American–owned company in Vermont that offsets carbon emissions for individuals, businesses, and organizations by investing (for a competitive price) in renewable energy projects (see the NativeEnergy website at *www.nativeenergy.com*).

Despite these advances, the film industry still needs to "focus on its own pollution" in pragmatic ways, so that regulations not only secure the safety of film personnel but of their locations' environments. The Chicago Artists Resource page includes a long article highlighting safe practices for pyrotechnics, fire, and explosion effects, but all the regulations Michael McCann outlines address the impact of these techniques on personnel, not on the environment. One guideline does highlight the amount of smoke allowed from effects, but the aim is again to keep personnel safe, explaining, "the quantity of smoke generated shall not interfere with visibility of exit signs or egress paths. There should be exhaust ventilation to rapidly remove the smoke (e.g., portable ventilators) since studies have shown that pyrotechnic smoke is alkaline and irritating to the eyes and respiratory system" (McCann).

The few carbon-neutral film productions pursued their environmentally sound practices voluntarily, even though The Environmental Media Association makes recommendations for pursuing environmentally friendly film content and production. It seems that because few regulations specifically address the environmental impact of the film industry, few film productions are eco-friendly.

Foregrounding and critiquing exploitation of both human and nonhuman nature in movies like *Hooper* and *The Stunt Man* provides an opening for a wider critique of the Hollywood film and television industry's contributions to air pollution and greenhouse gas emissions. Hollywood may represent both human and nonhuman nature as expendable, an attitude most evident in films like *Hooper*, but as in *Hooper*, Hollywood films may also interrogate the consequences of such attitudes about human life and the environment. Movies like *Hooper* and *The Stunt Man* astound audiences with impossible stunt work and spectacular explosions, but they also reveal the human sacrifices behind the filmmaking process. Taking this critique one more step—to the impact the filmmaking process has not only on humans but on nature—offers a more productive interrogation that may not only change our minds about the environment but change our actions.

10

Apocalypse as a "Return to Normality" in *28 Days Later* and *28 Weeks Later*

*2*8 *DAYS LATER* OPENS WITH A MONTAGE sequence of violent scenes from around the world. Mobs of people attack one another, run from police, and assault an officer. Crowds lynch a man and torture his swinging body. More crowds attack and then burn one another alive. The camera pulls back, and we see that the images are attached to a series of television sets and, as the shot widens, we see that a chimpanzee, buckled to a laboratory table and attached to probes and wires, is watching the violent scenes on the screens. Other monkeys struggle in small glass cages. It is animal lab hell. A group of masked invaders breaks into the lab—The Cambridge Primate Research Centre—and photograph and attempt to free the primates. A lab scientist discovers the activists and warns them that the chimps are infected, saying, "in order to cure, you must first understand." The activists ask, "infected with what," and he answers, "rage." The chimps have been sedated, but the infection is highly contagious. It's in their blood and saliva, and one bite can infect a human in fewer than twenty seconds. When a female activist is bitten after opening an enclosure, the scientist screams, "We have to kill her."

This opening scene sets up the premise for *28 Days Later*: Reiterated images of violence can infect primates with a rage virus that manifests itself in more rage, a rage that vomits blood and craves violence, especially against other primates, including humans. By exposing chimpanzees to innumerable scenes of violence, scientists have altered the chimps' genes, infecting them with a rage virus they have constructed with this immersion in displays of blood and gore. The virus resembles the Ebola hemorrhagic fever, linking it to a contemporary concern, but for many critics, this opening defines the film as a zombie movie that fails to achieve the "real soul" (O'Hehir "*28 Days Later* Review") of earlier zombie films like George A. Romero's *Day of the Dead* (1985), the film O'Hehir argues *28 Days Later* most emulates. According to O'Hehir, *28 Days Later* lacks the "primitive, intense depiction of a subterranean human community trapped in a zombie world" embraced by *Day of the Dead*. In fact, he dismisses the film, asserting that it has "lost any pretense of edge or originality it once had and has become a standard-issue smash 'n' slash with some cool cinematography" before it reaches its climax ("*28 Days Later* Review").

Roger Ebert also finds the film's ending "disappointing" ("*28 Days Later*") as a finale for a zombie movie, calling it a "standard ending" that lacks "nerve" ("*28 Days Later*"). But Ebert also broaches what we see as a crucial theme in both *28 Days Later* and *28 Weeks Later* (2007), the role of evolution in the preservation of Earth's ecology. Although Ebert asserts that audiences will not be "thinking much about evolution during the movie's engrossing central passages" ("*28 Days Later*"), we believe evolution serves an essential role in both films.

For us, the opening of *28 Days Later* also points to an environmental message beyond that of the activists who free the chimps and the virus they house: If we construct "rage" as a natural state in the form of a virus, it will destroy us. Both *28 Days Later* and *28 Weeks Later*, however, take this message further by aligning it with evolution. If humanity's destruction is an inevitable product of a constructed rage virus, then is it our presence or our absence that is a natural part of Earth's evolution? And how can humanity best ensure its survival, through extermination or accommodation?

These questions are broached during the third act of *28 Days Later* when, after the few survivors of the rage virus arrive at a military encampment, Sergeant Farrell (Stuart McQuarrie), one of the encampment's surviving soldiers, questions humans' role in "the whole life of the planet." Farrell asserts that humans have "only been around for a few blinks of an eye. So if the infection wipes us all out, that is a return to normality." Farrell's statement highlights the environmental issue explored in both *28 Days Later* and *28 Weeks Later*: an evolutionary battle over ecology.

In *28 Days Later*, uninfected humans battle zombielike infected humans in what looks like, at least on the surface, a battle for survival. For Major Henry West (Christopher Eccleston), Sergeant Farrell's commanding officer, this battle is a sign that all is normal, since warfare between humans is all that he knows. For Sergeant Farrell, the battle suggests humans' life on Earth has come to an end. But to the few civilians who escape, "staying alive" is no longer "as good as it gets." Instead, as Selena (Naomie Harris) explains, "All the death. All the shit. It doesn't really mean anything to Frank (Brendan Gleeson) and Hannah (Megan Burns) because . . . Well, she's got a Dad and he's got his daughter." For them, family and other connections provide something more than survival—loving community.

In *28 Weeks Later*, a genetic aberration provides the virus with human carriers, who spread the rage virus to the rest of the world. But here, too, familial relationships (now between a brother and sister) drive the film's narrative, this time in an evolutionary narrative that turns tragic because the goal is not accommodation but extermination. Because the brother is a carrier, he inadvertently destroys everyone around him, so he cannot build community with others. But the film heightens the tragedy by emphasizing the violent natures of both infected and uninfected humans. In *28 Weeks Later*, carriers of the virus, infected zombies, and violent soldiers annihilate everyone, rather than seek real community.

In the end, however, evolution in both films favors nature over rage-filled modern humanity. In *28 Days Later*, Jim (Cillian Murphy), Selena, and Hannah survive the virus, the violent soldiers, and the infected zombies, because they escape the violence of a modern urbanized world and recapture a premodern sense of community. In *28 Weeks Later*, the virus consumes most of humanity but is resisted by the few carriers with a genetic aberration that protects them from the rage virus and, at least symbolically, seems to separate them from the rage-filled modern world. Both films, in spite of their adherence to the genre expectations of zombie, horror, and science fiction films, embrace evolutionary narratives. *28 Days Later* adheres to a narrative that is embedded in the comic and communal, rather than tragic and individualized notions of species preservation. *28 Weeks Later*, on the other hand, embraces a tragic evolutionary narrative of "early Darwinism" (Meeker "The Comic Mode" 164) that supports extermination and warfare rather than accommodation.

According to Joseph Meeker, humans typically embrace a tragic evolutionary narrative that counters the climax communities of plants and animals, which are "extremely diverse and complicated" (162). But, this position comes at a price, and may cost humanity its existence. Meeker asserts, "We demand that one species, our own, achieve unchallenged dominance where hundreds of species lived in complex equilibrium before our arrival" (164). This attitude may not only lead to the destruction of other species but of humanity itself. Meeker believes humanity has "a growing need to learn from the more stable comic heroes of nature, the animals" (164).

The evolutionary narrative of *28 Weeks Later* illustrates the consequences of continuing down a tragic pioneer path. The evolutionary narrative of *28 Days Later* explores what might happen if humanity did learn from these more stable comic heroes, since, according to Meeker, effective "Evolution itself is a gigantic comic drama, not the bloody tragic spectacle imagined by the sentimental humanists of early Darwinism" ("The Comic Mode" 164). Meeker asserts:

> Nature is not "red in tooth and claw" as the nineteenth-century English poet Alfred, Lord Tennyson characterized it, for evolution does not proceed through battles fought among animals to see who is fit enough to survive and who is not. Rather, the evolutionary process is one of adaptation and accommodation, with the various species exploring opportunistically their environments in search of a means to maintain their existence. Like comedy, evolution is a matter of muddling through. ("The Comic Mode" 164)

For Meeker, successful evolution encourages communal action to ensure survival:

> Its ground rules for participants (including man) are those which also govern literary comedy: organisms must adapt themselves to their circumstances in every possible way, must studiously avoid all-or-nothing choices, must prefer any alternative to death, must accept and encourage maximum diversity, must accommodate themselves to the accidental limitations of birth and environment, and must always prefer love to war—though if warfare is inevitable, it should be prosecuted so as to humble the enemy without destroying him. ("The Comic Mode" 166)

Ultimately, despite the films' horrific narratives, they both embrace evolutionary narratives. The narrative of *28 Days Later* is based in a comic and communal view of survival, but the narrative of *28 Weeks Later* draws on a tragic and individually driven view that refuses to shed the pioneer role humanity sometimes seems to embrace and equates survival with extermination of all others.

After the film's opening exposition, *28 Days Later* highlights the comic evolutionary narrative driving the film. This narrative focuses primarily on

Figure 10.1. *28 Days Later*: Jim on the silent streets of London.

a bicycle courier named Jim and his search for community after waking as a Rip Van Winkle figure who has slept through twenty-eight days of the rage virus. His awakening is like a rebirth: He is in an empty hospital on a gurney and finds himself completely naked and attached to IVs. He finds hospital scrubs, dresses himself, and walks down stairs and through hallways yelling "hello" with every step. His entrance into a silent world foregrounds the consequences of the virus. From a balcony, London looks empty and quiet. The skies are completely clear. Wandering across the Tower Bridge, again yelling "hello," Jim steps over piles of plastic statues of Big Ben before the real Big Ben clock tower appears in front of him. Birds fly overhead. The sun sets over deserted buildings. And, when a car alarm sounds, the shattered silence reinforces how changed the city has become. Without cars, electricity, or mobs of people, the city of London becomes a silent landscape instead of a modern urban center and, perhaps, returns to its more natural state, a change that is reinforced by the digital camera work used in the film. According to the film's director, Danny Boyle, "Digital cameras are much more responsive to low light levels and the general idea was to try to shoot as though we were survivors too" ("*28 Days Later* Production Notes" 6).

  This pristine landscape is broken again when Jim reads newspaper headlines about the rage virus—an apocalypse with only one solution.

"Shoot to kill," a headline declares. And serenity is crushed when Jim enters a church and is attacked by a zombie, a priest stricken with the rage virus. The priest and a mob of other zombies chase him, but masked strangers protect him, throwing lit bottles of petrol at the crowd. An explosion erupts, destroying a building and lighting the dark city streets of London. The strangers adopt Jim and offer rules: Never go anywhere alone. Only travel in the daylight. And eat. They support him, even when he insists on finding his parents, a decision that results in three significant consequences: Jim discovers that his parents have committed suicide, leaving Jim a note on the back of a picture: "Don't wake up," it reads, a command that reinforces the Rip Van Winkle metaphor. Searching for Jim's parents results in the death of one of his protectors, Mark (Noah Huntley), when a zombie attacks the house. Finally, the decision provides Jim with a partner. The remaining protector, Selena, stays with Jim and becomes his connection to an Earth driven not by rage but by love.

Selena and Jim's community widens when they discover Frank and his daughter, Hannah, at the top of a high-rise apartment lit with Christmas lights. And together they drive off in a taxi on a quest to find "the answer to infection," a claim made in a radio broadcast from

Figure 10.2. *28 Days Later*: "Family" eats and watches horses.

Manchester. The film then centers on the group's communal road trip, highlighting scenes that bring them closer—escaping rats and zombies in a tunnel, gathering groceries by cartloads in a shop, and watching a herd of horses run freely beside a river. During this road trip, the digital video work of Anthony Dod Mantle highlights the pastoral quality of the silent and pristine landscape along the totally empty motorways.

According to A. O. Scott, Mantle's camera work "sometimes has an ethereal, almost painterly beauty. The London skyline takes on the faded, melancholy quality of a Turner watercolor; a field of flowers looks as if it were daubed and scraped directly onto the screen" and the survivors' journey "has a pastoral mood, and the actors, unwinding from the stress and panic of London, are allowed to be warm, loose, and funny" ("Film Review: Spared by a Virus But Not by Mankind"). Threats of danger are foreshadowed by tilted or low camera angles, but until the group sees Manchester in the distance, the English highways are clear and clean. Danny Boyle, the film's director, believed it was essential to shoot the film in digital video:

> The format felt appropriate to the post-apocalyptic landscape. This is very much an urban film, with the visit to the countryside aside, and I think DV has a grittiness about it that's magnificent for city movies. We're surrounded in all major cities by CC cameras; they're recording our every motion. This is now the way that we record our lives. ("*28 Days Later* Production Notes" 6)

Their arrival at the forty-second blockade near Manchester turns the tale. Frank loses control and throws a pebble at a bird to stop it from eating a corpse. When the bird flies away, its wings graze the corpse, and blood from the corpse falls into Frank's eye, infecting him. Then a soldier shoots Frank as he transforms, and Jim, Selena, and Hannah are "captured" by British soldiers seeking to procreate and thwart the virus. These soldiers seem almost as rage-filled as those infected with the virus, and they rejoice when they slaughter a zombie mob attempting to breach their castle. In fact, Major Henry West has promised women for his men because "women give them a future." He finds gowns for Hannah and Selena and sends Jim off to his death with a pair of soldiers when he resists the plan. The Major and his men seem to parallel the infected as their rage drives them not only to kill the infected but rape the two women the Major has brought them.

Jim, too, shows instances of rage, but his rage is contained and driven by love for both Selena and Hannah. He escapes the soldiers, sees a jet flying overhead and finds hope. That hope leads Jim to a primal transformation that is punctuated by the effective use of digital photography. Jim races to the forty-second blockade and blasts the distress horns in a downpour of rain that, in the graininess of the digital video, looks like an outpouring of tears.

The scene shows us a change in environment—it is finally raining in England after ten days of drought—and a change in Jim's character, all in the name of love. To save Selena and Hannah, Jim must destroy the soldiers, just as they destroyed the infected mob that attacked their fortress. When Jim slaughters the last soldier, who is holding Selena at gunpoint, he demonstrates how deep that rage might go when he shoves his thumbs into his victim's eyes—a scene repeated by the father in *28 Weeks Later*. But Jim recovers and tells Selena and Hannah, "It's not all fucked. We're going to be ok. I've seen someone."

The rage virus seems to have infected everyone—from the zombies and surviving soldiers to the vagabond warriors—Jim, Selena, and Hannah—reacting to the rage around them. But again Jim, Selena, and Hannah find peace and silence at the film's end, even after the Major shoots Jim from the backseat of their taxi. In the film's final scene, another twenty-eight days later, Selena sews on a treadle sewing machine, and,

Figure 10.3. *28 Days Later*: Jim, Selena, and Hannah greet a jet.

once again, Jim awakens like Rip Van Winkle, this time in a double brass bed. The rural scene outside the home is green and fresh. The aerial view reveals rocky cliffs and a clean river. Together the three lay out the fabric Selena has been sewing. From above we read, "Hello," so the film's message about evolution continues. Rage cannot sustain humanity. Connections with others in a premodern world without electricity and running water can. Once the rage virus has annihilated most of humanity except those willing to accommodate others, England returns to a state of normality in which the Earth can thrive.

28 Weeks Later draws on the rage virus premise of *28 Days Later*, but with a more powerful nod to the horror formula and an overwhelming polemic that changes the eco-evolutionary narrative broached in *28 Days Later*. The narrative of *28 Weeks Later* highlights the genre formula rather than philosophical questions about humanity's place on Earth and leads humanity to a tragic end. The film opens with a lit match in a dark room. The match lights up both a stove and the man and woman preparing a meal. They find the last can of tomatoes and five tins of chick peas but are most pleased by drinkable wine on a table and edible pasta on the stove. A picture of family members sent away hangs on the refrigerator: "They're far, far away and safe and sound," the man explains. They kiss, and then another woman steps into the kitchen, disrupting this happy family scene. Another shot reveals other residents, sitting in living room chairs and then moving into the dining room for dinner. A resident's boyfriend has disappeared and becomes the topic of discussion.

The residents all seem fearful about the boyfriend's fate. When one resident—the only non-white figure—warns them about the conflict between "us in here and them out there," the tone is reinforced. We hear banging on the door. After numerous knocks, a resident rises to check the door. The door is nailed shut, and after the resident tears off the boards and opens the door, sunlight blinds him. We now see that this is a house overlooking a field. There in front of the resident is a hungry child. The child is so hungry and wild, he eats with his hands. Between bites he explains how he got there. People were chasing him. His mum and dad were chasing him and screaming.

The child's explanation prepares us for the next scene, an attack on the house. The young woman, who has lost her boyfriend, stands too near an opening in a window, and someone from the outside claws and bites her through the gap. She changes almost immediately into a raging beast, and a resident kills her. Then they all run upstairs and away from the mob of violent attackers now crashing into the house. They keep running, but only the man from the kitchen escapes, leaving what we discover is his wife and most of the residents behind. The music rises.

The man's name is Don (Robert Carlyle), and he races off in a motorboat, killing attackers and another resident as he speeds away.

It is quiet in the motorboat after he escapes. The river and its banks set up what seems to be a pristine scene, free of danger. Then title cards show the passage of time. After five weeks, the titles claim the zombie victims of a virus have died of starvation. After eleven weeks, NATO forces arrive. Eighteen weeks later, Great Britain is free of infection. And twenty-four weeks later, reconstruction begins. Now it is twenty-eight weeks later, and survivors are returning to London. American soldiers guard the "Green Zone." Two children arrive, are checked for the virus, and admitted. The boy, Andy (Mackintosh Muggleton), has an aberrant iris, just like his mother. The girl, Tammy (Imogen Poots), looks like her mother without sharing this genetic aberration.

All around the Green (safe) Zone, soldiers gather waste in biohazard bags and burn corpses. But in the Green Zone, the electricity is back, and the trains are working. A voice on a loudspeaker tells the new arrivals, "Don't cross the river and leave the security zone. The United States Army is responsible for your safety." There are bodies still to be cleared outside the Green Zone, but in the zone there is hot and cold water, electricity, a supermarket, and even a pub. Aerial views of the city show empty streets and buildings but one moving train bringing the new arrivals to the Green Zone.

The children greet their father—Don, the only resident to escape the home at the beginning of the film. We see the family—father and two children—through a security camera and hear the chief medical officer object to the children's arrival. But her superior argues that the virus is not airborne and does not cross species, and the last victim died six months before. If it comes back they will implement Code Red and kill the infected. The children accompany their father to his penthouse apartment and learn about their mother's death and about their father's ordeal after his escape. Tammy tells him she's happy he's still alive. The father cries and apologizes, and the scene switches back to the armed forces guarding the zone.

After these first scenes, the premise for the film and the film's primary themes have been established. The premise for the film builds on *28 Days Later*: Most of Great Britain has been wiped out by a virus that turns its victims almost immediately into raging beasts, violent zombies still alive until they starve to death. Now, more than six months later, a Green Zone has been constructed that embodies the film's primary themes: One connects with a critique of the United States' policies in Iraq, and the other offers an exploration of the nuclear family unit.

The film's narrative and mise-en-scène parallel the Iraq situation in multiple ways. United States forces protect a Green Zone where expatriates return to the only electricity and running water in Great Britain. But the Green Zone is less secure than it seems. These forces, in spite of how equipped they appear, allow Andy and Tammy to escape the Green Zone and run away to their old home to find a picture and recapture memories of their mother. As Andy and Tammy race through the London streets on a stolen motor scooter, we see how little progress the military has made in their efforts to rebuild the city. Only after they discover their mother, Alice (Catherine McCormack)—still alive and cowering—in the back of the house do military personnel find them and escort them back to the zone. When the mother is prepared for quarantine, it looks like torture on the screen: She is stripped naked, blasted with water, and then tied down on a metal gurney.

The mother's entrance thrusts the film into a battle constructed like a war on terror. Her genetic aberration has protected her from the virus but turned her into a carrier. She infects her husband, Don, when he kisses her, and, as a raging beast, Don infects anyone near enough to grab, claw, and bite. The Senior Medical Officer (Philip Bulcock) calls a Code Red, and, as Bruce Diones asserts, "dramatic parallels to Iraq foreign policy" explode, "including equating raging zombies with Muslim terrorists" (19). Code Red has three levels: (1) Kill the infected, (2) containment, (3) extermination.

When neither killing the infected nor containing the survivors works, the Senior Medical Officer calls for extermination, raising the polemic to "stultifying" levels, according to Diones. As Diones argues, "In a film where U.S. military might is more menacing than flesh-eating zombies, there's little to cheer for" (19). The military fulfills this claim in the film, shooting anyone at ground level from helicopters, sniper perches, and balconies. Military aircraft bomb London avenues, strafe streets and tunnels with fire, and then drop chemical weapons whose gas and smoke kill all but a few infected survivors. These military actions are in themselves ecologically devastating acts, as well as brutal tactics against "targets," but evolutionary narratives drive this film almost as powerfully as they do *28 Days Later*.

The second theme regarding the nuclear family structure provides an opening for an eco-reading for the film that, as with *28 Days Later*, draws on the notion of evolutionary narratives. This time, however, the narrative is no longer comic. The evolutionary narrative asserted by *28 Weeks Later* is tragic and draws on war and extermination as its metaphors. The tragic evolutionary narrative driving *28 Weeks Later* in effect destroys humanity's chance for survival.

The family structure has disintegrated in *28 Weeks Later*. The father deserts his wife, leaving her to be killed, when the infected infiltrate their home after they open it for a lost boy. The children rebel against their father and military authority, rush to their former home for a picture, and bring their infected mother back to the Green Zone. Their mother infects her husband with a kiss, perhaps aware that her saliva will transmit the virus to him, since he lacks her genetic aberration. Then, after the father becomes infected, he stalks his children and attacks his son. The son survives because of his genetic aberration, but the daughter kills the father with a now dead medical officer's gun. Finally, the daughter and her brother escape to Paris with the help of a surviving American helicopter pilot, where, it seems, Andy's virus infects them all, destroying not only his own but others' families. Evolution's response to human rage causes the destruction not only of the nuclear family but also of society. The only humans who can survive the rage virus will inadvertently kill everyone who comes in contact with them, even those in their family.

Both the U.S. Iraq policy and the nuclear family structure are critiqued here. But the family at the forefront of the film's narrative points us back to Sergeant Farrell's question regarding humans' place in the life of the planet. Farrell argues that because humans have "only been around for a few blinks of an eye," their destruction would return the Earth to normality. But an effective evolutionary narrative calls for accommodation, not destruction, so only those humans with the rage virus and with a violent worldview that seeks to exterminate all other species should die.

In *28 Weeks Later*, on the other hand, extermination rather than accommodation is the goal, so the evolutionary questions, with which Farrell grapples, are reinforced and complicated. The infected may battle against the uninfected for territory in both *28 Days Later* and *28 Weeks Later*, but *28 Weeks Later* broadens the philosophical arguments broached in *28 Days Later* because it introduces the idea of an immune carrier for the virus into the evolutionary narratives on display. If humans continue to live on as carriers, then the rest of humanity, even those without the virus or violent tendencies, may be destroyed.

The environmental message in *28 Days Later* seems clear until the film's end. Humans and their explosive rage have constructed the virus that will annihilate all those with violent tendencies or infection and return Earth to its more "normal" state. *28 Weeks Later* counters that assertion, since at least two characters—a mother and her son—have evolved a genetic aberration that protects them from the virus while infecting all those they encounter. And the film's exposition, however flawed, suggests that the virus cannot survive except within these carriers. All other humans will destroy one another or die of starvation, leaving a pristine Earth like that in *28 Days Later* but one that excludes humanity, except, perhaps, a few remaining—genetically altered—humans.

28 Days Later and *28 Weeks Later*, then, build their case around evolution, two different evolutionary narratives. According to Meeker, "Warfare is the basic metaphor of tragedy, and its strategy is a battle plan designed to eliminate the enemy. . . . Comic strategy, on the other hand, sees life as a game. Its basic metaphors are sporting events and the courtship of lovers. . . . Comedy is the art of accommodation and reconciliation" ("The Comic Mode" 168). The evolutionary narrative of *28 Days Later* rests on such accommodation and reconciliation. *28 Days Later* ends with hope for humans who will be reconciled to living in a more natural, less invasive state.

The evolutionary narrative embraced by *28 Weeks Later* works toward species extermination, a failed plan, according to Meeker. In *28 Weeks Later*, family members have turned on each other, and the genetic accommodation that allows some members of the human race to survive kills everyone else. Although Anna Perleberg argues that *28 Days Later* leads humans back to Eden, a "post-apocalyptic paradise," we assert that Eden has nothing to do with the post-apocalyptic endings of either film.

While *28 Days Later* promises an idyllic state for humanity's survivors, both films ultimately argue that the natural world, not humanity, will return Earth to normality because normality for the Earth is a state where humanity is no longer in control. The post-apocalyptic world in *28 Days Later* does become pristine and natural, but only because the remaining humans accommodate themselves to the natural world. In *28 Weeks Later*, because both infected and uninfected humans seek to exterminate rather than accommodate others, normality for the Earth (except, perhaps, for the carriers) is a humanless world. After all, as Sergeant Farrell put it, "man has only been around for a few blinks of an eye." It is the life of the planet, not humanity's existence, that will return Earth to normality.

Conclusion

Al Gore's *An Inconvenient Truth* and its Skeptics: A Case of Environmental Nostalgia

ILMS WITH ENVIRONMENTAL POLITICS as their driving force have become more prevalent from the 1990s onward. The environmental content of Hollywood movies, for example, has become an item of interest in trade publications like *The Hollywood Reporter* and *Variety*, according to *The UCLA Environmental Report*. The report shows an increase from three to twelve articles between 1991 and 1993, and, after a drop back to three articles in 1996, a steady increase in articles focusing on environmental content in productions up to fourteen in 2004 (Corbett and Turco 11). What was missing, until 2004, were articles and Environmental Media Association Awards foregrounding environmentally sound film and television production practices (Corbett and Turco 11). Although this book focuses primarily on environmental content, especially less obvious content that is both obscured and revealed when read through an eco-critical lens, we also see the need to interrogate both content and production practices in relation to ecology. To demonstrate one way we can combine these eco-examinations, we end this book with an analysis of a film that both asserts a blatantly environmental message and presents it through means of an environmentally friendly production process, *An Inconvenient Truth*.

We begin with a reading of the rhetoric driving *An Inconvenient Truth*. Critics of *An Inconvenient Truth* base their negative reviews on what they see as Al Gore's inaccurate predictions. In an article claiming to respond to the film's science, "The Real 'Inconvenient Truth,' "

195

for example, JunkScience.com seeks to debunk predictions surrounding what has been called catastrophic planet warming, asserting instead that "activists and zealots constantly shrilling over atmospheric carbon dioxide are misdirecting attention and effort from real and potentially addressable local, regional and planetary problems" (13). Steven Milloy, the publisher of JunkScience.com, is a Fox News columnist with links to Phillip Morris and ExxonMobil with a B.A. in Natural Science, a Master of Health Sciences in Biostatistics from Johns Hopkins, and Law degrees from University of Baltimore and Georgetown. Ronald Bailey, science consultant for *Reason Magazine*, a libertarian magazine voted one of the "50 Best Magazines" three out of the past four years by the *Chicago Tribune*, asserts that Al Gore "exaggerate[s] the dangers by propounding implausible scenarios in which sea levels rise 20 feet by 2100" ("An Inconvenient Truth: Gore as Climate Exaggerator").

Instead, Al Gore's *An Inconvenient Truth* succeeds not because of its predictions but because of the eco-memories it evokes. Like eco-disaster films from the 1970s, Gore's film argues most powerfully when it draws on environmental nostalgia, a nostalgia we share for a better, cleaner world. Although environmental nostalgia is by definition limited, since a pure, untouched, and unpolluted past projected onto a now lost wilderness cannot recover its history, Gore's message gains rhetorical force when an environmental nostalgia with emotional appeal is evoked within a comparison and contrast mode.

Gore's Framework of Ecological Memories

An Inconvenient Truth argues powerfully for sustainable environmental policies by invoking both personal and universal ecological memories, as do *Silent Running* (1971), *Omega Man* (1971), and (even more closely entwined with Gore's narrative) *Soylent Green* (1973). The film opens with two scenes illustrating two historical memories of the world thirty years ago. One of those memories grows out of a meandering river that flowed near Al Gore's family farm, a river we see flowing clean and clear through a pristine green landscape. The year is 1973, and Al and wife Tipper float along in a canoe over gentle ripples of the Caney Fork River. Living nature is highlighted here by the river, the foliage that lines it and the fact that Tipper is close to giving birth to the Gores' first child. The footage shows its age, showing us that this is a memory, not a view of the present, and that it rests on personal history.

The other more universal historical memory is highlighted by images of Planet Earth shot from outer space, beginning with the 1968 shot from Apollo Eight and the 1972 shot from Apollo Seventeen (the last Apollo

Figure C.1. *An Inconvenient Truth* (2006): Collective memories of Earth frame the film.

mission) and continuing through a series of satellite images that show all Earth's continents and seas. In the 1968 and 1972 photographs, white clouds seem to swirl above clear blue oceans and, in the 1972 example, grasses and deserts on the African continent. The images serve as a starting point for a poignant slide presentation that shows us the impact humans have had on the Earth during the last thirty years especially. But beginning with thirty-year-old shots of a river and photographs of Earth shot in outer space from the Apollo missions also introduces the most powerful tool behind the documentary's success—environmental nostalgia or what we see as "eco-memory." The dates of both the river scene and the two Apollo photos become relevant here, since they coincide with the birth of the environmental movement and the EPA: Al Gore's *An Inconvenient Truth* harks back to a past that personalizes Gore and his message and memorializes an Earth less tainted by human exploitation, the Earth that was present when the first Earth Day was established in 1970.

The differences between Gore and his skeptics seem to respond to two issues: the amount humans contribute to global warming and answers to the question: "What, if anything, should we do about any future warming?" (Bailey "We're All Global Warmers Now"). Responses from both camps rest on eco-memory rather than future predictions. We contend, however, that the environmental nostalgia presented in *An Inconvenient*

Truth carries more force than the fair use mentality asserted by Bailey because it draws on both pathos—in relation to the personal memories Gore discusses—and logos—in relation to the slide show that prompted the documentary in the first place.

Personal Eco-Memories

Gore's personal memories not only add to his credibility by drawing empathy from his audience; they also serve as powerful environmental messages that connect tightly with the science on display in his slide show. The Caney Fork River footage frames the narrative, from the 1973 shots of Tipper and Al in their canoe to current scenes of the river that offer hope for a natural landscape. Both the 1970s and 2000s views of the river and its bank look lush and fertile, with the fecundity promised by Tipper's pregnancy in the earlier shots countered with evidence of continuing life along the river shorelines. The river also serves as a symbol of Gore and his family's journey as well as a journey we are taking here on Earth, suggesting that both as individuals and as a people we have choices we can make regarding the Earth's future.

In *An Inconvenient Truth*, Gore notes several experiences along that journey that remain poignant memories with lasting effects on his quest to share his views of global warming and ways to address its repercussions. The first of these personal experiences—his son's near-fatal accident—serves as a catalyst for his work as an environmentalist. In fact, Gore lines up what he calls the story of his son's accident with what he again calls a story—of the impact of global warming. According to Gore, while his son was recovering, he began writing *Earth in the Balance*. His son's accident had prompted him to reflect on not only his life but his priorities, making time for his family but also rethinking what it meant to be a public servant.

Other personal experiences coincide with his life on the family farm. When not living in a cramped Washington, D.C., apartment, Gore and his parents and sister lived on a farm where, he states, he learned about nature and caring for the land from his father, as they walked around and talked about the farm. He learned about the possible impact humans might have on nature from his mother, as she read Rachel Carson's *Silent Spring* to her two children. These scenes from the family farm in Tennessee, which connect Gore with the natural world, gain more force when he speaks emotionally about his sister Nancy's battle with lung cancer, because the chief cash crop for the Gores until the 1980s was tobacco. For Gore, the battle against tobacco parallels that against global warming, since scientists recognized tobacco's link to cancer and heart disease long before public opinion and public policy agreed. Gore sees the same disconnect between science and public policy in relation to global warming's dire repercussions.

These personal reflections establish Gore and his family's eco-memories, the memories that sparked Gore's crusade and the memories of the Tennessee farm and river that drives his nostalgia for what he sees as a better world environment. Such memories gain weight, however, because they are reinforced by science and by the universal experiences that have become a part of our collective memory. Gore's slide show, with the help of the film's director, Davis Guggenheim, draws on emotions as well as reason because it draws on our memories of Earth as a living world of green and blue, the earth of the Apollo space program photographs, eco-memories we all share.

Aligning Personal Eco-Memories with Universal Environmental Nostalgia

The film adeptly points to these memories, highlighting what we now have, what we have already lost, and what we can regain, if we take the small ecologically sound steps Gore outlines at the end of his film. In other words, the scientific slide show on display coordinates with the personal experiences Gore reveals, since they both hark back, drawing on the power of nostalgia—environmental nostalgia—to skillfully frame global warming as a problem we share but can solve together. And the solution takes us back to the environmentally sustainable world that, according to the film, may soon be lost.

An Inconvenient Truth's pictures of planet Earth shot from space provide not only a view of an eco-memory but of what some may see as the present state of our world—pristine and untouched. But the views also serve as a bridge to Gore's discussion of our thin atmosphere and how changing its composition has contributed to global warming and its repercussions. The juxtaposition of the shots of Earth from space with shots of a polluted Earth below draws further on our nostalgia for an environmentally sound world.

Gore reinforces this message by countering photographic evidence from thirty years ago with that from today, highlighting clear changes in the global environment. A shot of Kilimanjaro from 1970 sharply contrasts with photographs taken thirty years later, for example. The amount of snow capping the mountain has obviously receded, and in a shot from 2005, the mountain is nearly clear of ice and snow. Similar photographic evidence shows Glacier National Park losing more and more of its glaciers. And images around the world tell the same story of rapidly receding ice, snow, and glaciers. These images gain force in opposition to one another. The current views of parks and mountains, even those now without snow, mean nothing unless juxtaposed against earlier shots that show the devastating changes that have occurred there, at least partially because of our contribution to global warming.

Because of these earlier shots, we look back nostalgically on this world on which our own footprint might seem lighter. And then Gore shows us further evidence that we have made the negative impression those shots of glaciers imply. Ice cylinders taken from Antarctica paint a picture of earth's temperature over the past 650,000 years, pointing to 2005 as the hottest year in the cycles revealed there. Gore shows us some of the repercussions of this overall warming trend, focusing on heat waves and strengthening storms across the world. He reinforces his more general claims with a series of images highlighting the devastation in Hurricane Katrina's wake, images that not only remind us of the destruction there but also of our cry to save the city of New Orleans, our nostalgia for an untouched city prior to the hurricane and levee breaks.

The same pathos is in effect when Gore notes other consequences of global warming, including an increase in pests like pine beetles that destroy trees we yearn to save. Trees serve as reminders of a natural world we seem ready to preserve, and images of a treeless Haiti beside a tree-covered Dominican Republic again broach our environmental nostalgia. The images of the impact development has on the world add weight to the wish on which the film seems to rest, a wish for a return to a world like that of 1970. In fact, *Silent Running*, from 1971, sends a similar message regarding saving trees, but the film ends tragically, with hope for life other than humans in the hands of a lone robot. *An Inconvenient Truth*, on the other hand, ends with some effortless (and painless) ways we can change our future, without sacrificing ourselves.

The Strengths and Limits of Nostalgia

Nostalgia has been critiqued, reified, and recovered in the past few decades, with a resurgence of research in memory studies complicating negative views of nostalgia built on postmodern views. Postmodern responses to nostalgia critique its move toward essentialism. In her 1988 article "Nostalgia: A Polemic," Kathleen Stewart engages postmodern cultural critics' views that see nostalgia as a social disease. According to Stewart, "Nostalgia, like the economy it runs with, is everywhere. But it is a cultural practice, not a given content; its forms, meanings, and effects shift with the context—it depends on where the speaker stands in the landscape of the present" (227). Drawing on the work of Roland

Barthes, Jean Baudrillard, Walter Benjamin, Pierre Bourdieu, Jonathan Culler, Donna Haraway, Fredric Jameson, and Raymond Williams, Stewart elucidates why nostalgia is such a powerful rhetorical tool, as well: Stewart argues that "on one 'level' there is no longer any place for *anyone* to stand and nostalgia takes on the generalized function to provide some kind (any kind) of cultural form" (227, emphasis Stewart's).

According to Stewart, nostalgia serves as a powerful rhetorical tool that placates and paralyzes the disenfranchised: "Nostalgia is an essential, narrative, function of language that orders events temporally and dramatizes them in the mode of 'that's that happened,' that 'could happen,' that 'threaten to erupt at any moment' " (227). Stewart sees the seductive nature of nostalgia in a postmodern culture as not only culturally situated but reductively negative, resulting in what she calls mirages—either a "grand hotel" of affluence or a "country cottage" of romantic simplicity. For Stewart, then, nostalgia is a negative consequence of attempting to replace postmodern relativism (labeled good) with an essential past based in recovery of a "self" (labeled bad).

From the perspective of these earlier cultural critics, there is a vanishing point of striving and looking for the pure or untouched, unpolluted past, projected into the wilderness of the past of history. But that really is an ideological project. Much of the past, in terms of today's environmental issues, is substantially lost because of population explosion, irrevocable global warming, loss of biodiversity, and unknown effects of pollution. Each year people born will not remember the same past as previous generations. Our own literatures consider—through the lens of nostalgia—themes like the vanishing Indian, the disappearance of the buffalo, and the disappearing prairie, in relation to Frederick Jackson Turner's recuperative thesis of the frontier, a thesis that promotes progress at any cost, whether it be genocide or the expansion of industrialism in the United States.

More recent work, especially in anthropology and cultural studies, however, complicates visions of nostalgia as inherently and inescapably bad. In fact, it may itself prove not only a way to learn from the past but to recuperate real community. In Ethel Pinheiro and Cristiane Rose Duarte's 2004 article, "Loaves and Circuses at *Largo da Carioca*, Brazil: The Urban Diversity Focused on People-Environment Interactions," for example, nostalgia in the form of collective memory and appropriation is what "led *Largo da Carioca* to survive in spite of all the political and urban changes." Pinheiro and Duarte drew on both an historical evolutive approach and participant-observation data. Historical-evolutive research demonstrated that the open plaza maintains functions from Ancient Greece, Egypt, and Mesopotamia, especially those related to performance;

and participant-observation resulted in interview data that revealed how "people link social activity in the *largo's* physical structure."

Answers to a question asking respondents to "choose a word that could explain the place" illustrated the pull of nostalgia—one of the terms given to explain *Largo da Carioca*. Others were related, highlighting outdoor performances, culture, and tradition. The piece is esoteric but reveals the positive impact nostalgia might have, actually affecting the city's shape, ensuring that a people will appropriate a public space for performance and art because their collective memory draws them to it. The power of collective memory—of nostalgia—seems to be manifested in the continuation of *Largo da Carioca*. Recent cultural studies scholarship seeks to complicate earlier reductive cultural critiques of nostalgia, as well, noting that nostalgia need not always be constructed in negative terms. Situating nostalgia can minimize its essential draw, for example. According to Sean Scanlan's introduction to a 2005 special issue of *The Iowa Journal of Cultural Studies*, "In current work, nostalgia is no longer the programmatic equivalent of bad memory and the uses and limits of important theories from the 1990s are being reconsidered."

Although cultural critics critiqued nostalgia because it "abused individual and collective memory and . . . problematized the relations between producers and consumers," Scanlan suggests that nostalgia "can cross several registers simultaneously. It can be felt culturally or individually, directly or indirectly." According to Scanlan, "postmodernism's negative critique only partially illuminates its various links to memory, history, affect, media and the marketplace, only partially accounts for nostalgia's continuing power." Scanlan ends his introduction to this special issue with more positive conclusions about nostalgia:

> Nostalgia is often secondary or epiphenomenal, yet it can also be Proustian and epiphanic, generative and creative. Walter Benjamin's "Theses on the Philosophy of History" contains his vision of the angel of history—based on Klee's painting "Angelus Novus—in which the angel's face is [according to Benjamin] "turned toward the past," while a storm from Paradise "irresistibly propels him into the future to which his back is turned" (Benjamin 257–58). Benjamin is right to call this storm progress, but he does not describe what the angel might be feeling while looking toward the past. The angel of history . . . is nostalgic.

In fact, in the context of Gore's *An Inconvenient Truth*, nostalgia's rhetorical power gains force when contextualized both personally—through

Gore's own narrative—and historically—through our collective memory of Earth's changes from the 1970s to the present. Gore's message gains strength because it draws on both personal and collective eco-memories. It gains validity because it situates both science and personal history in particular cultural contexts. Current cultural critics have reappropriated nostalgia as both term and history. Gore reappropriates and expands it to include ecology. For Gore, it's not the cultural critics but the conservative scientists who most forcefully attack the rhetoric of *An Inconvenient Truth*.

Yet, like Gore, these critics draw on nostalgia to make their claims. Gore's film supports the claims made in these earlier eco-disaster films. Global warming has already impacted the Earth in ways predicted by such prophets, with loss of arable land, destruction of forests, and influx of natural disasters that resemble repercussions of biological warfare like that in *Omega Man* and eco-disasters in *Silent Running*. Environmental nostalgia works in both these 1970s eco-disaster films and in Gore's *An Inconvenient Truth*. The difference lies in the ways that nostalgia is evoked. Whereas the earlier disaster films drew on a current environment as the hope for a future world; Gore looks to a past, the past of these films' context, to demonstrate the destruction to which we have already contributed but which we now have the chance to overcome. Gore does not play the role of an apocalyptic prophet in his film. He serves as a personal example and a conveyor of hope.

An Inconvenient Truth as Carbon-Neutral Production

Gore does not only offer a general hope for earth's future if we as individuals make the changes he shows us during the film's credits (from changing to compact fluorescent light bulbs to planting trees). He also illustrates ways Hollywood can "green" the filmmaking and distribution process. The DVD packaging, for example, is 100% post-consumer recycled material, with no plastic case or wrapping to emit toxic waste into landfills.

The film is also, according to the official Web site's blog, the first carbon-neutral documentary: "Paramount Classics, Participant Productions, and NativeEnergy have joined forces to offset 100% of the carbon dioxide emissions from air and ground transportation and hotels for production and promotional activities associated with the documentary," according to the blog entry ("*An Inconvenient Truth* Website). The library record for the *An Inconvenient Truth* DVD even includes the descriptor, "a carbon neutral production." The Internet Movie Database's Trivia section for *An Inconvenient Truth* agrees with the commentary and extras

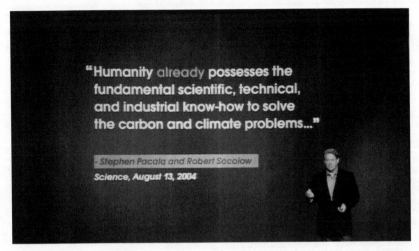

"Humanity already possesses the fundamental scientific, technical, and industrial know-how to solve the carbon and climate problems..."

- Stephen Pacala and Robert Socolow
Science, August 13, 2004

Figure C.2. *An Inconvenient Truth*: Al Gore offers signs of hope.

on the *An Inconvenient Truth* DVD. The site describes the carbon-neutral process used during and after the film production:

> NativeEnergy, which works with individuals and organizations to help them compensate for their contributions to global warming, calculated the "carbon footprint" from producing the film, including all travel, office, and accommodations related emissions. The company then offset emissions through renewable energy credits or green tags from new renewable energy projects. Paramount Classics and Participant will split the cost of these tags; the funds will go towards helping build new Native American, Alaskan Native Village, and farmer-owned renewable energy projects, creating sustainable economies for communities in need and diversifying our energy supply.

The film's executive producer, Jeff Skoll, who partnered with NativeEnergy to offset carbon dioxide emissions, explains that "these renewable energy projects offer options that will decrease our demand for fossil fuels and otherwise would likely not happen without these kinds of investments." Gore contributes a portion of the profits from both the movie and its accompanying book to a bipartisan educational campaign to combat global warming, as well. Gore's documentary, as well as recent film productions like *Syriana*, also a carbon-neutral film, illustrate one way Hollywood's film industry can "go green" not only in film content but in production practices. The turn away from film to digital production will enhance this environmental turn. For us, however, the messages of films from rhetorical documentaries like *An Inconvenient Truth* and *The River*, to action adventure films on wheels like *The Fast and the Furious*, can also offer hope as they move audiences to action, with (we hope) help from books like this one.

This book has attempted to show that an eco-critical analysis of films does not necessarily rest solely on outlining blatant environmental messages. It also involves a more studied look at the forms, discourse, and histories that helped define and obscure the possible ecological leanings shared by the films highlighted in our book, even when they represent multiple themes and cultural, historical, and political periods and standpoints. Although many of the films we read here seem to highlight and even promote environmental degradation, they also put that degradation on display, showing us the destruction, the eco-disaster, and the exploitation of resources that now seem in conflict with science, ideology, and media representations of ecology.

Despite their differences, these films, including Gore's *An Inconvenient Truth*, may inspire ecological action because they reveal much about the current state of environmental politics. The film industry has tackled environmental content, offering both blatant ("film vert") and more subtle examples (including those examined here) of films that convey environmental messages to audiences willing to pay for them. If Hollywood takes the next step toward linking ecology and popular cinema, "greening" its own industry, it will also show us some of the possibilities for eco-critical film studies. The "greening" of film studies through what Laurence Buell calls "environmentality," like the "greening" of the film industry, may not only address environmental content but stir readers to eco-action. As Buell argues, this "environmentality" may "help [. . .] instill and reinforce public concern about the fate of the earth, about humankind's responsibility to act on that awareness, about the shame of environmental injustice, and about the importance of vision and imagination in changing minds, lives, and policy as well as composing words, poems, and books" (133). We end this book with confidence that eco-critical film studies will, like the film industry, both examine the content of popular cinema and critique the film industry driving its production.

Filmography

11th Hour. Dir. Nadia Conners and Leila Conners Petersen. Co-written and produced by Leonardo DiCaprio. Tree Media Group and Warner Brothers, 2007.

2 Fast 2 Furious. Dir. John Singleton. Perf. Paul Walker, Tyrese, Eva Mendes. Universal Pictures, 2003.

28 Days Later. Dir. Danny Boyle. Perf. Cillian Murphy, Naomie Harris. Fox Searchlight, 2002.

28 Weeks Later. Dir. Juan Carlos Fresnadillo. Perf. Robert Carlyle, Rose Byrne, Catherine McCormack, Imogen Poots, Mackintosh Muggleton. Fox Atomic, 2007.

48 Hours. Dir. Walter Hill. Perf. Nick Nolte, Eddie Murphy, Annette O'Toole. Paramount, 1982.

10,000 B.C. Dir. Roland Emmerich. Warner Brothers, 2008.

Adaptation. Dir. Spike Jonze. Perf. Nicholas Cage, Meryl Streep, Chris Cooper. Sony, 2002.

Arachnophobia. Dir. Frank Marshall. Perf. Jeff Daniels, Harley Jane Kozak, John Goodman. Film Prod. Steven Spielburg. Buena Vista Pictures, 1990.

Artificial Intelligence: AI. Dir. Steven Spielberg. Perf. Hailey Joel Osment, Francis O'Connor, Jude Law. Warner Brothers, 2001.

The Badlanders. Dir. Delmer Daves. Perf. Alan Ladd, Ernest Borgnine. MGM, 1958.

Basic Training. Dir. Frederick Wiseman. Zipporah Films, 1971.

Batman. Dir. Tim Burton. Perf. Michael Keaton. Warner Brothers, 1989.

Bend of the River. Dir. Anthony Mann. Perf. James Stewart, Arthur Kennedy. Universal Pictures, 1952.

The Beverly Hillbillies. Created by Paul Henning. Perf. Buddy Ebson, Irene Ryan. CBS, 1962–1971.

The Birds. Dir. Alfred Hitchcock. Perf. Rod Taylor, Tippi Hedren, Jessica Tandy. Universal Pictures, 1963.

Bombing of Ploesti. *WWII Road to Victory*. Disk 4. Lions Gate Home Entertainment, 2004.

Born into Brothels: Calcutta's Red Light Kids. Written and Directed by Zana Briski and Ross Kauffman. Red Light Films, 2004.

Bowfinger. Dir. Frank Oz. Perf. Steve Martin, Eddie Murphy, Heather Graham, Robert Downey, Jr. Imagine/Universal, 1999.

Bride of Frankenstein. Dir. James Whale. Perf. Boris Karloff, Elsa Lanchester. Universal Pictures, 1935.

Bullitt. Dir. Peter Yates. Perf. Steve McQueen, Robert Vaughn, Jacqueline Bisset, Robert Duvall. Warner Brothers/Seven Arts, 1968.

Car of Tomorrow. Dir. Tex Avery. MGM, 1951.

Chang. Dir. Merian C. Cooper, Ernest B. Schoedsack. Paramount Pictures, 1927.

Children of Men. Dir. Alfonso Cuaròn. Perf. Clive Owen, Julianne Moore, Claire-Hope Ashitey, Michael Caine. Universal, 2006.

The China Syndrome. Dir. James Bridges. Perf. Jane Fonda, Jack Lemmon, Michael Douglas. Columbia Pictures, 1979.

Cimarron. Dir. Weley Ruggles. Perf. Richard Dix, Irene Dunne. RKO, 1931.

Citizen Kane. Dir. Orson Welles. Perf. Orson Welles, Joseph Cotton. RKO, 1941.

City on Fire. Dir. Alvin Rakoff. Perf. Shelley Winters, Leslie Nielsen, Ava Gardner, Henry Fonda. Astral Films, 1979.

Class of Nuke 'Em High. Dir. Richard Haines and Lloyd Kaufman. Perf. Janelle Brady, Gilbert Brenton, Robert Prichard. Troma Studios, 1986.

Class of Nuke 'Em High 2: Subhumanoid Meltdown. Dir. Richard Haines and Lloyd Kaufman. Perf. Janelle Brady, Gilbert Brenton, Robert Prichard. Troma Studios, 1991.

Class of Nuke 'Em High 3: The Good, the Bad and the Subhumanoid. Dir. Richard Haines and Lloyd Kaufman. Perf. Janelle Brady, Gilbert Brenton, Robert Prichard. Troma Studios, 1995.

Comes a Horseman. Dir. Alan J. Pakula. Perf. James Caan, Jane Fonda, Jason Robards, Mark Harmon. MGM, 1978.

Commerce Raiders. WWII Road to Victory. Disc 1. Lions Gate Home Entertainment, 2004.

Creature from the Black Lagoon. Dir. Jack Arnold. Perf. Richard Carlson, Julie Adams. Universal, 1954.

Crossfire. Dir. Edward Dmytryck. Perf. Robert Young, Robert Mitchum. RKO, 1947.

Dark City. Dir. Alex Proyas. Perf. Rufus Sewell, Kiefer Sutherland, Jennifer Connelly, William Hurt. New Line Productions. 1998.

Dark Days. Dir. Marc Singer. Wide Angle Pictures and Palm Pictures, 2000.

Dawn of the Dead. Dir. George Romero. Perf. Ken Foree, David Emge. United Film Distribution, 1978.

The Day After Tomorrow. Dir. Roland Emmerich. Perf. Dennis Quaid, Jake Gyllenhaal, Emmy Rossum, Sela Ward, Ian Holm. Twentieth Century Fox, 2004.

Daylight. Dir. Rob Cohen. Perf. Sylvester Stallone, Amy Brennaman, Viggo Mortenson. Universal, 1996.

The Day of the Dead. Dir. George A. Romero. Perf. Lori Cardille, Terry Alexander, Joseph Pilato. Lauren Entertainment, 1985.

The Day of the Triffids. Dir. Steve Sekely. Perf. Howard Keel, Kieron Moore, Janette Scott. Allied Artists, 1962.

The Defiant Ones. Dir. Stanley Kramer. Perf. Tony Curtis, Sidney Poitier. United Artists, 1958.

Die Hard. Dir. John McTiernan. Perf. Bruce Willis, Bonnie Bedelia, Alan Rickman. Twentieth Century Fox, 1988.

Dogtown and Z-Boys. Dir. Stacy Peralta. Narr. Sean Penn. Sony Pictures Classics, 2001.

Dragnet. Dir. Jack Webb. Perf. Jack Webb, Ben Alexander. NBC, 1951–1959.

Drift Society Volume I. Rise Above Entertainment, 2004.

The Dukes of Hazzard. Dir. Hollingsworth Morse. Perf. John Schneider, Tom Wopat, Catherine Bach. CBS, 1979–1985.

The Dukes of Hazzard. Dir. Jay Chandrasekhar. Perf. Johnny Knoxville, Seann William Scott, Alice Grecyn. Warner Brothers, 2005.

Eight Legged Freaks. Dir. Ellory Elkayem. Perf. David Arquette, Kari Wuhrer, Scott Terra, Scarlett Johansson, Doug E. Doug. Warner Brothers, 2002.

The End of Suburbia: Oil Depletion and the Collapse of the American Dream. Dir. Greg Greene. The Electric Wallpaper Co., 2004.

The Far Country. Dir. Anthony Mann. Perf. James Stewart, Walter Brennan. Universal, 1954.

The Farm of Tomorrow. Dir. Tex Avery. MGM, 1954.

The Fast and the Furious. Dir. John Ireland and Edward Sampson. Perf. John Ireland, Dorothy Malone. MGM/Palo Alto, 1955.

The Fast and the Furious. Dir. Rob Cohen. Perf. Paul Walker, Vin Diesel, Michelle Rodriguez. Universal Pictures, 2001.

The Fast and the Furious: Tokyo Drift. Dir. Justin Lin. Perf. Lucas Black, Bow Wow, Zachary Ty Bryan, Nathalie Kelley. Universal Pictures, 2006.

Fire at the Oil Gusher in Bibi-Heybat. Dir. A. Mishon. 1898.

Fires of Kuwait. Dir. David Douglas. Narr. Rip Torn. Imax, 1992.

Frankenstein. Dir. James Whale. Perf. Boris Karloff, Colin Clive. Universal Pictures, 1931.

Frogs. Dir. George McCowan. Perf. Ray Milland, Sam Elliott, Joan Van Ark. American International Pictures, 1972.

Fury. Dir. Fritz Lang. Perf. Spencer Tracy, Sylvia Sidney. MGM, 1936.

Giant. Dir. George Stevens. Perf. Elizabeth Taylor, Rock Hudson, James Dean. Warner Brothers, 1956.

Godzilla, King of the Monsters!. Dir. Ishirô Honda and Terry O. Morse. Perf. Raymond Burr, Takashi Shimura, Akira Takarada, Momoko Kôchi. Embassy Pictures Corp. and Toho Company, 1956.

Gone With the Wind. Dir. Victor Fleming. Perf. Vivien Leigh, Clark Gable, Olivia de Havilland, Leslie Howard. MGM, 1939.

Grass: A Nation's Battle for Life. Dir. Merian C. Cooper, Ernest B. Schoedsack. Paramount Pictures, 1925.

Gun Crazy. Dir. Joseph H. Lewis. Perf. John Dall, Peggy Cummins. United Artists, 1949.

Happy Feet. Dir. George Miller. Perf. Elijah Wood, Brittany Murphy, Robin Williams, Hugh Jackman, Nicole Kidman. Warner Brothers, 2006.

Hellfighters. Dir. Andrew V. McLaglen. Perf. John Wayne. Universal, 1968.

The Hidden. Dir. Jack Sholder. Perf. Michael Nouri, Kyle McLachlan. New Line Cinema, 1987.

High Plains Drifter. Dir. Clint Eastwood. Perf. Clint Eastwood, Geoffrey Lewis. Malpaso, 1973.

Hooper. Dir. Hal Needham. Perf. Burt Reynolds, Sally Field. Warner Brothers, 1978.

The House of Tomorrow. Dir. Tex Avery. MGM, 1949.

How the West Was Won. Dir. John Ford, Henry Hathaway, George Marshall, Richard Thorpe. Perf. Caroll Baker, Lee J. Cobb, Henry Fonda. MGM, 1962.

Humanoids from the Deep. Dir. Barbara Peters. Perf. Doug McClure, Ann Turkel, Vic Morrow, Cindy Wintraub. New World Pictures, 1980.

The Hurricane. Dir. John Ford. Dorothy Lamour, Jon Hall, Mary Astor. United Artists, 1937.

Ice Age: The Meltdown. Dir. Carlos Saldanha. Perf. Ray Romano, John Leguizamo, Queen Latifah. Twentieth Century Fox, 2006.

An Inconvenient Truth. Dir. Davis Guggenheim. Perf. Al Gore. Paramount Classics, 2005.

The Incredible Shrinking Man. Dir. Jack Arnold. Perf. Grant Williams, William Schallert. Universal, 1957.

In Old Chicago. Dir. Henry King. Perf. Tyrone Power, Alice Faye, Don Ameche. Twentieth Century Fox, 1937.

In the Kingdom of Oil and Millions (V Tzarstve Nefti I Millionov). Dir. Boris Svetlov. 1916.

The Invasion of the Body Snatchers. Dir. Don Siegel. Perf. Kevin McCarthy, Dana Wynter. Allied Artists, 1956.

Invasion of the Body Snatchers. Dir. Philip Kaufman. Perf. Donald Sutherland, Brooke Adams, Jeff Goldblum. United Artists, 1978.

Jarhead. Dir. Sam Mendes. Perf. Jake Gyllenhaal, Peter Sarsgaard, Jamie Foxx. Universal, 2005.

King Kong. Dir. Merian C. Cooper and Ernest B. Shoedsack. Perf. Fay Wray, Robert Armstrong, Bruce Cabot. RKO, 1933.

Kiss Kiss Bang Bang. Dir. Shane Black. Perf. Robert Downey, Jr., Val Kilmer, Michelle Monaghan. Warner Brothers, 2005.

Kiss of Death. Dir. Henry Hathaway. Perf. Victor Mature, Richard Widmark. Twentieth Century Fox, 1947.

The Last Man on Earth. Dir. Ubaldo Ragona. Perf. Vincent Price. American International, 1964.

Le Mans. Dir. Lee H. Katzin. Perf. Steve McQueen. Paramount/Solar Productions, 1971

Lessons of Darkness. Directed and narrated by Werner Herzog. Canal Pictures, 1992.

The Life of an American Fireman. Perf. Vivian Vaughan, Arthur White, James White. Edison Manufacturing Company, 1903.

Lumber Jerks. Dir. Friz Freleng. Warner Brothers, 1955.

The Lumière Brothers' First Films. Kino DVD, 1996.

The Matrix Reloaded. Dir. Andy and Larry Wachowski. Perf. Keanu Reeves, Carrie-Anne Moss, Laurence Fishburne. Warner Brothers, 2003.

The Matrix Revolutions. Dir. Andy and Larry Wachowski. Perf. Keanu Reeves, Carrie-Anne Moss, Laurence Fishburne. Warner Brothers, 2003.

Men at Work. Dir. Emilio Estevez. Perf. Charlie Sheen, Emilio Estevez. Epic Productions, 1990.

Metropolis. Dir. Fritz Lang. Perf. Gustav Frohlich, Brigette Helm. UFA, 1927.

Murder My Sweet. Dir. Edward Dmytryck. Perf. Dick Powell, Claire Trevor. RKO, 1944.

Mystic River. Dir. Clint Eastwood. Perf. Kevin Bacon, Sean Penn, Laura Linney. Malpaso, 2003.

Naked Gun 2½: The Smell of Fear. Dir. David Zucker. Perf. Leslie Nielsen, Priscilla Presley, George Kennedy, O. J. Simpson, Robert Goulet. Paramount Pictures, 1991.

Nanook of the North. Dir. Robert Flaherty. Royal Pictures (Home Vision Entertainment), 1922.

The New Frontier. Dir. Carl Pierson. Perf. John Wayne. Republic Pictures, 1935.

North Country. Dir. Niké Caro. Perf. Charlize Theron, Frances McDormand, Sean Bean, Woody Harrelson, Sissy Spacek. Warner Brothers, 2005.

Nosferatu. Dir. F.W. Murnau. Perf. Max Schreck. Film Arts Guild, 1922.

Oil Wells of Baku: Close View. Dir. Lumiere Brothers. Kino DVD, 1996 (1896).

Oklahoma Crude. Dir. Stanley Kramer. Perf. George C. Scott. Faye Dunaway. Columbia, 1973.

Omega Man. Dir. Boris Sagal. Perf. Charlton Heston, Anthony Zerbe, Rosalind Cash. Warner Brothers, 1971.

On Dangerous Ground. Dir. Nicholas Ray. Perf. Robert Ryan, Ida Lupino. RKO Pictures, 1952.

On the Beach. Dir. Stanley Kramer. Perf. Gregory Peck, Ava Gardner, Fred Astaire, Anthony Perkins, Donna Anderson. United Artists, 1959.

The Outlaw Josie Wales. Dir. Clint Eastwood. Perf. Clint Eastwood, Sandra Locke. Warner Brothers, 1976.

Out of the Past. Dir. Jacques Tournier. Perf. Robert Mitchum, Jane Greer. Warner Brothers, 1947.

Pale Rider. Dir. Clint Eastwood. Perf. Clint Eastwood, Carrie Snodgrass, and Michael Moriarty. Warner Brothers, 1985.

The People of the Cumberland. Dir. Elia Kazan. New Deal Programs, 1937.

Piranha. Dir. Joe Dante. Perf. Bradford Dillman, Heather Menzies. New World Pictures, 1978.

Planet of the Apes. Dir. Franklin J. Schaffner. Perf. Charlton Heston, Roddy McDowell, Kim Hunter, Linda Harrison. Twentieth Century Fox, 1968.

Power and the Land. Dir. Jons Ivens. RKO, 1940.

Rebel Without a Cause. Dir. Nicholas Ray. Perf. James Dean, Natalie Wood. Warner Brothers, 1955.

Riding Giants. Dir. Stacy Peralta. Sony Pictures, 2004.

The River. Dir. Pare Lorentz. Perf. Thomas Chalmers (voice). Farm Security Administration, 1937.

Roger & Me. Dir. Michael Moore. Dog Eat Dog Films/Warner Brothers, 1989.

Salesman. Dir. Albert Maysles, David Maylses, Charlotte Mitchell Zwerin. Maysles Films, 1968.

San Francisco. Writ. Robert E. Hopkins and Anita Loos. Perf. Clark Gable, Jeanette MacDonald, Spencer Tracy. MGM, 1936.

Shane. Dir. George Stevens. Perf. Alan Ladd, Jean Arthur, Van Heflin. Paramount, 1953.

Silent Running. Dir. Douglas Trumbull. Perf. Bruce Dern, Cliff Potts, Ron Rifkin, Jesse Vint. Universal Pictures, 1971.

Silkwood. Dir. Mike Nichols. Perf. Meryl Streep, Kurt Russell, Cher. Twentieth Century Fox Pictures, 1983.

Silver City. Dir. John Sayles. Perf. Chris Cooper, Richard Dreyfuss, Michael Murphy, Kris Kristofferson, Daryl Hannah, Thora Birch, Tim Roth, Maria Bello. Anarchist's Convention Films, 2004.

The Sixth Sense. Dir. M. Night Shyamalan. Perf. Bruce Willis, Haley Joel Osment. Hollywood Pictures, 1999.

Skeeter. Dir. Clark Brandon. Perf. Michael J. Pollard, William Sanderson, Tracy Griffith. New Line Cinema, 1994.

Something for the Birds. Dir. Robert Wise. Perf. Patricia Neal, Victor Mature. Twentieth Century Fox, 1952.

Soylent Green. Dir. Richard Fleischer. Perf. Charlton Heston, Edward G. Robinson, Leigh Taylor-Young. MGM Pictures, 1973.

Spoilers of the Plains. Dir. William Witney. Perf. Roy Rogers, Penny Edwards. Republic Pictures, 1951.

Star Wars: Episode IV, A New Hope. Dir. George Lucas. Perf. Mark Hamill, Harrison Ford, Carrie Fisher. Twentieth Century Fox, 1977.

The Stunt Man. Dir. Richard Rush. Perf. Peter O'Toole, Barbara Hershey, Steve Railshack. Twentieth Century Fox, 1980.

The Swarm. Dir. Irwin Allen. Perf. Michael Caine, Katherine Ross, Richard Widmark, Olivia de Havilland, Richard Chamberlain, Patty Duke, Fred MacMurray, Henry Fonda. Warner Brothers, 1978.

Syriana. Dir. Steven Gaghan. Perf. George Clooney, Matt Damon, Chris Cooper, Amanda Peet. Warner Brothers, 2005.

Symphony of Oil. Dir. Pumpyanski. Azerbaijan, 1933.

Tarantula. Dir. Jack Arnold. Perf. John Agar, Mara Corday, Leo G. Carroll. Universal Pictures, 1955.

Terminator 2: Judgment Day. Dir. James Cameron. Perf. Arnold Schwarzenegar, Linda Hamilton, Edward Furlong, Robert Patrick. Columbia/TriStar, 1991.

Them! Dir. Gordon M. Douglas. Perf. James Whitmore, Edmund Gwenn, Joan Weldon, James Arness. Warner Brothers Pictures, 1954.

They Live By Night. Dir. Nicholas Ray. Perf. Farley Granger, Cathy O'Donnell. RKO, 1948.

The Time Machine. Dir. George Pal. Perf. Rod Taylor, Alan Young, Yvette Mimieux. MGM Pictures, 1960.

T-Men. Dir. Anthony Mann. Perf. Dennis O'Keefe, Alfred Ryder. Eagle Lion, 1947.

To Be or Not To Be. Dir. Alan Johnson. Perf. Mel Brooks, Anne Bancroft, Christopher Lloyd. Twentieth Century Fox, 1983.

Toxic Avenger. Dir. Michael Herz and Lloyd Kaufman. Perf. Andree Maranda, Mitchell Cohen, Jennifer Babtist, Cindy Manion, Robert Prichard. Troma Studios, 1985.

Toxic Avenger, Part 2. Dir. Michael Herz and Lloyd Kaufman. Perf. Ron Fazio, John Altamura, Phoebe Legere, Rick Collins, Rikiya Yasuoka. Troma Studios, 1989.

Traffic. Dir. Steven Soderbergh. Perf. Benicio Del Toro, Michael Douglas, Catherine Zeta Jones, Don Cheadle, Benjamin Bratt, Erika Christensen, James Brolin, Dennis Quaid, Salma Hayek. Bedford Falls Productions/USA Films, 2000.

Tulsa. Dir. Stuart Heisler. Perf. Susan Hayward, Robert Preston, and Pedro Armendariz. Eagle-Lion, 1949.

Twilight Zone: The Movie. Dir. Joe Dante and John Landis. Perf. Dan Akroyd, Albert Brooks, Vic Morrow, John Lithgow, Kathleen Quinlan. Warner Brothers, 1983.

U Boat War. WWII Road to Victory Disc 2. Lions Gate Home Entertainment, 2004.

Unforgiven. Dir. Clint Eastwood. Perf. Clint Eastwood, Morgan Freeman. Warner Brothers, 1992.

V For Vendetta. Writ. Andy and Larry Wachowski. Dir. James McTeigue. Perf. Natalie Portman, Hugo Weaving. Warner Brothers, 2005.

When the Levees Broke: A Requiem in Four Acts. Dir. Spike Lee. 40 Acres & A Mule Filmworks/HBO, 2006.

White City/Black City. Azerbaijan, 1908.

Who Framed Roger Rabbit. Dir. Robert Zemeckis. Perf. Bob Hoskins, Christopher Lloyd, Joanna Cassidy. Buena Vista Pictures, 1988.

Who Killed the Electric Car?. Dir. Chris Paine. Electric Entertainment/Sony, 2006.

Wild Hogs. Dir. Walt Becker. Perf. Tim Allen, John Travolta, Martin Lawrence, William H. Macy, Ray Liotta, Marisa Tomei. Buena Vista, 2007.

Wild River. Dir. Elia Kazan. Perf. Montgomery Clift, Lee Remick. Twentieth Century Fox, 1960.

Woodstock. Dir. Michael Wadleigh. Warner Brothers, 1970.

Works Cited

"*28 Days Later* Production Notes." *28 Days Later*. Dir. Danny Boyle. Perf. Cillian Murphy, Naomie, Harris, Christopher Eccleston, Megan Burns, and Brendan Gleeson. Fox Searchlight Pictures, 2002.

Abbey, Edward. *The Monkey Wrench Gang*. New York: Harper Perennial Modern Classics, 2000.

"Academy Statement re: Green Initiative Announcement." 25 Feb. 2007 <www. oscars.org/press/pressreleases/2007/07.02.25.html>.

Apte, Mahadev. *Humor and Laughter: An Anthropological Approach*. Ithaca, NY: Cornell UP, 1985.

Armstrong, Derek. "*Eight Legged Freaks* Review." *All Movie Guide*. 2002 <http://www.allmovie.com/cg/avg.dll?p=avg&sql=1:260297~T1>.

Babbitt, Bruce. "Preface." *Sand County Almanac and Sketches Here and There*. London: Oxford UP, 2000.

Badalov, Rahman. "Oil, Revolution, and Cinema." *Azerbaijan International*. 5.3 (Autumn 1997) <http://www.azer.com/aiweb/categories/magazine/53_folder/53_articles/53_revolution.html>.

Bailey, Ronald. "Earth Day, Then and Now." *Reason* (May 2000). 11 May 2004 <http://www.reason.com/news/show/27702.html>.

———. "An Inconvenient Truth: Gore as Climate Exaggerator." *Reason* (16 June 2006) <http://www.reason.com/news/show/116471.html>.

———. "Inconvenient Uncertainties and Moral Ambiguities." *Reason*. (May 2006) <http://www.reason.com/blog/show/113924.html>.

———. "We're All Global Warmers Now: Reconciling temperature trends that are all over the place." *Reason*. (11 Aug. 2005) <http://www.reason.com/news/show/34079.html>.

Barry, John. *Rising Tide: The Great Mississippi Flood of 1927 and How It Changed America*. New York: Simon and Schuster, 1997.

Baxter, Ellen. *Private Lives/Public Spaces: Homeless Adults on the Streets of New York City*. New York: Community Service Society of New York, Institute for Social Welfare Research, 1981.

Baudrillard, Jean. *America*. Trans. Chris Turner. New York: Verso, 1998.

————. "Simulcra and Simulations." *Selected Writings*. Ed. Mark Poster. New York: Stanford UP, 1998. 166–84.

Bennett, Michael. "Manufacturing the Ghetto: Anti-urbanism and the Spatialization of Race." *The Nature of Cities: Eco-criticism and Urban Environments*. Eds. Michael Bennett and David W. Teague. Tucson: U of Arizona P, 1999. 169–88.

Bennett, Michael and David W. Teague. *The Nature of Cities: Ecocriticism and Urban Environments*. Tucson: U of Arizona P, 1999.

Biskind, Peter. *Easy Riders, Raging Bulls: How the Sex-Drugs-and-Rock 'N' Roll Generation Saved Hollywood*. New York: Simon and Schuster, 1998.

Black, Ralph W. "What We Talk about When We Talk About Ecocriticism." 29 March 2004 <http://www.asle.umn.edu/conf/other_conf/wla/1994/black.html>.

Bordwell, David and Thompson, Kristin. *Film Art: An Introduction*. 2nd ed. New York: Knopf, 1986.

Bourget, Jean-Loup. "Social Implications in the Hollywood Genres." *Film Genre Reader II*. Ed. Barry Keith Grant. Austin: U of Texas P, 1995: 50–58.

Bradshaw, Peter. "The Day After Tomorrow." *The Guardian*. 28 May 2004 <http://arts.guardian.co.uk/fridayreview/story10,1225933,00.html>.

Browne, Nick. "The 'Big Bang': The Spectacular Explosion in Contemporary Hollywood Film." 28 Oct. 2006 <www.cinema.ucla.edu/strobe/bigbang/bang1.html>.

Brussat, Frederic, and Mary Ann. "Silent Running: Movie Review." *Spirituality and Health: Spiritual Practices for Human Being*. 1980–2003. 1 Dec. 2003 <www.spiritualityhealth.com/newsh/items/moviereview/item_5071.html>.

————. Film Review: "The Day After Tomorrow." *Spirituality and Health: Spiritual Practices for Human Being*. 1970–2006. 5 May 2007 <http://www.spiritualityandpractice.com/films/films.php?id=8506>.

Buell, Lawrence. *The Future of Environmental Criticism: Environmental Crisis and Literary Imagination*. Malden, MA: Blackwell Publishing, 2005.

Burne, David. *Get a Grip on Ecology*. London: The Ivy Press, 1999.

Buffum, Edward G. *Six Months in the Gold Mines: From the Journals of Three Years' Residence in Upper and Lower California. 1847-8-9*. Philadelphia: Lea and Blanchard, 1850.

Carson, Rachel. *Silent Spring*. Boston: Houghton Mifflin, 1962.

Chase, Donald. "Watershed: Elia Kazan's *Wild River*." *Film Comment*. 32.6 (1996): 10–17.

Cleese, John. "Synopsis of Humour and Psychoanalysis conference." London: Freud Museum. 5 Nov. 1994 <http://www.freud.org.uk/Humour.htm>.

Corbett, Charles J., and Turco, Richard P. "Film and Television Industry." *Southern California Environmental Report Card*, 2006. 5–11, 40.

Crockett, Harry. "What is Ecocriticism?" <http://www.asle.umn.edu/conf/other_conf/wla/1994/crockett.html>.

Crouch, Craig E. "Hydraulic Mining in California." *Hydraulic Mining—CPRR Photographic History Museum*. 10 Aug. 2003 <http://cprr.org/Museum/Hydraulic_Mining/>.

Detwyler, Thomas. "Selling the Car Culture through Advertising." *University of Wisconsin.* 7 Feb. 2001 <www.uwsp.edu/geo/courses/geog100/CarCult-Ideol.htm>.

———. "U. S. Culture and the Environment." *University of Wisconsin.* 4 January 2001 <www.uwsp.edu/geo/courses/geog100/USAutoCulture&Env.htm>.

"The Development of the Oil and Gas Industry in Azerbaijan." *AzerMSA.* 21 June 2004 <www.members.tripod.com/azmsa/oil.html>.

Diamond, Jared. *Collapse: How Societies Choose to Fail or Succeed.* New York: Viking, 2005.

Diones, Bruce. "*28 Weeks Later.*" *The New Yorker.* 28 May 2007: 19.

Ebert, Roger. "*28 Days Later.*" 27 June 2003 <http://rogerebert.suntimes.com/apps/pbcs.d11/article?AID=/20030627/REVIEWS/306270301/1023>.

———. "Dark City." *Roger Ebert's Movie Yearbook 2001: Every Single New Ebert Review.* Kansas City: Andrews McMeel Publishing, 2001: 127–28.

———. *The Day After Tomorrow.* 28 May 2004 <http://rogerebert.suntimes.com/apps/pbcs.dll/article?AID=/20040528/REVIEWS/405280303/1023>.

Ehrlich, Paul. *The Population Bomb.* New York: Ballantine Books, 1968.

Erickson, Hal. "*Tulsa* Review." *All Movie Guide.* 31 Mar 2004 <www.allmovie.com>.

Flink, James J. *The Car Culture.* Cambridge. Cambridge UP, 1975.

Frayling, Christopher. "Eastwood on Eastwood." Eds. Kapsis, Robert E., and Coblentz, Kathie. *Clint Eastwood: Interviews.* Jackson: UP of Mississippi, 1999: 130–36.

Freud, Sigmund. *Jokes and Their Relation to the Unconscious.* New York: W. W. Norton, 1963.

Glotfelty, Cheryll. "What is Ecocriticism?" 24 Mar. 2004 <http://www.asle.umn.edu/conf/other_conf/wla/1994/glotfelty.html>.

Goff, Phillip. "Car Culture and the Landscape of Subtraction." *Monocular Texts.* December 2003 <www.monoculartimes.co.uk/texts/ architexts/carculture_1.shtml>.

Goodman, Amy. "INTERVIEW: *Dark Days*: The Ultimate Underground Film." *indieWIRE.* 3 Oct. 2003 <www.indiewire.com/people/int_Singer_Marc_000830.html>.

Gore, Al. *Earth in the Balance: Ecology and the Human Spirit.* New York: Plume Reprint, 1993.

Grant, Nancy L. *TVA and Black Americans: Planning for the Status Quo.* Philadelphia: Temple UP, 1989.

Hastings, Michael. "*2 Fast 2 Furious*: Overview." 25 Apr. 2005 <http://movies.msn.com/movies/movie.aspx?m=537055>.

Haver, Ronald. *David O. Selznick's Hollywood.* New York: Alfred A. Knopf, 1980.

Hayles, N. Katherine. "Searching for Common Ground." Abstract. *Reinventing Nature? Responses to Postmodern Deconstruction.* Eds. Michael E. Soule and Gary Lease. Washington, D.C.: Island Press, 1995: viii.

Heider, Karl G. *Ethnographic Film.* Austin: U of Texas P, 1976.

"*Hellfighters* Production Notes." *Hellfighters.* Dir. Andrew V. McLaglen. Perf. John Wayne. Universal DVD, 1968.

Hladik, Tamara. "The Omega Man." *Classic Sci-Fi.* 1998. 14 May 2004 <www. scifi.com/sfw/issue68/classic.html>.

———. "Soylent Green." *Classic Sci-Fi.* 1997. 10 May 2004 <www.scifi.com/sfw/ issue55/classic.html>.

"Howe, Desson. "Fires of Kuwait Review." *Washington Post.* 4 Dec. 1992 < http:// www.washingtonpost.com/wp-srv/style/longterm/movies/videos/firesofku-waitnrhowe_a0af4e.htm>.

Hubbard, Preston J. *Origins of the TVA: The Muscle Shoals Controversy, 1920–1932.* New York: W. W. Norton and Company, 1961.

Ingram, David. *Green Screen: Environmentalism and Hollywood Cinema.* Exeter, UK: U of Exeter P, 2000.

Jackson, Abraham V. W. *From Constantinople to the Home of Omar Khayyam.* Piscataway, NJ: Gorgias Press, 2002 (1911).

"Jarhead Production Notes." 2 May 2007 <http://www.cinemareview.com/produc-tion.asp?prodid=3171>.

Johnson, Rebecca. "Car Culture: How American Got Hooked by Little Bugs and Monster Trucks—and Everything in Between—and Why it's Time to Park Our Automobile Obsession." *walkinginfo.org.* December 2003 <www. walkinginfo.org/insight/features_articles/carcult/>.

Kaminski, Stuart M. "Comedy and Social Change." *American Film Genres.* 2nd ed. Chicago: Nelson-Hall, 1985. 135–70.

Kazimzade, Aydin. "Celebrating 100 Years in Film, Not 80: Cinema in Azer-baijan: The Pre-Soviet Era." *Azerbaijan International.* 5.3 (1997) 24 Mar. 2004 <http://www.azer.com/aiweb/categories/magazine/53_folder/53_ articles/53_100years.html>.

Keane, Stephen. *Disaster Movies: The Cinema of Catastrophe.* London: Wallflower, 2001.

Kellert, Stephen R. "Concepts of Nature East and West." *Reinventing Nature? Responses to Postmodern Deconstruction.* Eds. Michael Soule and Gary Lease. Washington, DC: Island Press, 1995. 103–22.

Kiester, Edwin Jr. "Turning Water to Gold: Confronted with a Hill Full of Gold, Miners Removed the Hill and the Gold—and Left a Mess Behind. *Smithsonian.* August 1999: 18.

King, Geoff. "Spectacular Narratives: *Twister, Independence Day,* and Frontier Mythology in Contemporary Hollywood." *Journal of American Culture.* (1999): 25–39.

Klein, Norman M. *Seven Minutes: The Life and Death of the American Animated Cartoon.* London: Verso, 1993.

Kolodny, Annette. *The Lay of the Land: Metaphor as Experience and History in American Life and Letters.* Chapel Hill: U of North Carolina P, 1975.

Korth, Joanne. "NASCAR history awaits." *St. Petersburg Times Sports Online.* 4 July 2004 <www.sptimes.com/2003/07/04/Sports/NASCAR_history_awaits. shtml>.

Lease, Gary. "Introduction: Nature Under Fire." Ed. Soule, Michael, and Lease, Gary. *Reinventing Nature? Responses to Postmodern Deconstruction.* Washington, DC: Island Press, 1995. 3–15.

Legler, Gretchen T. "Ecofeminist Literary Criticism." *Ecofeminism: Women, Culture, Nature.* Ed. Karen J. Warren. Bloomington: Indiana UP, 1997: 227–38.

Leopold, Aldo. *Sand County Almanac Almanac and Sketches Here and There.* London: Oxford UP, 1949. 2000.

Lichtneker, David. "Recovered Classic: Silent Running." *The Z Review.co.uk.* 1 Dec. 2003 <www.thezreview.co.uk/features/silentrunning.htm>.

Li, Ken. "Racer X." *Vibe Magazine.* May 1998.

McCann, Michael. "Pyrotechnics, Fire and Explosion Effects." *Chicago Artists Resource Page.* 2 May 2007 <http://www.chicagoartistsresource.org/?q=node/15369>.

McGilligan, Patrick. *Clint: The Life and Legend.* New York: St. Martins Press, 1999.

McKay, John P. "Baku Oil and Transcaucasian Pipelines, 1883–1891: A Study in Tsarist Economic Policy." *Slavic Review,* 43.4 (Winter 1984): 604–23.

"Making of *Dark Days.*" *Dark Days.* Dir. Marc Singer. Wide Angle Pictures and Palm Pictures, 2000.

Matheson, Richard. *I Am Legend.* New York: Orb Books, 1997.

Meeker, Joseph W. *The Comedy of Survival: Literary Ecology and the Play Ethic.* Tucson: U of Arizona P, 1997.

———. "The Comic Mode." *The Eco-criticism Reader: Landmarks in Literary Ecology.* Ed. Cheryll Glotfelty and Harold Fromm. Athens: U of Georgia P, 1996. 155–69.

Moore, John R. *The Economic Impact of TVA.* Knoxville: U of Tennessee P, 1967.

Morton, Margeret. *Fragile Dwellings.* New York: Aperture, 2000.

———. *The Tunnel.* New Haven: Yale UP, 1995.

Mumford, Lewis. *Highway and the City.* London: Secker and Warburg, 1964.

Murphy, Patrick, et al. "Forum on Literatures of the Environment." *PMLA.* 114.4 (1999): 1089–104.

Murray, Rebecca. "Ellory Elkayem Talks About 'Eight Legged Freaks.' " 2004 <romanticmovies.about.com/library/weekly/aa071702g.htm>.

Nelson, Gaylord. "Earth Day '70: What It Meant." *U.S. Environmental Protection Agency.* 11 May 2004 <http://www.epa.gov/history/topics/earthday/02.htm>.

———. "How the First Earth Day Came About." *Envirolink: The Online Environmental Community.* 11 May 2004 <earthday.envirolink.org/history.html>.

O'Hehir, Andrew. "*28 Days Later*" *Salon.com.* 27 June 2003 <http://dir.salon.com/story/ent/movies/review/2003/06/27/28_days_later/index.html>.

———. "The Fast and the Furious: Fast cars! Hot chicks! Pointless thrills!" *Salon.com.* 22 June 2001 <http://archive.salon.com/ent/movies/review/2001/06/22/fast_furious/index.html>.

Osborn, Fairfield. *Our Plundered Planet.* Boston: Little Brown, 1948.

Pavlides, Dan. "*Hellfighters* Review." 31 Mar 2004 <www.allmovie.com>.

Pearleberg, Anna. "Lurching Towards Eden: Post-Apocalyptic Paradise in Danny Boyle's *28 Days Later. The Image of the Road in Literature, Media, and Society.* Ed. Will Wright and Steven Kaplan. Pueblo, CO: Society for the Interdisciplinary Study of Social Imagery, Colorado State University—Pueblo, 2005: 64–65.

Phillips, Dana. "Is Nature Necessary?" *The Ecocriticsim Reader: Landmarks in Literary Ecology*. Ed. Cheryll Glotfelty and Harold Fromm. Athens: U of Georgia P, 1996: 204–22.

Pinheiro, Ethel, and Cristiane Rose Duarte. "Loaves and Circuses at *Largo da Carioca*, Brazil: The Urban Diversity Focused on People-Environment Interactions." *Anthropology Matters Journal* 6.1 (2004) <www.anthropologymatters.com>.

Price, Jenny. "Thirteen Ways of Seeing Nature in L.A." *The Believer*. April 2006 <http://www.believermag.com/issues/200604/?read=article_price>.

Proyas, Alex. "Commentary." *Dark City*. Dir. Alex Proyas. Perf. Rufus Sewell, Kiefer Sutherland, Jennifer Connelly, William Hurt. New Line Productions. DVD. 1998.

"The *Real* 'Inconvenient Truth.' " *JunkScience.com*. 26 April 2006 <www.junkscience.com/Greenhouse>.

Remschardt, Ralf. "Comedy and Comic Performance in Theory and Practice." Spring 2003 <www.arts.ufl.edu/theatreanddance/comedy/4930syllabus.htm>.

Ross, Andrew. *The Chicago Gangster Theory of Life: Nature's Debt to Society*. London: Verso, 1994.

———. (Interviewed by Michael Bennett). "The Social Claim on Urban Ecology." *The Nature of Cities: Eco-criticism in Urban Environments*. Ed. Michael Bennett and David W. Teague. Tucson: U of Arizona P, 1999: 15–30.

Rothman, Hal K. *Saving the Planet: The American Response to the Environment in the Twentieth Century*. Chicago: Ivan R. Dee, 2000.

Sarris, Andrew. *"You Ain't Heard Nothin' Yet": The American Talking Film History and Memory, 1927–1949*. Oxford: Oxford UP, 1998.

Scanlan, Sean. "Introduction: Nostalgia." *Iowa Journal of Cultural Studies*. 5.1 (2005) <www.uiowa.edu/~ijcs/nostalgia/nostint.htm>.

Schickel, Richard. *Clint Eastwood: A Biography*. New York: Alfred A. Knopf, 1996.

Scott, A.O. "Film Review; Spared by a Virus But Not by Mankind." *New York Times*. 27 June 2003.

Searight, Sarah. "Region of Eternal Fire: Petroleum Industry in Caspian Sea Region." *History Today* 5.8 (2000): 45–51.

Shabecoff, Phillip. *Fierce Green Fire: The American Environmental Movement*. New York: Hill and Wang, 1993.

Slotkin, Richard. *Gunfighter Nation: The Myth of the Frontier in Twentieth-Century America*. Norman: U of Oklahoma P, 1998.

———. *Regeneration Through Violence: The Mythology of the American Frontier, 1600–1860*. Norman: U of Oklahoma P, 2000.

Sontag, Susan. "The Imagination of Disaster." *Against Criticism*. New York: Picador, 1966. 209–225.

Soule, Michael, and Lease, Gary, eds. *Reinventing Nature? Responses to Postmodern Deconstruction*. Washington, DC: Island Press, 1995.

"*Southern California Report Card 2006*: UCLA Institute of the Environment Urges More 'Green' Practices by Film and Television Industry." 18 Mar 2007 <www.ioe.ucla.edu/report-card-06-pr.html>.

"*Soylent Green*." *Home Theater*. 2 May 2005 <http://www.hometheaterinfo.com/soylent_green.htm>.

Stewart, Kathleen. "Nostalgia—A Polemic." *Cultural Anthropology*. 3.3 (1998): 227–41.

"Study: Television, Filmmaking Industries Are Big Polluters." *nbc4.tv* 14 Nov. 2006 <www.nbc4.tv/print/10315943/detail.html>.

Tashiro, Charles S. "The *Twilight Zone* of Contemporary Hollywood Production." *Cinema Journal*. 41.3 (Spring 2002): 27–37.

Tavernier, Bertrand. "Commentary." *Lumiere Brothers: First Films*. "Oil Wells of Baku: Close View." Kino DVD, 1896.

Tepper, Sheri. *The Gate to Women's Country*. New York: Doubleday, 1988.

Thai, Tang. "The Mustang Was It." *St. Louis Dispatch*. 7 Jan. 2004: F1.

Urry, John. "Automobility, Car Culture and Weightless Travel: A discussion paper." *Department of Sociology, Lancaster University*. January 1999.

Vogt, William. *Road to Survival*. New York: William Sloane Associated, 1948.

Wilson, Alexander. *Culture of Nature*. Toronto: Between the Lines, 1992.

Wolfe, Tom. "The Last American Hero is Junior Johnson, Yes!" *Esquire*. March 1965. Reprinted in *Esquire: 40th Anniversary Celebration* (October 1973): 211–22, 436, 438, 442, and 446.

Worster, Donald. "Nature and the Disorder of History." *Reinventing Nature? Responses to Postmodern Deconstruction*. Ed. Michael Soule and Gary Lease. Washington, DC: Island Press, 1995. 65–86.

Yacowar, Maurice. "The Bug in the Rug: Notes on the Disaster Genre." *The Genre Film*. Ed. B.K. Grant. Baltimore: Scarecrow Press, 1977. 90–107.

Index

223